T0348965

I Regret Almost
Everything

I Regret Almost Everything

Keith McNally

G

GALLERY BOOKS

New York   Amsterdam/Antwerp   London
Toronto   Sydney/Melbourne   New Delhi

G

Gallery Books
An Imprint of Simon & Schuster, LLC
1230 Avenue of the Americas
New York, NY 10020

First Gallery Books hardcover edition May 2025

GALLERY BOOKS and colophon are registered trademarks of Simon & Schuster, LLC.

Simon & Schuster strongly believes in freedom of expression and stands against censorship in all its forms. For more information, visit BooksBelong.com.

For information about special discounts for bulk purchases, please contact Simon & Schuster Special Sales at 1-866-506-1949 or business@simonandschuster.com.

The Simon & Schuster Speakers Bureau can bring authors to your live event. For more information or to book an event, contact the Simon & Schuster Speakers Bureau at 1-866-248-3049 or visit our website at www.simonspeakers.com.

Interior design by Carly Loman

Manufactured in the United States of America

10 9 8 7 6 5 4 3 2 1

Library of Congress Control Number: 2024950334

ISBN 978-1-6680-1764-7
ISBN 978-1-6680-1766-1 (ebook)

For my children: Harry, Sophie, Isabelle, George and Alice

Autobiography is only to be trusted when it reveals something disgraceful. A man who gives a good account of himself is probably lying, since any life when viewed from the inside is simply a series of defeats.

GEORGE ORWELL

I Regret Almost Everything

1.

In early August 2018, I tried to commit suicide. I was in our summer house on Martha's Vineyard with my wife and two young children. For the previous five weeks I'd been stockpiling sleeping pills and pain-killers, which I planned to take when my family went to Boston. The day before they were set to leave, the fifty-three pills went missing. After a frantic search, I found them tucked behind some books on my desk. Fearing that someone knew about my plan, I decided to take the pills that night, with my family still in the house.

For the past year my wife, Alina, and I had been sleeping in separate rooms. I went to bed early, locked the door and transferred the thirty-eight Ambien and fifteen Percocet from plastic vials into a wooden bowl. In handfuls I scooped all fifty-three pills into my mouth and washed them down with water, swallowing the lot in under two minutes.

Having always considered myself a coward, I was shocked at how little I hesitated before taking such a lethal dose. As I drifted into oblivion, I remember thinking that it had been so easy. My suicide attempt had worked.

Only it hadn't.

There was a time when everything worked. Twenty months earlier I'd been happily married and the owner of eight successful Manhattan restaurants, including Balthazar in SoHo. In 2004, the *New York Times* had called me "The Restaurateur Who Invented Downtown." I had everything going for me. And then on November 26, 2016, the clock stopped.

I was living in London. One Saturday morning I coaxed my youngest children, George and Alice, into seeing a Caravaggio exhibition with me at the National Gallery. George was thirteen, Alice eleven. While looking at a painting of Jesus being betrayed by Judas, *The Taking of Christ*, I sensed my body beginning to show signs of betraying me: a strange metallic tingling started to pinch my fingertips. It was an odd feeling, but as it stopped after five or six seconds, I didn't give it another thought. Soon afterward, to the relief of my children, we left the museum.

Two hours later, when I was back home by myself, the metallic feeling returned. Only this time it was in earnest. Within seconds the horrific tingling shot up my left arm and, like some malignant jellyfish, clasped itself onto my face. Terrified, I phoned Alina, who rushed back with the kids and instantly called an ambulance. George, fists clenched, was panic-stricken as medics examined my convulsing body. Within minutes I was being hoisted into the waiting ambulance. Alina, George and Alice looked on.

I woke up several hours later in Charing Cross Hospital. The first thing the doctor told me was that I'd had a stroke. The second thing was that my brain would never be the same again. Perhaps his bluntness was necessary for legal reasons, but from where I stood—or lay—it was a brutal awakening.

After the doctor left, I tried wriggling my arms and legs to check that I wasn't paralyzed. I wasn't, thank God. To test my memory, I wrote the alphabet on the back of the nurse's chart. I then tried saying the letters aloud, but here there was a problem. The words wouldn't conform to my efforts. They exited my mouth in such a slurred and disorderly way that I sounded like a stage drunk. But this was a small price to pay for my stroke. My *first* stroke, that is. Because the next day the artillery arrived and gave me such a hammering that in one fell swoop I lost the use of my right hand, right arm and right leg. And my slurred speech, perhaps in fright, went AWOL. Overnight I was confined to a wheelchair and deprived of language.

So much for The Restaurateur Who Invented Downtown.

* * *

I shared a ward with five other men whose ages ranged from forty to eighty. At night, with words inaccessible to me, I'd listen in awe to them talking. Speech suddenly seemed like a divine accomplishment. Even everyday words had an element of poetry to them.

I dreaded the moment when the men would stop talking and I'd be left with my own thoughts. Sleepless, half-paralyzed and unable to speak, I felt buried alive. More than anything, I wished the stroke had killed me.

Bereft of speech and right side unusable, I wondered how my relationship with Alina might change. And with George and Alice also.

All children exaggerate their father's strength. Most sense it ebbing away imperceptibly over twenty or so years. Generally, a father's decline appears natural, tolerable even. It wasn't going to be like that for my children.

My new life seemed ungraspable. It existed, but was outside of me.

On my second day in the hospital, Alina arranged for George and Alice to visit. An hour before they were due, I became so ashamed of them seeing me disabled that I canceled the visit. The next day I could hold out no longer.

Hospitals are a great leveler. Like soldiers at war, patients lose all distinctiveness. As they entered the ward, George and Alice failed to recognize me. I was lying at the end of a row of identical beds, assimilating into the world of the sick and dying. Although it had only been three days since I last saw them, they looked years younger. They stood by the door, small eyes darting from one sick man to the next, searching for some identifiable sign of their father. After a few seconds they rushed to my bed.

Alice seemed happy to see me, but George looked angry and said less than usual. He'd behaved in a similar way a year earlier after watching me lose a match in a squash tournament. Back then, I found his anger confusing. Now it made sense.

3

Alina put on a brave face but was so shell-shocked she said little. I managed to gurgle out a few words, and in between the long silences the heavy breathing of the man in the next bed entered uncomfortably into our space. Alina told the children I was going to regain my voice and would soon be walking out of the hospital.

Neither responded.

When the three of them left, I wept for the first time in twenty years.

2.

Although my restaurants were taking in $80 million a year before my stroke, my reason for building them was never the pursuit of money. It was partly to gain the admiration of those I respected, and partly the satisfaction I received from seeing an idea realized. But whatever satisfaction the restaurants gave me was fleeting—which is probably why I can't stop building them.

I ran my places conscientiously, but with a sense of humor. My staff got a kick when I insisted on pricing a double espresso at half the price of a single and described an expensive Bordeaux as undrinkable. This was less an attempt to be funny than a feeble effort to sabotage a system I'd spent years assembling. This minor subversiveness has always been a trait of mine. When customers ask me where the bathroom is, I often say we don't have one.

My stroke brought those cavalier days to a halt. I was now about to pay a massive price for not having set up my businesses more conventionally: with a hierarchy of partners and managers in position to replace me in case I died or became incapacitated. Riding a bicycle with no hands only works if you don't fall off.

Before my stroke, I'd gone for three and a half years without a checkup. Considering I was sixty-five, it now seems the height of madness to have waited so long. The reason wasn't due to my being busy. It was simply that I didn't want to see my GP until I was in perfect health. I have the same attitude about tidying my apartment before the cleaner comes. But at my age, the longer I went without a checkup, the greater the chances of having terminal cancer. And because there's no cure for cancer, there was no point in having a checkup. It was a catch-22.

During my sensible period of having annual checkups, I'd invite my doctor and his family to Balthazar for a free dinner a week before my appointment. I did this not because I liked the man but because I was convinced that giving him a complimentary meal a week before my checkup would guarantee me a clean bill of health. I also have a crazed belief that flying first class reduces the chances of my plane crashing. And so far this mad theory has been proved correct—at least as far as flying goes.

As a boy I skipped over the sidewalk's grout lines to avoid serious illness. You always think it won't be you. Cancer, strokes, heart attacks. These things happen to other people. Not me. You always think it won't be you.

There are two types of strokes: hemorrhagic and ischemic. Mine were the more common: ischemic. There are many conditions that bring about an ischemic stroke. High on the list are elevated blood pressure, heart disease, high cholesterol, diabetes and smoking. I had none of these and had never smoked a cigarette in my life. For this reason my neurologist was at a loss to understand what triggered my two strokes. On paper I was an extremely fit sixty-five-year-old.

Strokes are caused by a lack of oxygen to the brain. The two I had occurred within twenty-four hours of each other, and both were the result of a blockage in one of my neck's arteries. The arteries convey blood from heart to brain, and their obstruction starves the brain of oxygen. Every minute it's denied oxygen, the brain loses two million cells. If the left side of the brain's oxygen supply is cut off, the right side of the body is affected, and vice versa. Because the left side regulates language, a stroke on this side—as mine were—is likely to affect speech, as well as limit physical movement on the right side.

Every four minutes someone dies from a stroke. I was one of the lucky ones, but my speech and body were now so alarmingly foreign that I started to doubt my own identity.

Sleepless in the dead of night, my thoughts bordering on the hallucinatory, I was desperate to know that the *real* me still existed. Though paralyzed and voiceless, I had to be certain that the sliver of human matter that was irreducibly me hadn't changed. That it was still there. The core, the centerpiece. The fucking bull's-eye. At the same time, I yearned for sleep. And more sleep.

It's said that if you want a good night's sleep, stay away from hospitals. By my third day at Charing Cross I understood why. What little sleep I could muster was constantly interrupted by nurses drawing my blood, taking my temperature and checking my vital signs. I was often woken and transferred to a movable bed without explanation. A porter would then wheel me along a fluorescent-lit corridor to an elevator, where we'd ascend three stories to a floor where electrocardiograms and MRI and CT scans took place. It was odd how adamant the nurses were that only porters, and *positively* nobody else, be allowed to push the gurneys. On account of their sanctity, I often found myself stranded mid-corridor waiting for this trolley specialist to appear. Apparently, no passing neurologist or heart surgeon possessed the correct qualifications to even touch the gurney, let alone move it.

On average, the brain employs a hundred trillion neural connections to send and retrieve information—"memos"—to and from parts of the body. A stroke causes severe damage to a number of these pathways. Although brain damage can never be totally reversed, a process called neuroplasticity can help repair sections of these damaged pathways. Believing that neuroplasticity is only effective during the first six months following a stroke, neurologists recommend that rehabilitation begin the second one leaves the hospital. They also recommend plenty of unbroken sleep.

In those turbulent early days, all I thought about, and longed for, was sleep. My waking hours were such a torture that sleep was my only reprieve.

Despite being an atheist, I began to think my stroke was possibly retribution for a life shot through with questionable behavior. Perhaps unnatural troubles *are* caused by unnatural deeds. How else to explain my mangled body?

For the first two days I was unable to talk, but on the following day my voice reappeared. Like a soldier after battle, it returned a specter of its former self. Weary and spiritless, it limped into view. A voice that had once been clear and concise was now leaden and sluggish. At best, I sounded like someone speaking underwater. I still do.

Three days after my stroke, relief arrived. My three older children, Harry, Sophie and Isabelle, flew from New York to London to be with me. Their mother, my first wife, Lynn Wagenknecht, came with them.

Although we'd been divorced for twenty-four years, Lynn and I remained close. Being the daughter of a nurse and a doctor gave her a familiarity with hospitals that, in my present condition, I found reassuring. Having Lynn and our three children at my bedside in the daytime made it easier to forget the changes in my body. Nighttime was different. Lying in my bed, unable to sleep, I was racked with shame. Shame that my body was now so debilitated that I was going to be forever dependent on other people. And the current shame of having no control over my bowel movements. Luckily, there was an orderly kind enough to deal with the mess.

Freddy was a gangly Jamaican agnostic who'd begin the cleanup by stressing the importance of dignity in these degrading circumstances. In his thick Jamaican accent, Freddy would claim that dignity's loss came from within. As with many wise maxims, I believed this to be true about other people, but not myself.

Freddy had some wonderful homespun turns of phrase. One was "sufferation": "That man, he got a lot of sufferation." Another was "beyond the sandbar," which described something desirable but unattainable. Although Freddy didn't speak the Queen's English, his language was fresher and far more original than the late Queen's ever was, and I was fascinated by it. I was also grateful for his willingness to clean up after me. While some of those more senior to Freddy, who were often religious, exhibited an impatience with my mess, this friendly agnostic on the bottom of the nursing hierarchy displayed only goodness. Such a pity that "uneducated" goodness such as Freddy's is seldom rewarded in the corporate world. The last time I inquired about Freddy he was still on the bottom rung.

Like many patients who suffer an ischemic stroke, I now found it hard to calculate simple math. Even basic addition was difficult. If there were twenty large plates on a table, it would take me at least fifteen minutes to count them. With schoolboy sums now beyond me, it was clear that someone else should take over the financial side of my restaurants. I chose my oldest daughter, Sophie.

Sophie knew the restaurant business well from having worked closely with me for six years. Four months before my stroke, she'd married Adam Pritzker and they'd moved to Los Angeles to begin their new life.

From my hospital bed, I asked Sophie if she'd be willing to take over operating the finances of my eight restaurants. She agreed. Three weeks later Sophie and her immensely considerate husband moved back to New York.

Sophie's first task was to try to free me from a lease I'd signed two years earlier. I'd agreed with a landlord called Bobby Cayre to rebuild a former restaurant of mine, Pastis. Like the original, the new Pastis was to be in New York's Meatpacking District. However, in drawing up the fifteen-year lease, I'd foolishly signed a million-dollar personal guarantee. This guarantee would only be enforced if I failed to build the new restaurant. Seeing as I was fit and healthy, the chances of me not building Pastis at the time had been practically zero. Practically, but not quite.

Ordinarily, landlords don't allow tenants to relinquish their leases, but in this case, with the tenant being an echo of the man he was when signing the agreement, I was sure Cayre would care enough to make an exception.

* * *

A few days after arriving in London, Lynn felt that her presence un-settled Alina and she decided to return to the US. Sophie and Isabelle, feeling the same way, left with her. Only Harry remained.

Although I sympathized with Alina for feeling overwhelmed by the arrival of my first family, I wished she could have understood the com-fort they brought me.

But nobody thinks straight the day after Armageddon.

3.

I first met my second wife, Alina, in the basement of Balthazar during
its construction in the winter of 1997. Sorting through stacks of
hundred-year-old mirrors, I caught the misty reflection of an Asian-
looking woman with a sultry gaze. She was accompanying her friend
to a job interview. Although we scarcely talked to each other, Alina
cast such a powerful mix of tenderness and sensuality that I couldn't
look at her.

During the thirty minutes she was there, we barely exchanged two
words.

The next time we met was two weeks later at Pravda, a subterranean
vodka bar I owned. It was raining heavily that night and the place was
packed and steamy. I was helping the maître d' seat customers when
Alina walked in with some girlfriends. I took a break and sat down with
them. After twenty minutes we were sitting alone together.

Alina was half Japanese. Although born in Hawaii, she'd grown up
in Alaska with her mother and three siblings. In her early twenties she'd
moved to New York to work as a model. She was now twenty-nine and
working as the maître d' of a fashionable Vietnamese restaurant. Despite the outgoing nature of her job, Alina was soft-spoken and reticent,
which only increased my attraction to her.

Sitting in a booth, Alina said it was pure chance she saw me that
night because she only came into the bar to avoid the rain. Although I
don't believe in fate, I thought this was a good sign. But then again, I
would think that. When first having a crush on someone, people tend to

interpret coincidences as good omens. We also exaggerate the things we have in common. Just before closing time, the DJ played a Cat Stevens song, "Moonshadow." Alina said she loved Cat Stevens because he had such integrity. To bring us closer, I lied and said I agreed.

Though we hadn't touched, I left Pravda that night with Alina very much under my skin.

It's hard to say whether love distorts or intensifies the qualities of those we fall for, but talking to Alina that night at Pravda, I thought she was the most sensual woman I'd ever known. The most contradictory also. Although she was shy and introverted, Alina not only had a permanent boyfriend when she agreed to date me but also had a lover, someone with a prestigious title at Condé Nast. I'm surprised I didn't get lost in the shuffle.

Eventually Alina left her boyfriend (and lover) and began dating me exclusively.

Our five-year courtship proved a stormy mixture of desire and jealousy, but the non-stormy times were so extraordinary they led me to propose. We were married on 2/2/02. An auspicious date—or so I thought.

Since my divorce a decade earlier I'd missed being a full-time father. Within three years, Alina and I had two children, George and Alice. This was a busy time for us. We bought a five-bedroom house in Greenwich Village and renovated it together while, at the same time, I was cowriting a cookbook, operating four restaurants and planning others. Over the next seven years I built and opened Schiller's on the Lower East Side, Morandi and Minetta Tavern in the West Village and Pulino's on the Bowery.

The James Beard Awards are the American restaurant industry's equivalent to the Oscars, and equally repulsive. I had first attended one of the ceremonies in 1998 and loathed everything about it. Watching chefs and restaurateurs I admired act so sycophantically toward self-important food critics made me think twice about being in the same business. And the winners' acceptance speeches were so self-indulgent and humorless that I vowed never to attend one again.

When I was nominated in 2010 for the country's outstanding restaurateur, I stuck to my promise and refused to go to the ceremony. I sent my daughter Sophie instead. Surprisingly, I won. Sophie collected the medal on my behalf and handed it to me the next day. A week later, disgusted with myself, I threw it in the garbage.

This kind of self-loathing had gnawed at me for years, and the more successful I became, the worse it got. It seemed that my entire life in New York was based on deception. I'd flourished as a maître d' not through hard work but as a result of an eagerness to tailor my character—Zelig-like—to fit the customer. I won the guest over with superficial charm or phony self-deprecating humor. When building my own restaurants, I designed them to deceive just as meticulously as I'd designed my character.

It hadn't always been this way.

Before moving to New York at twenty-four, I'd had a measure of integrity, but once there, I squandered it. Whether this was due to the restaurant business I couldn't say, but winning the Outstanding Restaurateur award was my breaking point. I just had to get out.

A week after winning the award, I made plans to quit restaurants and move back to England. Alina was more than happy to live in London. I told friends I was taking a five-year sabbatical to give our two kids a European education. (Not that I knew what a "European education" was.) The real reason was more selfish. I was going back to London to search for something from my past. What that was, I didn't have a clue.

Six months later we bought a Victorian house in Notting Hill, a stone's throw from Portobello Market. I then spent a year flying between New York and London doing what I'm addicted to doing: renovation. I spent fifty-two weeks renovating the house from top to bottom. Finally in August 2011, Alina, George, Alice and I packed all our possessions and moved to England.

Our house on Blenheim Crescent backed onto a communal garden where eight-year-old George and I would play soccer after school, and six-year-old Alice had the freedom to roam unsupervised in the garden's luscious five acres. We enrolled the kids in Notting Hill Prep, a private school ten minutes from the house. Being working class, I should have felt deeply hypocritical sending my kids to private school, but instead it gave me fictitious feelings of having escaped my upbringing.

During my second week in London, I took the underground to Bethnal Green, the working-class district where I'd grown up. I hoped that by immersing myself in the streets and buildings of my youth, I could recognize the boy I was at six and somehow reconcile him with the person I'd now become at sixty.

Emerging from the underground station, I experienced a moment of intense remembering, but that flicker of my remote past was gone in less than a second, and the more I saw of my old neighborhood, the more elusive the past became. It was like watching the development of a photograph in reverse: the moment my boyhood sensations became identifiable was the instant they disappeared.

Fifteen years after arriving in New York, I had written and directed a feature film, *End of the Night*, which revolved around a married man whose life spirals out of control. It was no masterpiece but did contain a sequence that now, in London, seemed relevant. Toward the end of the film, the main character stares at a photograph of himself as a child and slowly cuts it to shreds. I hadn't seen the film in twenty years, but that scene shot through my bones when I returned to Bethnal Green.

4.

After ten days in Charing Cross Hospital, I was told my bed was needed for another patient. It seemed odd that after putting so much effort into saving my life, the doctors made only a cursory attempt to reassemble it. It's hard to imagine how stroke patients without the finances I was lucky to have are able to repair their fragmented lives after leaving the hospital. The fault lies not with the National Health Service but with the British government for underfunding this remarkable institution.

On being discharged, I paid a small fortune to enter a private rehabilitation clinic. The St. John & St. Elizabeth Hospital in affluent West London had the appearance of a plush boutique hotel, with similarly outrageous fees. It served as a stark reminder that in the Western world, health is more often than not a business.

My new surroundings were more polished than those I had left, but comfort was less vital to me than having my own room. When privacy was required at Charing Cross, a nurse had pulled a thin, washed-out curtain around my bed. The relief one feels from closing a door to the outside world is unquantifiable. Especially when the outside world appears as threatening as mine now did.

Unable to sleep more than an hour a night, I was given the sleeping pill Ambien. To the insomniac, there's nothing as exquisite as sleep, and after ten nights of near sleeplessness, taking an Ambien each evening gave me the most blissful feeling. If I had known then that I'd later use this drug to try to end my life, perhaps I would have thought twice about taking it. Or perhaps not.

After ten days of rehabilitation, my right hand, right arm and right leg remained paralyzed. Fortunately, my private parts still functioned, but taking pleasure from this was like totaling a car and performing cartwheels because the windshield wipers still worked. Most humiliating was having to pee into a bottle at night. Unable to use my more dominant hand made this procedure quite complicated, and once or twice I tipped over the bottle. Sleeping the night reeking of urine was one of my less pleasant experiences at St. John's.

Since ninety percent of all improvements occur within the first six months of rehab for most post-stroke patients, the chances of reclaiming my health were dwindling with each passing minute. Aware of time running out, those responsible for the rehab program made it as relentless as boot camp.

Despite the intensity of my sessions, it was still impossible for me to move my right leg. It didn't feel like part of my body. There was no kinship, no connection, and I feared I'd never walk again. A grim prospect at the best of times, but since I was an obsessive hiker, it felt even more horrific. The previous summer I'd walked 115 miles across Devon. The summer before that I'd hiked 185 miles over ten days in the north of England. At St. John's, I couldn't walk one step.

Each day my physical therapist wheeled me to the gym and for several hours encouraged me to put my right foot in front of the other. It felt pointless, like trying to resuscitate someone with no pulse. My leg just wouldn't move. Then, after nearly three weeks of continually practicing the exact same exercise for two hours a day, a miracle occurred—my leg actually *moved*. Over the next hour, with the aid of a cane, I took six steps. I couldn't believe it. I actually walked. My physical therapist burst into tears.

In almost every hospital I've stayed in since my stroke, there's been someone whose kindness has prevented me from falling off the edge. At St. John's it was a male nurse named Abi. Like many exceptional nurses, Abi came from the Philippines. He had a self-effacing manner and an uncanny awareness of my moods. Whenever he sensed I was down, Abi would come and talk to me. Always sympathetic, but without a trace of sentimentality, Abi cared about his patients without making a fuss about caring. Above all, he exuded a quiet moral virtue, which, though hardly part of my own character, is a quality I'm at least able to recognize in others.

Abi once told me that in the Philippines it was normal for most families to care for the sick or disabled. Growing up in a small town, where grandparents were a respected part of the community, Abi had become familiar with the infirmities that accompany aging in ways that many in the West have not. He explained how the benefits of a strong relationship with one's grandparents went both ways. Listening to Abi describe how they helped form his character made me realize what little impact my own grandparents had made on my life, and how perfunctory a role my parents had played in my children's lives. Like many of my generation, this was a result of moving far from home in my twenties. And once away, I stayed away. After talking to Abi, I wished my parents had seen my children more often. If only life were a rehearsal for the real thing.

Although the improvement in my leg wasn't the breakthrough I'd been hoping for, at least it meant that with the aid of a cane I could go to the bathroom at night. My right hand and right arm showed no such improvement. After three weeks of nonstop therapy, my arm was as intractable as when I'd arrived, and, worryingly, my hand even seemed to be getting worse: excessive spasticity was causing it to tighten into a clenched fist.

The clinic's occupational therapist tried to shock my damaged nerves into life by performing bouts of electrical stimulation. Like a Stalinist interrogator, she connected electrodes to my wrist and forearm and shot electrical currents through them. If the stimulator was turned too high, I'd receive the most fearsome shock. Other than that, the currents had no effect.

Demoralized over my lack of improvement, I asked the neurologist at St. John's if he honestly thought I'd ever be able to use my right hand again. If you have to preface a question with the word "honestly," the answer is pretty obvious. He replied that, in all likelihood, I'd never be able to use it again. I thanked him for being straightforward and changed the subject.

Despite my nonchalant response, I found the doctor's news hard to take, not least because I harbored pretenses of being a writer and my unusable hand was the one I wrote with. The next day I began teaching myself to type with my left hand and within a month I was typing slowly but adequately.

This meant that after sixty-five years of being right-handed, I effectively became left-handed.

Before the twentieth century, left-handedness was thought to be an affliction, with many children forced out of the habit. Although statistically, left-handed people are more prone to suffer from dyslexia and psychotic disorders, many of the recent US presidents have been left-handed—including Obama, Clinton, Bush Senior and Reagan. A disproportionately high number of Nobel Prize winners have been left-handed too, and it's widely believed that left-handed people, on the whole, are better problem solvers than their counterparts. Perhaps from having to adapt early on in life to objects designed for right-handed people, left-handed people have a wider scope of learning.

In the unlikely event I take up boxing, one redeeming aspect of being left-handed would be to call myself, with some legitimacy, a southpaw. There's something ruggedly appealing about the word "southpaw."

Three weeks after entering St. John's, I discovered the cause of my stroke. Since I didn't fit the normal profile of a stroke sufferer, neurologists at both Charing Cross and St. John's were unable to work out what triggered it. When a doctor at St. John's mentioned that, on rare occasions, an abrupt jerking of the head could cause a tear in one of the neck's arteries, I remembered a convulsive coughing fit I'd had the day before my stroke.

For years I'd experienced bouts of violent coughing whenever I opened a new restaurant. These episodes struck around the opening and lasted no more than four or five days. Chances are they were a reaction to the pressure I was under at the time. The difference between the fits in the past and the one that probably activated my stroke was that this one was far more savage. It kicked in shortly after I opened the restaurant Augustine in the fall of 2016.

Despite Augustine taking two years to construct and going a million dollars over budget, it ended up being the most dazzling restaurant I've ever built. But achieving this dazzle cost me three million brain cells.

With Augustine up and running, I intended to take a year off from work. A few weeks after the restaurant opened, I flew back to London to be with Alina, George and Alice.

The day after I returned, the four of us drove to the countryside to visit my older brother Peter, who was dying of cancer. Later that morning, I was seized by a vicious coughing attack. After ten minutes it was over. Only it wasn't. Without knowing it, I had torn an artery in my neck.

We spent the rest of the day with Peter, then drove home.

That night I fell asleep in George's bed. I remember lying down and stroking his back and beginning a story about the Second World War before my increasing drowsiness from jet lag steered the tale into complete gibberish. As I lay happily sleeping beside George, a menacing chain of events was unfolding inside my slumbering body that, twenty-four hours later, would change my life forever.

Soon after being admitted to St. John's, I heard about a masseur with unique healing powers. Normally, I wouldn't buy into this sort of drivel, but when you have a serious disability that conventional medicine can't remedy, you become surprisingly vulnerable to any encouraging alternative. At least I did.

Dr. Ali had a beguiling Indian accent that he used to the hilt as he massaged my enfeebled limbs, making seductive assurances that I'd "soon be up kicking a soccer ball." Dr. Ali was a capable masseur, but no miracle worker. He wasn't cheap either. Even so, I succumbed to his flattery and half believed him. That is, until I left the clinic several weeks later in a wheelchair, with no soccer ball in sight.

Against my neurologist's advice, I took a short break from the hospital and spent Christmas that year at home in Notting Hill. My homecoming was a complicated affair, and Alina had worked overtime organizing it: she had rented a hospital bed, an ambulance, two medics, a wheelchair and a steel ramp. She'd also made the living room extraordinarily festive, with bundles of wrapped presents around a Christmas tree adorned with tons of decorations and glowing fairy lights. Despite the embarrassment of entering the house in a wheelchair, I felt quite emotional to be home again, even more so because it was Christmas Eve. It was like a scene from *It's a Wonderful Life*.

That night, Alina, George, Alice and I sat around the fire, eating caviar and blinis and watching one of our favorite films: *The Naked Gun*.

After the children went to bed, Alina and I talked for a while, then awkwardly made love on the rented hospital bed in the living room. It was the first time we'd made love since my stroke. It was followed by an uncomfortable silence.

Lying there by the dying fire, we were probably each wondering what the other was thinking. It was now Christmas Day, and our world was no longer the same.

After twenty minutes, Alina went upstairs for the night. Left there alone, I couldn't sleep. Thoughts of leaving Alina and the children and returning to the hospital left me feeling hopelessly adrift. The last line of the David Bowie song "Space Oddity" kept repeating itself in my mind: "Can you hear me, Major Tom? . . . Can you hear me, Major Tom? . . . Can you . . . ?"

5.

I hate New Year's Eve celebrations. Like most people who can't let go, I'm a coil of contradictions. I love dancing but have never been on a dance floor. I hate exhibitionism yet was once an actor. I dislike parties but organize one every night. However, listening to London's street revelers from my hospital bed during the last hours of 2016, I would have given anything to be part of those festivities.

The new year began badly. Sophie emailed from New York to say she'd met with the Pastis landlord Bobby Cayre and he'd decided not to free me from the lease. This meant that if I didn't build the restaurant, I'd lose my million-dollar guarantee. According to Sophie, Cayre and his partner Jared Epstein had been prepared to let me out, but a third partner would not. This was the first I'd heard of a third partner. When negotiating the lease, I'd dealt exclusively with Cayre and Epstein (whom I found obnoxious); a third partner had never been mentioned. This unnamed person was adamant that I either build Pastis or forfeit my million-dollar guarantee. I couldn't possibly afford to lose a million dollars, yet I was in no condition to build a restaurant.

There's never a good time to have a stroke, but mine came at the very worst time. I had young children and my finances were wobbling. Three of my restaurants were struggling and in the next two years would close, cutting my earnings in half. I'd also recently bought a house in the English countryside that I could not afford. To help pay for the house—and its drastically high renovation costs—I was depending on my latest restaurant, Augustine, succeeding. When a business has to do well to pay off another debt, you know you're in trouble. It's just a pity it took a stroke to make me realize this.

After Sophie's bad news, the only thing that prevented me from hitting rock bottom was the presence of my older son, thirty-two-year-old Harry. After Lynn, Sophie and Isabelle returned to New York, Harry stayed in London and was with me every day of the five weeks I stayed at St. John's. Returning from physical therapy and seeing Harry's backpack hanging on my door was more uplifting than the therapy itself.

Although Harry and I used to be very close, we were less so at the time of my stroke. During my stay at St. John's, that closeness began to return and I'd wake up every morning longing to see him.

One morning, I asked Harry if he'd consider working with me. As he was a photographer and an aspiring filmmaker, the last thing Harry needed was to work in the restaurant business with his father. The fact that he said yes without a moment's hesitation says a lot about Harry. The fact that I didn't fully appreciate it until years later says even more about me.

I taught Harry to play chess at seven years old, and at St. John's we played most evenings—often late into the night. Before my stroke, I'd beat Harry comfortably, but that was no longer the case. At St. John's I lost every game bar one. A chess player's skill is determined by how many moves he or she can think ahead. The damage to the left side of my brain reduced this ability.

Hard as it was accepting a damaged and spiritless body, it was far harder to live with my scrambled speech. My interest in words began early. Being the smallest in my class at school, I used them to defend myself the way my tougher friends used their fists. (Although in my neighborhood, if you dared use a word with more than three syllables, you risked getting a broken nose.) While I hated the phrase "love of language," words were crucial to me and the older I became, the more I judged people by their language and less by their looks and behavior. Not by how "well" they spoke, but by how free of cant and clichés their phrases were. In life and onscreen, I've always been attracted to people as much by their language as anything else. The theater critic Kenneth Tynan famously remarked, "I doubt if I could love anyone who did not wish to see *Look Back in Anger*." I doubt that I could love anyone who uses the phrase "reach out to," or the equally odious "learning curve."

Harry spent hours every day helping me improve my speech, trying to extract the right words from my uncomplying lips. It's hard to convey the frustration you feel when your mouth disobeys your mind's directives. It's like asking a taxi driver to take you to the White House and instead he takes you to Alcatraz. If I had to choose between my voice returning to normal or having full use of my arms and legs, I'd choose my voice.

When Harry was young, we used to go hiking once a year. The first time was in Switzerland when he was six. There's nothing that bonds a father and son like sleeping in a small tent together after a long day's hike. When he was eleven, we joined a hiking group on a five-day trek in Montana's Glacier National Park. Before the hike, the group was required to watch a thirty-minute video on how to respond if confronted by a grizzly bear. I didn't need a thirty-minute video to advise me to run away as fast as fucking possible.

We didn't see a bear on the trip, but we found traces of one, in the form of humongous piles of bear excrement. (It's odd that no matter how unpleasant the idea of stepping into animal dung is, the thought of treading in human excrement is horrific.) At dusk Harry and I would pitch our tent and fall asleep instantly. When Sophie and Isabelle each turned ten, they joined us on the Montana hikes.

Before Montana, I hadn't realized how dignifying walking long distances could be. But although it was magnificent, Montana wasn't as conducive to reflection as hiking in more gentle countryside. The landscape was so breathtaking there was little room for introspection. Given the choice, I'd rather hike in unspectacular countryside than in the Himalayas. A writer friend once told me travel narrows the mind. It took me a long time to understand the meaning of this.

Like many divorced fathers, I spent most of the time I had with my kids in or around sports.

Without any encouragement from me, Harry learned to play ice hockey at twelve years old. After a year of skating lessons and hockey camps, he was good enough to qualify for a prestigious Manhattan team called the Cyclones. Their first match was against a Staten Island team with a reputation for violence—a reputation more than justified, as most of the twelve- and thirteen-year-olds were sons of mobsters.

Seeing these teenage hooligans barreling onto the ice, one of the Cyclones peed himself and the rest of the team froze in terror. They lost badly that day. Luckily, the team's future opponents were all sons of dentists and accountants.

Over the next two years I took Harry to all his games. On Friday nights we'd pack a duffel bag the size of a Buick and at six the next morning drive silently to distant suburbia. The towns had names I'd never heard of—Mamaroneck, Long Beach, Hackensack—and, after Harry quit hockey, would seldom hear of again. On these arctic mornings, traveling to places like Montclair and Paramus, Harry and I forged an intimacy that was incidental to ice hockey. Sadly, this closeness slipped away after he graduated from high school.

Around the same time, I began to feel a distance from Sophie and Isabelle, too, which was probably due to my remarrying and having a second family. After my first divorce I longed to have more children—not least because the custody agreement with Lynn left me feeling superfluous. Although officially I had joint custody, like many single fathers I only saw my children on weekends and half the holidays. My role as a parent was diminished, and I felt like little more than a benchwarmer.

The distance between Harry and me increased further when he decided to drop out of college. I was disappointed, and he knew it. Coming from someone who left school at sixteen, this was the height of hypocrisy. Regrettably, I fit the cliché of many successful working-class fathers who are determined that their children be better educated than they were. I didn't want Harry to end up like me, missing the starter's gun and spending the rest of his life struggling to catch up with the pack. Though I've spent fifty years trying to compensate for this, I sweat bullets every time I'm with a group of people and the conversation turns to college.

A year before my stroke, I was invited to lunch at the house of the English architect Norman Foster, alongside such eminent guests as an ex–poet laureate, two famous writers and a former Australian prime minister. Despite my anxiety at being part of this august group, I managed to hide my lack of formal education by staying silent most of the time and tossing in the occasional clever reference to suggest my reticence came from deep thinking and not ignorance. This "performance" went well until the ex–poet laureate asked me which university I'd attended. In the excruciating silence that followed, I felt like the whole of Harvard was staring at me and I began stuttering. Thankfully, Foster threw me a lifeline by saying that universities were overrated and that he'd left school at sixteen. Whether true or not I never knew, but Foster's sensitivity to my predicament, and courage in hoisting me out of it, was a deed that only someone truly educated could carry off.

While knowing in my bones that real education doesn't spring from having attended university, I also know there's an ineradicable part of me that believes the opposite and, sadly, always will. Whatever their education and wealth, no one fully escapes the class they were born into. I know I haven't.

6.

I was born into a working-class family in the East End of London in 1951. The East End of my childhood was a world away from the gentrified, hip place it's since become. War permeated everything in the fifties. Most men between thirty and forty-five had fought in the Second World War, and most over sixty in the First World War. Former soldiers with peg legs hobbled along unpaved streets, and bomb sites pockmarked the neighborhood. These vivid reminders of the Luftwaffe's attacks on the East End were part of everyone's lives. Oblivious to the danger of unexploded bombs, kids my age found the dirt-filled craters ideal for playing in and far more enjoyable than anything later designed by city planners.

London was in black and white in the fifties, closer to Victorian England than to the pizzazz of the sixties. My East End world was one of street fights, farthings, polio, double features at the cinema and, occasionally, fog so thick you needed a flashlight to see ten feet ahead.

I grew up in Bethnal Green in a one-story house known as a prefab, half a million of which were slapped together in working-class areas after the war to compensate for the country's housing shortage. Though the exterior walls were cast in reinforced concrete, the interior walls were made of a material so thin you could punch a hole through it. But unlike some of my friends' more substantial brick houses, prefabs had bathrooms and indoor toilets. They also had wraparound gardens, which was unusual in the East End. Despite these comforts, we had only one coal fire to heat the whole house. In winter the place turned as cold as Leningrad. When I was young, only the poverty-stricken lived in prefabs. As a teenager, this caused me no end of shame.

My mother hated living in a prefab. But buying a house or flat was out of the question for people of our means. As a result, she would always be in the process of sending long, handwritten letters to the local council requesting a move. She spoke of some mythical "waiting list" she was on, as if reaching the top was like entering the antechamber to heaven. "I'm nearing the top of the list," she would say, like a character from Beckett.

My father, Jack McNally, was born in 1920 and was the youngest of five. His grandparents on his father's side had left Ireland in the mid-nineteenth century. His grandmother on his mother's side was Jewish, which I didn't discover until I was sixty. I thought it had been pure coincidence that in my twenties I'd lived on a kibbutz several times and that many of my close friends were Jewish. (Two of my children later married Jews, with one of them converting to Judaism.)

After leaving school at thirteen, my father took a job in a wine merchant's shop. On weekends he played soccer for a decent London team and showed such promise that, if he hadn't been called up for the Second World War, he might have played professionally. Instead, he was drafted into the Royal Navy at nineteen and spent the entire six years of the war as a stoker, serving a country that, largely, didn't give a toss about its working classes.

Jack was an excellent boxer. One of the few benefits of spending six years at sea was that it gave him a chance to box regularly. He passed on his fighting skills to my two older brothers, Peter and Brian, but not to me. Growing up, my brothers were always getting into fights. Usually with each other. One morning they tore into one another so fiercely my mother couldn't separate them and had to use a neighbor's phone to call my dad, who was at work. He rushed home and beat them unsparingly with his leather belt. I'm not sure whether Peter and Brian's eagerness to fight came from being belted regularly by our dad, but he rarely beat me, and I became such a coward that if you wanted someone to name names at the McCarthy Hearings you'd choose me.

Unless pushed to his limits, my father possessed a gentleness that was rare in a man of his background. Yet until the end of his life, whenever he bumped into an old friend, instead of shaking hands, he'd instantly jump into a boxer's stance and playfully spar. I never saw my dad shake hands. Not once. Nobody from my background ever did. Nor did they talk about being happy or unhappy. Discussing emotions was no more a part of my world than Pontius Pilate.

After being discharged from the navy at the end of the war, my father became a stevedore—a waterfront laborer who loads cargo on and off ships. Unsurprisingly, his favorite film was *On the Waterfront*, starring Marlon Brando.

Around this time Jack met my mother, Joyce Woodroof, who'd grown up on Columbia Road, just a mile away from where he was born. Five months after they met, they got married, on Christmas Day, 1946, at the church of St. John in Bethnal Green. He was twenty-six and she was twenty-two. For the next fifty years they would endure a grim and joyless marriage.

Despite being working class, my mother considered herself a rung above my dad on the social ladder. Her father was a French polisher who came from a two-hundred-year line of such craftsmen, one of whom bore the name Napoleon. French polishing is a wood-finishing technique that involves brushing endless layers of a shellac-like finish patiently onto wooden furniture. This subtle accruing of texture corresponds so closely to my approach to restaurant design that it's not a stretch for me to feel a link with these distant relatives.

Although my mum excelled at school, she was forced to leave at thirteen by a domineering mother intent on her daughter working and contributing to the family's income. My mother read continuously all her life and taught herself to speak Spanish at forty-five. Her interest in books underscored my dad's ignorance in literary matters, and this made for an incompatible marriage.

My father was a strong, persevering man, much like Boxer, the horse in *Animal Farm*, of whom George Orwell writes: "He was not of first-rate intelligence, but he was universally respected for his steadiness of character and tremendous powers of work."

My dad was far from articulate, which my mother only made worse by mentioning every day in front of us children.

Although he had trouble expressing himself, my father was basically a happy man. After nine hours of backbreaking work on the docks, he wasn't hankering for much other than a peaceful life. My mother felt differently. A day of domestic drudgery only intensified her desire for something more stimulating, and not receiving it from my father, she nagged him to death.

One argument stands out. Frustrated by my dad's silence during dinner, she goaded him:

"Well, you're not saying much."

"What d'you mean? I haven't said a bloody word!"

The subsequent row was so ferocious my mother locked herself in the bathroom and threatened to commit suicide. Or "do myself in," as she would say.

Though my parents argued regularly, my mother only threatened to do herself in when there was additional pressure from Christmas or bank holidays. Family weddings were particularly stressful, which is probably why I detest them today.

In hindsight, I realize that for most of her marriage my mother—perhaps like many women of her generation—was chronically depressed. She despised my dad—and his family even more. She thought they were rough and uncouth, and their tendency to settle arguments with their fists intimidated her. Even so, my dad never hit my mother. The idea was unthinkable.

Most of my mother's behavior was dictated by the phrase "what would the neighbors think?" She was paranoid of them knowing our "business," and rarely let my friends into the prefab because she was terrified of them discovering *our business.* It was as if my dad were in the living room secretly constructing a nuclear warhead.

Despite hearing from his friends that he was a competent boxer, I never saw my father hit another man. My mum wasn't remotely violent, but I did see her in a fight one time. I was seven years old, and she'd just dropped me off at school when I suddenly heard her screaming. I quickly turned and saw my mother being struck in the face by a neighbor. She tried to hit the woman back, but the blow didn't connect. They kicked and scratched each other in front of me until a passerby intervened. Witnessing my mother fighting with another woman was so traumatic that I've had a fear of physical violence ever since.

My mother worked most of her life as an early-morning office cleaner. She also shopped, cooked, washed and ironed clothes for our whole family, never taking a day off. How she found time to read her novels and hefty books on history, I've no idea. Nor can I imagine how she managed to learn new languages. Amazingly, after mastering Spanish, she took a stab at German. Of course, she would rather have taken a stab at my dad.

Along with foreign languages, my mother became obsessed with German history. Perhaps this was because her happiest times had been during the war. While German planes were bombing London, my teenage mother was out dancing and flirting with glamorous American soldiers. I believe that to prolong her happiness, she would have paid the Luftwaffe handsomely to continue bombing London.

When I was ten, my mother would tell me stories in confidence about her nights dodging bombs and dancing with attractive GIs. There was one she talked about repeatedly called Stan, who had a Clark Gable mustache. She wondered aloud about Stan's fate, as the last time she saw him he was being shipped off to France as part of the Allied invasion force. At a young age, seeing my mother so happy at recalling these memories brought me a kind of heightened pleasure I've seldom experienced since. It also triggered an interest in storytelling.

Decades later, while visiting me in New York, my mother decided that she and my dad would take a Greyhound bus 1,800 miles to San Antonio, Texas. At the time, this trip mystified me. It was only after they returned from Texas that I understood the reason. Stan was from San Antonio. By visiting his hometown, my mother could breathe the same air that this American GI had once breathed. It was the closest she would ever come again to the soldier with a Clark Gable mustache on whom she'd had a crush forty years earlier. True love cut off at infancy becomes truer every day.

In the summer of 1984, my mother and I took a four-day trip to Berlin. Looking back, it's not the city I remember most but the hotel where we stayed. Due to a mix-up on arrival, we had to share a room with two beds, which I found excruciating. We hadn't slept so close to each other in over thirty years. Turning off the light, I felt intensely self-conscious. Why it feels more intimate talking to someone in the dark, I've no idea, but after the light went out and she started talking, I felt so uncomfortable I pretended to be asleep. I've felt guilty about this ever since.

I'm relieved my mother wasn't around when I had my stroke. The sadness I feel at the thought of my children seeing me in my present condition would be doubled at the idea of my mother seeing me. At her core—perhaps the core of every mother—was the need to alleviate the suffering of her children. For all her faults, she loved me. For her to have seen me in a wheelchair would have been unbearably sad for both of us.

Despite her intelligence, my mother had some unwelcome traits. The worst was her persistent habit of feeling slighted. There was always someone she felt "snubbed" by. And she dealt with it by giving this "ungrateful person" the cold shoulder. For long periods she wouldn't be speaking to her best friend, her sister-in-law, my grandmother, her late brother's wife, our next-door neighbor—the list was endless. There was always somebody gnawing away at her peace of mind, which is a trait I've somewhat inherited, having once gone eight years without speaking to my brother Brian.

I never saw my parents show any affection toward each other. The only time I saw them touch was on holiday when my mother instinctively took my father's hand as he helped her cross a wide puddle. Within seconds she quickly pulled her hand away, as if she'd suddenly remembered he had the bubonic plague.

Aside from her children, the only people my mother truly loved were her father and her brother, Ronnie. Her father died of cancer when she was twenty-six. Ronnie, a modest, soft-spoken man three years her junior, was my mother's only sibling and she doted on him.

At seventeen, Ronnie worked as an air raid warden during the Second World War. One night, while he was standing on the roof of a building on the lookout for enemy planes, two bombs exploded close by, knocking him unconscious and peppering his teenage body with hundreds of glass shards. After two weeks in intensive care, Ronnie began to recover, but the incident had a devastating effect on my mother and was perhaps the beginning of her chronic depression. A year later, Ronnie developed diabetes.

After the war, Ronnie worked as a milkman, often taking his morning break at our prefab. I remember that as he and my mother talked, she would lean in close to him in a way she never did with my dad, suggesting a warmth that was absent in her marriage. Over tea and cream doughnuts, they would talk about their father, whom they adored far more than their mother. When Ronnie later died of a heart attack at thirty-eight, it hit my mother hard. She never recovered and her relationship with my father became unsalvageable.

After fifteen years of nonstop letter-writing to the local council, one of my mother's dispatches broke through enemy lines to get to the top of the pile and we moved to a modern, soulless flat in Hackney, three miles away. Within a month, my mother convinced herself there was a rat living in the kitchen and wrote to the local council requesting another move. The council replied that, as the flat was brand new, a rat in the kitchen was highly unlikely. Knowing my mother had a phobia of vermin, I agreed. Three years later, I saw a rat in the kitchen myself, and not long after that, other tenants reported seeing rats in their flats. It turned out my mother had been right all along.

At seventy-two, my mother divorced my father. By coincidence or not, this happened at the same time she finally found a flat she was comfortable in, which was three blocks from the prefab where we had all grown up. No longer living under the same roof as the man she detested, she found a measure of contentment that brought her compulsive letter-writing to a close.

In 1998, my mother died. She was seventy-four. Although she rarely drank, the cause was cirrhosis of the liver. She spent the last two weeks of her life in the austere public ward of the London Hospital. I was in England at the time, staying at a friend's with my nine-year-old daughter, Isabelle. Dutifully, I visited my mother for an hour every day. At the entrance to her Gothic-style hospital, my most pressing thought was how to show affection to my mother without kissing her. I hadn't kissed either of my parents since I was ten and, I regret to say, it remained that way until they died.

Early one morning I received a phone call from the hospital to say my mother had passed away. The caller, no doubt trained to deliver bad news sensitively, ran through the same rehearsed script she must have recited to thousands of strangers. The first thing that came to my mind were the opening words of Albert Camus's *The Stranger*, "Mother died today" . . . and the realization that this was the only day of my life when I could say these words legitimately. Before my stroke, I did everything to keep genuine emotion away, and substituting a fictitious death for a real one was my way of avoiding the discomfort of grief. I rarely lived in the present. I felt I had only the anticipation of an event or its memory. I'd often repeated Camus's words "Mother died today" in jest, subconsciously numbing myself for the day when it would really happen. And it worked. The day my mother died, I didn't feel a thing.

In 2002, four years after my mother died, I invited my dad to come and live with me in Greenwich Village. Emigrating to New York at eighty-two seemed to invigorate him. Being something of a Dickensian character, my dad made friends easily. He'd visit my restaurants each morning, and I'd often find him sitting in the dining room having coffee with one of the managers. This irritated me because my managers were supposed to be working in the morning, not sitting down with my dad enjoying a coffee together. I'd give anything to see this now.

Having worked all his life, my dad found it difficult not having a job in New York. He asked me to try to find him one. When I mentioned needing someone to separate garbage in the basement of Balthazar, he jumped at the idea. Although the job pleased him, I must say it felt a little odd for me to be hobnobbing upstairs with fancy customers in Balthazar's dining room while my dad was slaving away in the basement below. I wondered what my mother would have made of it. She probably would have thought that was where he belonged.

My dad loved watching films. One rainy afternoon he went to see *Brokeback Mountain*, expecting a traditional Western, and was shocked out of his mind watching two cowboys French-kissing.

Apart from boxing and football, the only other sport my dad enjoyed was horse racing. Once in New York, he'd often spend the mornings with his eyes glued to a newspaper, scrutinizing the racing form as though studying for a Cambridge entrance exam. With his cramming done, he'd nip down to the local OTB stand and place a chunk of his life savings on a horse. Invariably, it lost. He would have had more luck picking his horses blindfolded.

In 2003 I took my dad to see the famous Breeders' Cup horse race in Los Angeles. We first flew to San Francisco to visit my son Harry, who was at university there. (Hopefully not studying the form of racehorses.) My dad adored his nine grandchildren, and Harry was no exception. He lavished affection on him in the way grandparents who have difficulty expressing love to their own children do. I often think parents empty all their neuroses onto their own kids, allowing them the luxury of a complication-free relationship with their grandchildren. That was certainly the case with my dad and Harry, and I was envious.

On leaving Harry, I rented a Mustang convertible and my dad and I headed onto Highway 1 for the four-hundred-mile drive to Los Angeles. Although we didn't talk much on the way, I believe the journey's unforced silences brought us a little closer. Five years later, he died.

At eighty-eight, my dad had lived longer than anyone else in our family. Unlike my mother—and me—he didn't regret a thing about his life. I was glad he'd gotten to know his grandchildren and was able to spend summers on Martha's Vineyard with them and Alina. Even so, I hadn't always enjoyed his presence on the Vineyard and am painfully aware of how churlishly I occasionally behaved toward him. Unfortunately, I could never see my dad happy without being conscious of how angry this would have made my mother. She never understood why most people preferred his company to hers when clearly she was the more expressive and the cleverer of the two. The truth was, he was simply easier to be with. Perhaps, growing up with low expectations, my father felt he had more than fulfilled his potential, whereas my mother, starting out with greater expectations, never came close to realizing hers. Her prospects had been stymied by the two people she disliked most: her mother and my father. I wish I had done more for her. A lot more.

When somebody close to you dies, there's always regret at not having spent more time with them. With my mother, I felt the additional guilt at having spent more time with my father than with her. I find this hard to understand now, as I was much closer emotionally to my mother. I could also talk to her about history and current affairs, which my dad didn't have a clue about. But no matter how interesting she was to talk to, my mother felt compelled to step out of the conversation periodically in order to malign my father. She just couldn't stop herself. In an effort to alienate her four children from him, she drummed into us how inarticulate our father was and I grew up bitterly aware how difficult my dad found it to express himself.

Ironically, since my stroke, I now have trouble expressing myself, and my inarticulacy is far worse than my dad's ever was. I often wonder if my children feel the same way about their dad as I did about mine. It seems the dog has returned to bite me.

7.

Although psychologists bang on about the effect parents have on children, they rarely mention the impact that siblings have. Much of my behavior has its roots in my relationship with my two older brothers. And not necessarily for the better.

Peter was four years older than me. Brian three. I have a sister, too: Josephine, who's eight years younger than me. Peter, Brian and I attended the same elementary and high school and, like most kids in our neighborhood, we each left school at sixteen. Going to the same school as my two older brothers, whom I feared as much as I admired, left its mark, and growing up in their shadow prompted me to form a very close relationship with Josephine.

I remember bumping into Peter at an open-air swimming pool when I was nine and, perhaps as a substitute for hugging me, he grabbed my head and forced it under the water. It lasted less than seven seconds but felt like an eternity. From then on I was scared to death of running into either of my brothers outside the house.

One day Brian decided to play truant and asked me to lie to our parents and say I'd seen him at school. That evening, sensing Brian hadn't been to school, my parents asked me if I'd seen him that day. Fearful of a beating from my brother, I lied and said I had, on the school playground. Having set me up, Brian then sold me down the river: "He's lying! He didn't see me! He couldn't have. I was at a school cricket match all day!" When I blurted out that Brian had forced me to lie, he looked daggers at me and mouthed: "Just wait until we're alone." I don't remember if he hit me later, but living under the threat of violence is often more damaging than the violence itself. It's not only your mum and dad who fuck you up.

Brian often clashed with our mother, adored our father and received the best genes from both. Like our mother, he was an obsessive reader; until his early twenties, he was also an aggressive street fighter. He was a talented footballer and cricketer as well. He was our dad's favorite. Peter had less charm than Brian but more integrity and was closer to my mother and often at odds with my father. Peter was slightly out of step with the world.

Having tough brothers did have its occasional benefits and certainly gave me a degree of protection at school. Since I was small for my age, I was a target for older boys. In my first week, I remember standing on the playground eating an ice cream when a cocky older kid called Samways ripped it from my hand and threw it to the ground.

"You know whose brother that is?" his friend said.

"No, and I don't care either," Samways replied.

But when his friend said, "McNally," Samways bolted to the ice cream van parked outside the school and came back with a new one for me.

Although closer to my two brothers in age, I was more like my sister in temperament. Josephine and I were devoted to each other and, despite our age difference, spent as much time together as possible. Perhaps we were exceptionally close because we both felt somewhat isolated within our family. But like many of my intimate relationships, our closeness would be undermined by my moving away. When I moved to New York at twenty-four, Peter and Brian were already living abroad, and Josephine, at sixteen, was left alone in London with parents she felt little connection to. She would never forgive me for the sense of abandonment she felt and we hardly spoke over the next thirty years.

When I was a child, it was compulsory in England for all eleven-year-olds to take a daunting exam called the eleven-plus. Even today, the two words still make me shudder. Unlike my brothers, I had barely read a book outside the classroom, but after just about passing this test, I joined them at a school for "clever" boys called Coopers' Company. This academic grammar school was the pride of my working-class neighborhood.

Despite being small for my age, it didn't bother me until the second year at Coopers', when during communal showers after gym class, I noticed that, unlike me, most of my classmates had pubic hair. I was mortified. Embarrassed to be seen naked, I began devising countless ways to avoid taking my weekly after-gym shower. If I'd put as much effort into my schoolwork as I did into not being seen naked, I could have gone to Oxford. As it was, out of this elaborate process of avoiding detection, another ability was hatched: a knack for leading two lives.

When not evading showers, I discovered I was quite good at English, which was lucky since I was a disaster in all other subjects, none more so than physics. My interest in English was entirely due to one teacher: Paul Williams, nicknamed "Bill" Williams by his pupils.

The charismatic Mr. Williams was strict and precise and, much to the thrill of the boys, often tossed in the word "fuck" when discussing Shakespeare. This had the twofold effect of making us pay instant attention while shooting down the halo above the word "literature."

Without soft-pedaling the rigors of language or making too much of the playwright's humor (which he didn't care for), Mr. Williams taught us not to be intimidated by Shakespeare, prefacing his introduction to the Bard—a term he hated—by claiming it would be "fucking hard work but . . . if you stick with it, it'll be worth it." We stuck with it because we enjoyed the swearing, plus the fact that Williams never shied away from explaining Shakespeare's sexual innuendos.

Williams came down hard on boys who tried to impress him, particularly those who used unnecessarily long words. He hated clichés and pretension, and once slapped a boy twice on the back of the head for boasting that he was an avid reader. Twice slapped, because Williams saw two evils in the phrase "avid reader"—it was both pretentious and a cliché.

At fifteen, I wrote an essay, mostly plagiarized from my brother Brian, on the disadvantages of growing up working class. Williams liked it enough to send it to the director of a BBC radio arts program, who suggested I come to the studio and read it on the air. I arrived at the BBC on a school day and was less nervous about reading into a microphone than elated at missing double physics. My first two readings were cut short and dismissed. I knew my third reading was acceptable because Herr Director allowed me to finish it. At this point, the arts were like a foreign language to me. I had no idea that a year from this recording I'd be fully immersed in them.

My "speech" aired the following month, but I didn't listen to it. I was too embarrassed. At fifteen, my voice still hadn't broken and was about sixty octaves higher than those of all my friends. Forty years later, Mr. Williams sent me a tape of the recording. Hearing my fifteen-year-old self speak was so unsettling that halfway through I couldn't take any more and had to stop it. This had nothing to do with the content of the essay or my high voice; I was disturbed because I didn't recognize the person talking.

One night, five years after leaving school in 1967, I bumped into Mr. Williams at an Old Vic production of *Long Day's Journey into Night* starring Laurence Olivier. My old English teacher was there with another man, his lifelong partner, Bertie. Although it wasn't a shock to discover that Mr. Williams was gay, his choice of companion surprised me. Then again, I'm often surprised—and invariably disappointed—by the partners of people I admire. (Aren't most people?)

Bertie was a small man with a name that spoke volumes. I've never understood why an adult whose youth is long gone continues to use the diminutive form of their first name, such as Mikey or Kimmy. Regrettably, Bertie compounded the offense by being physically diminutive himself. He was just millimeters over five feet. As if to compensate, he used excessively long words, pronounced with such affectation that he would have gotten a terrific slap on the head in Mr. Williams's class in 1964. But Williams seemed besotted with his partner and charmingly unaware of any pretentiousness—proof that loving someone makes us blind to habits and language we would find insufferable in other people. As Guy de Maupassant wrote in *Bel-Ami* (one of my favorite novels), "Loving words, which are always the same, take their flavor from the lips by which they are uttered."

I left school at sixteen with just one O level—the barest minimum of qualifications—and took a job as a bellhop at London's Hilton Hotel on Park Lane. On my second day, I was asked to escort Marlon Brando to his room. Like most movie stars, Brando was shorter in person than on the screen. He had a boxer's broad shoulders and a surprisingly high, nasal voice. In the elevator, he asked me what I intended to do with my life. I had no idea and said as much. (I still have no idea.)

In the hotel's ballroom one night, I watched the Beatles listen to a lecture given by the guru Maharishi Mahesh Yogi. This was August 1967, two months after they'd released the *Sgt. Pepper's* album. Ringo was missing but John, Paul and George sat in the third row, looking spellbound as the Maharishi talked about "raising the consciousness of man." Soon afterward the Beatles visited the Maharishi at his retreat in India, where they discovered that instead of raising the consciousness of man, he was having sex with many of the women in their entourage. Perhaps for the Maharishi, it was the same thing.

In my third month at the hotel, an American guest who was a producer asked me to try out for a role in his film. I hadn't a clue what "trying out" meant, but prayed to God it didn't involve taking off my clothes. Thankfully, it just meant reading a script aloud. Which I did and was immediately offered the role.

A month later, I was being chauffeured to the film studio. My working-class neighbors had never seen a limousine before, and many stood on their doorsteps in awe as the black Bentley purred to a stop outside my home in Bethnal Green. Making my way from the prefab to the limousine, I felt on top of the world, but realizing I had a small audience of neighbors watching me, I quickly feigned modesty in front of them. I've been feigning modesty ever since.

I spent three days filming *Mr. Dickens of London* at London's Pinewood Studios, in which I was cast as a street urchin befriended by Dickens, who was played by Sir Michael Redgrave.

Having enjoyed this dip in theatrical waters, I left the Hilton to pursue a career as a boy actor. I was sixteen, but looked all of twelve. After two months of unemployment, I read about an open call for the relatively large role of John Darling, Wendy's older brother, in a production of *Peter Pan*. The play was set to tour the eight dullest cities in the Midlands, the cream of which were Hull, Birmingham and Wolverhampton. I passed the audition and we rehearsed the play for three weeks. Our first night was in Hull, which in February 1968 felt as far from London's Swinging Sixties as Gdańsk.

My digs in Hull consisted of a damp, dreary room with discolored wallpaper curling at the edges. To fend off the miserable cold, there was a small gas heater on the floor, operated by a coin meter placed illogically close to the ceiling. I was obliged to stand on a chair and feed it a shilling every four hours.

The boardinghouse was run by a landlady who was fiercely protective of Hull's resistance to London's sexual revolution. Around midnight, she'd prowl the hallways in search of its evidence in her tenants' bedrooms. I often heard her rapping on the doors, asking, "Have you got anybody in there? I thought I heard a woman. Are you sure?" Even if you'd been bold enough to smuggle a woman into your room, the beds were so aggressively narrow that even Flat Stanley himself would have had trouble fucking in them.

As if living in the Midlands for two months wasn't misery enough, I was made to feel even worse when the seven teenage actors playing the Lost Boys initiated a campaign to blackball me. Unlike them, I hadn't attended drama school, and they saw me as an interloper who'd entered the acting profession illegitimately. As a result, they ostracized me for the length of the tour, which meant I had a very unpleasant eight weeks. Despite this, I was determined to look for more acting roles when *Peter Pan* ended.

Once back in London, I began searching for a theatrical agent to represent me. With my limited experience, the only agency willing to take me on had the curious name of Plant & Froggatt, giving the impression they represented botanists rather than actors. After signing up to their cringe-inducing motto "See and be seen by as many people as possible," I went on scores of auditions, many of which were for parts I was way too young for, including a role in Stanley Kubrick's *A Clockwork Orange*. In front of Kubrick and Malcolm McDowell, I gave a choirboy's reading for the role of a psychopathic thug. The moment I began, I saw Kubrick roll his eyes. I wanted to bang my head against the nearest wall.

Two weeks after the disastrous audition, I landed the role of Ronnie Winslow, the fourteen-year-old hero in Terence Rattigan's *The Winslow Boy*. This 1940s play about a young cadet expelled from naval college for a theft he didn't commit was being restaged in York by its repertory company. Traveling the two hundred miles north by train, I began reading the play for the first time. To my horror, I discovered the role was immense. After getting through the first half, I turned each page tentatively, praying that Winslow's name wouldn't appear again. Another actor would have been thrilled by the size of the role, but I was sixteen, inexperienced and terrified.

Arriving at the theater alone, I received an affectionate welcome from the play's director and cast. Although the first day of rehearsals can feel like arriving in a foreign city blindfolded, there's nothing more satisfying than when the blindfold comes off and the unknown becomes navigable. The satisfaction, however, is tempered by the anxiety one feels in the lead-up to opening night. As *The Winslow Boy* edged closer to its first performance, rehearsals went on late into the night, emotions heightened and friendships intensified. It was a blissful period, and one never to be repeated once the play opened.

I spent ten weeks in York. My performance received good reviews, although it's hard not to shine when you're playing a boy unjustly accused of a crime. It didn't surprise me that no one from my family came, but I was annoyed that none of them asked me anything about my experience. After all, I was sixteen and playing the lead in a prestigious play. I think my parents and brothers were embarrassed by my being an actor.

In those days, people from my background associated the theater with homosexuality. In this case, they would have been right, because during my time in York I had an affair with a male cast member. The experience reinforced my feelings of living in two worlds.

When the run ended, I was sad to leave the other actors. As a repertory company, it had only so many plays with parts for young boys. But my next show, in London's West End, would have roles for twenty boys.

Forty Years On was written by English playwright Alan Bennett. The play would run for a year at the Apollo Theatre on Shaftesbury Avenue and starred theater legend Sir John Gielgud, with Bennett himself playing the second lead.

The first day of rehearsals was at the Drury Lane Theatre on a hot August bank holiday in 1968. I'd recently turned seventeen and was still living with my parents. I took the Tube from Bethnal Green to Holborn and walked through the deserted streets of Covent Garden to the theater. Feeling apprehensive, I had no idea that the twelve months I'd spend in *Forty Years On* would shape the rest of my life.

The play was set in a British public school—a private school, that is—and my minor character was a public schoolboy. I'd impersonated middle-class characters in other roles and was comfortable playing someone whose diction and pronunciation were way different from mine. The longer I worked in this middle-class profession, in which I seemed to play mostly public schoolboys, the more I absorbed the manner of speaking of those around me. Over time, I unintentionally lost my working-class accent. There are many times when I wish I hadn't.

When I broke the news to my mother that I was about to work alongside Sir John Gielgud, she became hysterical and cried out: "But John Gielgud's a homosexual!" It was only a year after homosexuality had been decriminalized in England. It still seems incredible that until 1967 it was unlawful and "an act of gross indecency" to have sex with someone of the same gender.

The fictitious school in *Forty Years On* was staging an end-of-term play for the boys' parents. In one scene, my character is seen being put to bed by his nanny, played by an imperious stage actress called Dorothy Reynolds.

On the third day of rehearsals, the director asked me to take off my shoes to do the scene more realistically. In doing so, I revealed enormous holes in my socks. Reynolds winced and the other actors laughed. My two worlds had collided. Angry and ashamed, I cursed my working-class parents.

Underneath her lordly presence, Reynolds had a sensitive heart. Without saying a word, she came over to me and put her hand on my shoulder. That small gesture taught me a lot.

Forty Years On opened in October 1968 and, despite my embarrassing socks, received enthusiastic reviews and ran for just over a year.

Back then, actors performing in a West End theater could attend matinee performances of other plays for free; this policy also extended to West End cinemas. Having my days free until 5 p.m., I took full advantage and saw a different film almost every day for the entire run of *Forty Years On*, including practically every film made before 1969 by Truffaut, Godard, Antonioni, Pasolini and Bergman.

The foreign film I liked most that year was Claude Chabrol's *Les Biches*. As I was a relatively innocent seventeen-year-old, this worldly French film with trysts, lesbians and betrayals satisfied all my sexual and artistic longings in one shebang. (I saw *Les Biches* again recently and winced at its pretentious dialogue.)

The year I spent onstage in the West End—October 1968 to October 1969—turned into a momentous one for the world. Nixon became president. Neil Armstrong walked on the moon. Sirhan Sirhan was convicted of killing Robert Kennedy and James Earl Ray pleaded guilty to assassinating Martin Luther King Jr. New York's Stonewall riots triggered the gay rights movement. Chappaquiddick, Woodstock, anti-Vietnam rallies and the Manson murders all occurred during those frantic twelve months. However, I was so caught up in my own minuscule world of films and plays that I regret to say not one of these pivotal events had a shred of impact on me.

That same year I went alone to London's Old Vic and paid five shillings to sit in the gods (the nosebleeds) to watch Tom Stoppard's dazzling

Rosencrantz and Guildenstern Are Dead. Although I barely understood a word, I still enjoyed it and was quite aware that it was a groundbreaking play. What I didn't know was that some forty years later I'd become friends with Stoppard. When Alina and I moved to London in 2011, we saw Tom and his wife, Sabrina, often, and occasionally the four of us would go to the theater. I don't claim to know him well, but Stoppard has an uncanny ability to make those around him feel smarter than they are—me especially. In the summer of 2012, Tom and Sabrina invited me to see Shakespeare's rarely performed tragedy *Timon of Athens* at the National Theatre, along with David Hare and his wife, Nicole Farhi. As the curtain rose, I couldn't believe I was in a London theater seated between Tom Stoppard and David Hare, two of the most brilliant playwrights of the past half century.

In the first few months after my stroke, Stoppard took the extraordinary step of sending me detailed accounts of plays he'd recently seen. It's a reflection of his greatness that he always wrote more graciously about the plays he didn't like than those he did. He's one of the two kindest and most sensational playwrights I've ever known. (The other is Euripides.)

I've seen most of Stoppard's plays and found them remarkable. All but one, that is. I saw *The Hard Problem* the week it opened in 2016 but didn't enjoy it. By coincidence—a theme of the play—I bumped into Stoppard two days later and we got round to discussing it. I wriggled out of admitting that I hadn't liked it by saying I hadn't understood it. Tom was so alarmed that I hadn't understood *The Hard Problem* that he gave me an even harder problem by offering me a free ticket to see it again that very night. I ended up seeing the only Tom Stoppard play I didn't like twice in three nights. As usual, by not being straightforward, I'd twisted myself in knots.

8.

I've had two homosexual relationships in my life. The first was with an actor when I was sixteen. The second and more serious one was with English playwright Alan Bennett.

Although Alan and I became friends when sharing the stage in his play *Forty Years On*, it wasn't until after the play ended that our relationship developed into something else.

Forty Years On ran at the Apollo Theatre in London's West End for just over a year. Several weeks after it closed, Alan invited me to go to the theater with him. I don't remember the play's name, but once it was over, he invited me back to his house in Camden Town for supper. After eating lightly and talking about the play, Alan drove me home. At the time I was living with my parents in Hackney.

The following week, we did the same: theater, supper at Alan's house and then the long drive back to Hackney. We fell effortlessly into a weekly routine, which I very much enjoyed.

Supper was always simple: a light salad and a chunk of pâté or cold chicken that Alan had roasted before the theater. During the meal, we'd talk about that night's play, but to avoid getting serious too quickly, Alan would preface his thoughts on the play by gossiping about the actors. He was quite funny about short actors, with Edward Fox often his main target.

When discussing a play, Alan was always careful to keep one foot in the shallow end. If he felt he was veering toward the academic, he'd quickly make fun of himself. I didn't contribute much to a play's assessment, but what little I did add—and considering my ignorance, I'm surprised I added anything at all—was always listened to without interruption.

When Alan took me home to Hackney, I always asked to be let out several blocks from my parents' flat. At this point our relationship was purely platonic, but I was fully aware of what my family and friends would think. There was only one thing they would think. I was eighteen and the playwright was thirty-five and unmarried. I kept my friendship with Alan completely secret.

Six weeks after our theatergoing routine began, Alan drove me to see a small Anglican church in the countryside. On our return, we stopped the car at a rest stop to eat sandwiches and drink tea from a flask. It was a dreary day and Alan seemed unusually melancholy. It was then that I sensed he was in love with me. Not long after that, I stayed the night at his house.

Sleeping with Alan felt like a natural progression of our friendship. It was uncomplicated, and I never once felt guilty about it. After that first night, I'd stay over two or three times a week. While I loved Alan, the attraction was never physical, and our nights together were more intimate than passionate. Soon after our relationship began, Alan told me that before meeting me he'd never slept with someone he was in love with.

Over the next nine months, Alan and I would go to the theater at least once a week seeing every stripe of play—from experimental to Shakespeare. Even regarding plays he didn't care for, Alan always discovered something of merit. The only plays he had no time for were those that lectured the audience or did nothing but confirm their beliefs.

My relationship with Alan enriched my life in ways I find hard to explain. I can't imagine how my life would have turned out without it. I suppose many people feel this way about one specific person. I think those who don't have something inherently missing from their lives.

One of the things I most admired about Alan was his instinct to distrust the gratification he received when proven right. He was highly suspicious of certainty. (Turning down a knighthood in the eighties, he would even question the glimmer of pleasure he felt by refusing it.) Alan was the only man I've known who gained no satisfaction from being in the right.

Alan's Camden Town house was on Gloucester Crescent, an attractive, tree-lined street that in the late sixties and early seventies became a haven for London's intelligentsia, one of whom was his close friend, the theater director Jonathan Miller. I loved the house and even had a minuscule hand in its renovation. Two weeks after *Forty Years On* opened, Alan invited several of us from the play to help scrape off years of paint from a plaster frieze. When I saw the house a year later, I was shocked by its transformation, mainly the walls of Alan's sitting room. He had stripped them of decades of wallpaper, then rubbed a mix of colored waxes and paints onto the hundred-year-old plaster until it turned an extraordinary deep mustard color. (The same color I've been trying—mostly unsuccessfully—to reproduce on my restaurants' walls for almost fifty years.) Hanging salon-style on his sitting room walls were about thirty twentieth-century paintings, including some by Vanessa Bell, Roger Fry, John Minton and Robert MacBryde. I'd never been to an art gallery in my life, so the names meant nothing to me. In fact, a few of the unadorned frames meant more to me than the artworks. (Even today I often prefer the frame to the picture.)

Alan sparked my interest in paintings by talking about them in the same way he did books and plays: modestly and unassumingly, with an opinion tacked on almost as an afterthought. Although he was an established writer and I was a fairly uneducated teenager, Alan never consciously tried to educate me. Whatever interests I developed from our friendship—and there were many—were absorbed by me more than imparted by Alan. In all the time I knew Alan, he never once recommended a book to me.

When we first started going to the theater, Alan was writing his sec-

ond play, *Getting On*, and when we'd return to his house, he'd immediately pull the half-finished—and half-frozen—manuscript from the
fridge, where he'd cleverly hidden it from potential thieves. His eight
years at Oxford hadn't been *entirely* wasted.

Getting On was the first of Alan's various plays in which there's a
minor character loosely based on me.

Keeping my liaison with Alan from my family and friends didn't require much effort. The five years spent desperately avoiding my school's
communal showers had prepared me well for this kind of deception. It's
been said that in the 1950s, when homosexuality was illegal in England,
homosexuals often made the best spies because they were conditioned to
leading double lives. I'm sure I took so readily to my own double life as
a result of having to conceal my embarrassment in the school showers as
a late-developing thirteen-year-old.

The early seventies was an exceptionally fertile period in the English
theater. Alan regularly took me to the Royal Court to see new plays by
John Osborne, David Storey, Edward Bond and Christopher Hampton.
The National Theatre was then at the Old Vic, with Laurence Olivier
as its artistic director and Alan's friend Jonathan Miller its associate director. I saw most of Miller's productions, including *Danton's Death*, *The
School for Scandal* and *The Merchant of Venice*. Though the majority flew
over my head, the brilliance of Miller's staging did not. His production of
The Merchant of Venice with Olivier as Shylock was a revelation. Setting
the play in the late nineteenth century, Miller persuaded Olivier to play
Shylock not as the Fagin-like "stage Jew" but as a greed-driven businessman who just happens to be Jewish. It was a brilliant interpretation.

I first met Miller in the fall of 1968, just after *Forty Years On* opened.
I was at Alan's house with two other boys, scraping the paint from
the living room walls, when Miller, an intellectual of vast learning,
walked in and casually announced, "I'd *really* love to fuck Judi Dench."
Though pure bravado, it was—and still is—the best introduction I've
ever heard.

Once I began staying over at Alan's, I got to know Jonathan Miller and his wife, Rachel, well. I regularly ate dinner at their house opposite, usually with Alan but also on my own. Rachel was a terrific cook—the type who's able to improvise a great meal out of leftovers in the fridge. I got to be as fond of her as I was of Jonathan. Though they knew about my relationship with Alan, we never talked about it openly.

Miller was a true polymath—a doctor of medicine, a theater and opera director, and a documentary filmmaker. He was the most articulate man I've ever known. With Peter Cook, Dudley Moore and Alan Bennett, he'd written and starred in the satirical review *Beyond the Fringe*, which opened in London in 1961 and on Broadway the following year. Today, it's hard to grasp the impact that this antiestablishment show made on England in the sixties. It was the first time anyone dared ridicule the royal family and the British government. It was also the forerunner to *Monty Python's Flying Circus*.

Visiting Jonathan's and Alan's houses at eighteen, I was struck by how different they were from the prefab where I had grown up. No floors laid with cheap linoleum, no freezing-cold bedrooms, no outdoor coal shed. These houses had heating in every room, paintings on the walls and hundreds of books on the shelves. I returned to my family's flat in Hackney more aware than ever how common and uneducated my parents were, and I have to admit I resented them for it.

Bennett's and Miller's houses had a Bloomsbury feel, with unaffected interiors and predominantly twentieth-century paintings on the walls. I'd never seen wooden Venetian blinds before, but both had them installed in every window. I was riveted by them (and still am).

Bennett had the more interesting paintings, Miller the more interesting sculptures. When seen close-up, these "sculptures" were often everyday objects. Miller had such a unique eye he was able to extract the extraordinary from the commonplace. On a trip to Florence to look at Renaissance art, Miller was more interested in junk shops than in the Uffizi. In one, he bought a rusting padlock for less than a dollar. What looked like corroding garbage in a Florentine junk shop was transformed into an oxidized gem when displayed in his London study. It was this attentiveness to the apparently negligible that made Miller a remarkable theater director.

Paradoxically, Miller seldom went to the opera or theater himself. He preferred art galleries, he said, because his plays and operas were based on people's unconscious behavior: the tapping of a pencil, the scratching of an ear, a grieving mother's twisting of her hair. Through studying classical paintings—and his training as a doctor—Miller had learned that involuntary action could often be more revealing than calculated action.

Miller occasionally asked me to join him on visits to London's National Gallery. Looking at paintings with him was like watching films with Orson Welles. Miller's witty and strikingly perceptive explanations breathed such dynamism into five-hundred-year-old artworks that they'd burst into life. It was astonishing the way he could draw links between two seemingly disparate subjects. Listening to Miller talk about paintings gave me the confidence to visit art galleries without feeling like a trespasser.

I appreciated Miller taking me under his wing, but there was occasionally turbulence on the journey. He loved Dickens and regularly encouraged me to read his books. Desperate to please, I secretly read all of Dickens's novels over one summer—all except one: *Bleak House*. Boasting of my achievement, I found myself quickly cut down to size: "What?" said Miller. "You didn't read *Bleak House*? But that's the best one!" Another time, on his suggestion, I combed Tuscany for paintings by Piero della Francesca but apparently missed one, as I discovered on returning to London, when I received the same admonition: "What? You didn't see the *Madonna del Parto*? But this is the most interesting Piero della Francesca in the world!"

For all his brilliance, Miller could be infuriating, but it was worth it. The man was a genius.

While Miller was at the height of his success in the seventies, Bennett—thanks to a rough period during the rehearsals of his play *Getting On*—was at his lowest. The lead, Kenneth More, didn't fully understand his character and, in Alan's eyes, was ruining things by overacting. Alan wanted less from More. Before long, More wanted less from Alan, and banned him from the theater. Being prevented from attending rehearsals of his own play brought Alan close to a breakdown. One night, the cast gathered at his house to discuss the crisis, among them a young and slender Brian Cox, who, forty-five years later, would become best known for playing Logan Roy in HBO's *Succession.*

Alan's suffering increased as Jonathan's success grew. The two of them had a complicated relationship. As well as having vastly different personalities—one was a great talker, the other a great listener—they were close friends at the top of British theater who happened to live opposite each other. While Alan was shy and spoke only after careful consideration, Jonathan was confident and assertive, a linguistic genius whose phrases appeared fully formed without effort. Alan often told me he never mentioned to Jonathan the subject of any play he was working on for fear the polymath would know more about the topic than he did. However, he did take Miller's suggestion to write a play about King George III's illness. The astonishing *The Madness of King George* would be one of Alan's most successful plays and be made into an equally successful film starring Helen Mirren.

The happiest times I saw Alan and Jonathan enjoy together were in Miller's kitchen, both hysterical with laughter from something the other had said. There were also prolonged periods when Alan couldn't come to terms with Jonathan's brilliance, or with the success that appeared to come so easily to him. The time of the rehearsals for *Getting On* was the worst of these episodes.

Given how often Alan was irritated by Jonathan, I find it hard to understand why for thirty years he lived across the road from him. It was either the ease with which he could show up unannounced for meals, selflessly provided by Rachel, or perhaps it's related to the old Woody Allen joke: "You know, this guy goes into a psychiatrist's office and says, 'Doc, my brother's crazy! He thinks he's a chicken.' And the doctor says, 'Why don't you turn him in?' And the guy says, 'I would, but I need the eggs.'"

Reputations are fickle. In the sixties, seventies and eighties, Miller's reputation was much greater than Bennett's. Today, it's the reverse. Plays and books have the potential to thrive after the writer dies. The theater director's productions have no such luck. Who now remembers the director of John Osborne's *Look Back in Anger* or the director of Arthur Miller's *Death of a Salesman*? After a director dies, his or her specific staging can never be seen live again. After a writer dies, his or her books can be reread and plays restaged.

It seems unjust, but Miller's standing is likely to diminish because his extraordinary staging cannot be reproduced. His spellbinding creations have vanished into thin air. However, their impact on people fortunate enough to have experienced them has not. Especially not on me.

9.

Eight months after my relationship with Alan began, I read Hermann Hesse's *Siddhartha*. This 1922 novel takes place in ancient India and follows the life of a young Brahmin, Siddhartha, and his odyssey to distant lands in search of spiritual enlightenment. I was so mesmerized by the book that two months after reading it, I left home to take a long journey myself: I hitchhiked five thousand miles from London to Kathmandu. But my journey was more in search of moral insight than anything as lofty-sounding as spiritual enlightenment.

However, there was another reason for taking this long trip. Although I was still very close to Alan, I no longer wanted to continue a physical relationship with him. His feelings had become much stronger than mine and I felt overwhelmed—almost suffocated—by them. Having long identified with W. H. Auden's words "If equal affection cannot be, let the more loving one be me," it had made my relationship with Alan—and many future relationships—difficult to sustain.

I paid for my trip to Nepal with money I'd earned starring in a television play called *Twenty-Six Efforts at Pornography*. This sixty-minute drama was based on the relationship between an aging teacher and a free-spirited pupil who'd written a harmless essay with the title "Twenty-Six Efforts at Pornography." Believing the essay to be obscene, the teacher planned to expel the boy. I played the boy.

The night the play aired on the BBC I was home with my parents. As the title rolled onto the screen, my mother stiffened and gave a pronounced huff—an indication she was just as offended by the title as the teacher in the play. Seconds before I appeared onscreen, she got up from her high-backed chair and changed the channel. Not one reference was made to the play ever again, neither by my parents nor my siblings. (And I, too, have never seen it.)

I left London for Kathmandu in September 1970 with a friend I'd grown up with, Jimmy Andrews. I was nineteen, with shoulder-length hair and a face that had never seen a razor. Alan was sad when I left but understood my need to travel. Before leaving, I gave him the names of the major cities on my route so that he could write to me, care of *poste restante*. It sounds incredible now, but in those days it was possible to send mail anywhere in the world simply by adding the words *poste restante*—"general delivery"—to the city or town and recipient's name.

On our third day hitchhiking, Jimmy and I reached Luxembourg. Staying at the same youth hostel as us was an attractive Dutch woman, Monique. The two of us got on so well that I stayed an extra day in Luxembourg. Although we were both quite taken with each other, nothing physical happened. On parting, I promised to visit her in Holland on my return from Kathmandu. Over the next nine months I'd receive an affectionate letter from Monique every ten days. I'd reply immediately.

Reaching Munich, I ran out of money but found a job as a dishwasher at an American army base. Another dishwasher told me of a warm basement in an industrial plant nearby where I could sleep at night. After work, I'd steal into this vast boiler room with my sleeping bag and remain there until daybreak. Although I was never caught, I'm sure my lungs took a beating from inhaling the noxious fumes from the two gigantic boilers close by.

I've often found that the more menial the job, the happier I am on payday. After washing dishes twelve hours a day for six days, my pay packet seemed enormous. On my first day off I planned to eat off a plate instead of washing one. I also wanted to see something of Munich. After wandering around the city by myself (always the best way to get to know a city), I ended up alone at a bar eating my first schnitzel. Though the schnitzel was delicious, I had trouble enjoying it because I couldn't stop thinking about the dishwasher who'd have to clean my plate afterward. Just as images of the road monopolize the mind after driving twelve hours straight, images of unwashed dishes now consumed mine.

Despite my being the bar's only customer, the place was very festive. A wedding party of about fifty middle-aged Germans had rented the small dining room opposite the bar. With a three-piece jazz band playing in the middle of the room, the party became increasingly lively as the night wore on.

Although it made me happy watching the wedding guests enjoy themselves, I was more than glad I wasn't among them. (I feel the same way about the sun. I can only enjoy its presence when sitting in the shade.).

I don't think the pleasure I was receiving from sitting alone at the bar was clear to others because pretty soon a couple from the party, in a gesture of kindness to a young foreigner, invited me to join them. I was suddenly caught—as I often am—between doing what I wanted to do at the risk of upsetting others or upsetting myself by pleasing others. As usual, I chose to please others.

Perhaps it was the beer, but sitting at a table full of strangers made me feel surprisingly content. I had drunk just enough to make me smile at nothing.

After an hour or so, I became overwhelmingly tired. I put on my coat and began saying *auf Wiedersehen* to the guests at my table, when a woman sitting opposite looked panic-stricken and began shouting. I had no idea what she was saying, but the band stopped and everybody seemed flustered. Words were spoken and the whole room began staring at me. The husband of the couple who'd invited me to join the party came over and, looking quite shamefaced, told me that the woman at the table was missing her purse. There was an awkward pause before he politely asked permission to search me. Though taken aback, I agreed. As he rifled through the deep pockets of my overcoat, the revelers were eerily silent and the band, out of embarrassment, pretended to inspect their instruments. Suddenly, there was an almighty scream and the woman whose purse had been stolen began shouting in German and holding a purse above her. Apparently, she'd found it in the bathroom.

The man quickly withdrew his hand from my coat pocket and apologized so profusely that I began to feel sorry for him. After all, it wasn't his fault and I would probably have done the same thing if positions had been reversed. The music started and the place livened up again. I didn't know what to do. I was desperate to leave, but if I fled that second, the wedding guests might think I was making too much of being wronged. So I hung around in a sort of holding pattern for five or six minutes and then edged quietly out the door.

After a month of washing dishes, I packed my rucksack and continued on toward Kathmandu. Jimmy and I hitchhiked to Brindisi in the south of Italy and took a ferry to the island of Corfu. A couple of weeks later, we made our way to Athens, where Jimmy unfortunately ran out of money and had to return home. After four days of hitchhiking alone, I reached Istanbul. I'd never experienced anywhere so alien or beautiful. With its mysterious domes and minarets, and streets through which the Crusaders had once marched, the city had me immediately under its spell. Exotic smells of paprika, cumin, sumac and cinnamon—spices that were completely foreign to me—filled the marketplaces.

Seeing sacks of these spices, freshly ground, lining the aisles of the city's main bazaar sparked an interest in cooking, which, until then, meant nothing to me.

In 1970, Istanbul's Pudding Shop was the most famous hippie café in Europe. This mecca for long-haired travelers served traditional Turkish food and played hip Western music. It also had stacks of Penguin paperbacks you could read without spending a cent. Every hitchhiker on the road knew the Pudding Shop. For hippies passing through Istanbul, it was a rite of passage to eat there. Its casual dining area had worn armchairs and a huge bulletin board covered with pinned-up notes for fellow travelers. One of them was the famous open love letter from a woman called Megan to "Malcolm," in which she asked for his forgiveness and apologized for "the business down in Greece."

I stayed a week in the city, spending every night in the Pudding Shop, eating alone and thumbing through old Graham Greene paperbacks. (*The Quiet American* was my favorite, and still is.) Despite pursuing some kind of spiritual awareness, I tended to side with those who were skeptical of enlightenment in contrast to those seeking it, which is probably why I made so few friends on the road. One friend I did make, however, was a long-haired Frenchman who'd just returned to Istanbul from Kathmandu, traveling along the route I was planning to take: the hippie trail. He told me there was such cheap transport between Turkey and Nepal that hitchhiking was totally unnecessary.

Eventually I left the security of the Pudding Shop and with $250 in my pocket began the four-thousand-mile journey across Asia. Like most teenagers, I was oblivious to the risks of traveling alone so far from home. Apart from somebody trying to steal my watch, I faced few dangers during my time abroad. I was a traveler, not a tourist, and my youth and Jesus-length hair made me a recognizable member of that friendly constituency—hippies—whom locals generally accepted. Unlike most Westerners they met, hippies didn't seem to display the entitled behavior of their ancestors who had once tried to colonize this part of the world. This was especially true in Afghanistan.

Landlocked and bordering six different countries, Afghanistan is the size of Texas and was, in 1970 at least, way safer. It was also much friendlier to strangers. Whereas Texans are naturally suspicious of outsiders, being welcoming to strangers is a crucial part of Afghan culture. (Experiencing this firsthand would later help shape my values in the restaurant business.)

I loved Afghanistan, and traveling penniless through its harsh countryside I was treated lavishly by its poor inhabitants. No matter the circumstances, I was always invited into their houses and offered tea. And very often this would turn into dinner, consisting of no fewer than four or five dishes. As I rose to leave well satiated, my Afghan host would gesture wildly, as if to say, "But, surely, you have not eaten enough?"

Afghans were among the kindest people I've ever met. Most of the homes I entered were elaborate mud huts, with no discernible plumbing or sewage system. (It was a far cry from Alan Bennett's Bloomsbury-like house.)

Eight years after my visit, Afghanistan would be invaded by the Soviets, the beginning of a war that would last from 1979 until 1989, when the

Soviets, like many before them, discovered the country was unconquerable and withdrew in humiliation. Two million Afghan civilians were killed during those horrific years. I've often wondered how many of those who went out of their way to befriend a young hippie were among them.

Throughout my nine-month trip I would find long letters from Alan waiting for me in such cities as Mashhad, Lahore and Kathmandu. He must have been the only Yorkshire playwright to send a letter to the main post office in Kandahar. It was there, in the southernmost city of Afghanistan, that I smoked marijuana for the first time. And the last. It took a lot of marijuana to have any effect, but what effect it did have was calamitous, making my heart beat three times faster than normal. In my desperation not to lose control, I began to have a panic attack. I remember going up onto the roof of my shanty hotel, looking at the night sky and thinking my heart was about to explode. It took forty-eight hours for my pulse to return to normal and forty years for me to get over the experience.

After a few weeks in Afghanistan, I took a ramshackle bus through Pakistan's Khyber Pass. Ten days later, I reached the capital of India, New Delhi, where I stayed for a week, collecting my mail and recovering from a serious bout of "Delhi belly." Once well enough to walk around the city, I was struck by how much of its new section reminded me of an imperial England I had traveled halfway around the world to escape. Considering that Britain had ruled India for close to a hundred years, this should have come as no surprise.

Walking through New Delhi one sweltering afternoon, I saw in the distance the shimmering outline of a spectacular building. Or rather, a building designed to be spectacular: Rashtrapati Bhavan. Known locally as "the Empire in Stone," it was built for the British governor-general of India, but today is the official residence of India's prime minister. Designed in 1929 by the architect Edwin Lutyens, it was intended to symbolize the permanence of British rule in India. Less than twenty years later, India gained independence, and that rule was over. Some permanence.

I remember the moment I first saw Rashtrapati Bhavan well because

I had just collected a letter from my eleven-year-old sister, Josephine. She had written to tell me about studying for her eleven-plus exam, which she would soon be taking.

Since leaving London five months earlier, I'd allowed nothing to distract me from reaching Nepal. My objective had been to travel five and a half thousand miles overland from London to Kathmandu and I was determined to achieve it. But the closer I got to Kathmandu, the more I questioned my reason for traveling there. Thirty miles from the Nepalese border I abruptly changed course, and instead rode random trains throughout northern India. This was the beginning of what would turn out to be an eternal habit of mine: abandoning goals once they became graspable.

Of all forms of transport, traveling by train is the one that's most conducive to reflection. The slower the train, the richer the introspection. Those I took in India in February 1971 lumbered along so tentatively that I could sit by an open door with my legs dangling outside, staring at the vast plains beyond. But it wasn't the mysterious landscape ahead that I was thinking of, but the back streets of London's East End where I grew up. Magnificent views don't necessarily prompt magnificent thoughts. Usually, it's the opposite.

On one overnight journey, I sat in third class next to a family from southern India who were migrating north. All their possessions, including four live chickens, were crammed into our small compartment. In the middle of the night, sixty miles between stations, the father of the family left his seat and went to the bathroom but returned instantly, screaming in Hindi. In broken English, he told me that he'd been to the toilet—which was just a hole in the floor—and when he crouched down, the wallet carrying his life's savings had fallen onto the tracks. I pulled the communication cord and the train sluggishly ground to a halt. An officious-looking guard arrived and the hysterical father explained his predicament. The guard was unmoved but gave the man a flashlight and thirty minutes to find his missing wallet.

By now, a crowd of curious Indians had surged into the corridor outside our compartment, chattering and eager to know the news. The four chickens in their wire cage were standing bolt upright, making the anxious, clipped sounds of birds in fear. I helped the man clamber out of the compartment and watched him being swallowed up by the starless Indian night.

Thirty minutes passed and he still hadn't returned. His raggedy children were in tears and begged the guard to give their father more time. The guard was adamant. The train *had* to stay on schedule. Suddenly the whistle blew, and the grinding apparatus of valves, pistons, cylinders and connecting rods set the steam train's giant metal wheels in motion. The carriage lurched forward and we slowly pulled away. I never saw the man again.

Echoes of the incident stayed with me. Just after my stroke, I was haunted by thoughts of this man, forsaken in the middle of the night, watching his family vanish from sight. I once read that one of the survivors of the *Titanic* found the silence following the ship's sinking the most harrowing sound he'd ever heard. I wonder if the man with the lost wallet felt the same way when he could no longer hear the fading sounds of the train carrying his wife and children away.

Images of the man alone on the tracks disturbed me so much that the appeal of idling my time away on trains disappeared and I craved the stability of a schedule. The next day I traveled to the Nepalese border town of Birgunj.

Six months after leaving Bethnal Green, I had arrived in the country where Buddha was born.

From Birgunj I took an eight-hour journey on a rickety bus that staggered its way up four thousand feet to the Land of the Gods, Kathmandu. The bus dropped me off at daybreak. Stepping into this beautiful, ancient city, I felt as if I were standing on top of the world. With its two thousand temples and air of serenity, this Himalayan utopia seemed more mythical than real.

First impressions exist in their own world. Though indelible in the mind, they're almost impossible to re-create. At dawn on that first morning, Kathmandu had an extraordinarily medieval feeling.

At that hour I seemed to be the only foreigner on the streets. Olive-skinned Nepalese women, carrying bundles of clothes on their backs, were scurrying to the city's open washing areas. Scores of men on bicycles were making their way along narrow streets, and the fine, barely perceptible rain was slowly turning the dirt alleyways into mud. Despite the activity, I remember there being precious little sound on the streets. It was as if Buddha had imposed a curfew on noise for the day's first hour.

Having not slept on the bus, I walked the streets of Kathmandu in a fog. In India, one was constantly badgered by children asking for *baksheesh*. Here no one bothered you, which was part of its appeal. Around eight that morning I looked for somewhere to sleep.

In Nepal in 1971, you could live comfortably on less than a dollar a day. Lodging was cheap. Dirt cheap if you were willing to share a room. That night I shared one with an American in his late twenties. He had ginger hair, a red goatee and lips so narrow they hardly registered. His bed was two feet from mine and beside it he had a stack of books—all political—none of which I'd heard of. He introduced himself and asked if I knew who Mikhail Bakunin was. To hide my ignorance, I jokingly asked if he was the same Bakunin who played right wing for Dynamo Kyiv. My roommate forced a thinnish smile, more in an attempt to overlook my unfamiliarity with Bakunin than in reaction to my joke. Appreciating this encouraged me to listen more intently when, minutes later, he launched into a spiel about communism, quoting Marx and Trotsky, and about how society needed to become a better place—one where the world's wealth would be shared equally by everyone. This made a lot of sense to me and I went to sleep regretting how little I knew about politics.

I didn't know how cold the nights could be in Nepal, and I woke up a few hours later shivering and in need of some more blankets. Seeing as my communist roommate had a huge pile on top of his sleeping body, I gently nudged him and asked if I could borrow one. He woke, stared at me for a few seconds and then screamed, "Fuck off!"

So much for sharing the wealth.

I stayed in Kathmandu for six weeks, spending some of my days reading in the British Council Library, but most of the time loafing around the city. Before email, there was nothing as thrilling as collecting an overseas letter from a city's main post office. Checking for mail in Kathmandu became part of my daily routine. If handed a letter from Holland, I knew it would be from Monique. Though we'd only spent one whole day together, it was uncanny how similar our views were. I was aching to see her.

In those days, it was customary in working-class homes for the mother of the family to write all the letters. Mine wrote to me regularly while I was traveling. To save money, my mother used a razor-thin sheet of baby blue paper called an aerogram, and in her clear and sturdy handwriting (which was way superior to mine) would cram hundreds of words on every square millimeter to get her money's worth—then she'd fold and gum it on three sides, sealing it so tightly it was impossible to pry open without ripping out vital sentences. Though my mother's letters could be mundane, as with all good writers, it was unquestionably *her* voice that came across. Looking back, I wonder how it was for my mother having her youngest son living so far from home in a country she'd never heard of.

Alan Bennett wrote often. In one letter, he mentioned that he'd finished writing his play *Getting On* and when it was published, he was going to dedicate it to me. I was flattered but embarrassed. I can't bear my first name and seeing it in print makes me cringe. Consequently, I've never seen Alan's dedication.

Waiting in line at the post office one day, I saw a long-haired American reading Joseph Heller's *Catch-22*, a book every other backpacker seemed to be reading. When I asked him about it, the young man simply gave the book to me. This generous gesture was typical of long-haired travelers at the time.

The man's name was Joe, and he was bumming around India and Nepal for a year before returning home to plunge himself into the family business, which he was dreading. In nine months, Joe was the only fellow traveler I became good friends with. We met each morning at a

Tibetan tea shop close to the post office. Tibetans make their tea with salt and yak butter. Not quite the way it's made in Bethnal Green, but proof that habit is the basis of all taste.

My new friend and I got on so well we decided to take a week's hike outside Kathmandu. Two hours after leaving the city, we were deep in a Nepalese countryside that had barely changed in a thousand years. On our third night, I couldn't sleep. I lay on the floor of a wooden hut beneath the towering Himalayas, starting to feel frighteningly remote. Whether I felt remote from home or my true self I couldn't say, but just before daybreak, the same frenzied heartbeat I'd experienced in Afghanistan returned. It affected me so much I cut the hike short, said goodbye to Joe and returned to Kathmandu. The next day it got worse. My pulse was racing so fast I thought it would trigger a heart attack. Panicking, I boarded the first of fifteen different buses that would take me back the four thousand miles to Istanbul. I scrambled from bus to bus along the same hippie trail I'd taken so optimistically just months before, but this time I was so delirious that at sundown one day in Pakistan I mistook a field of sheep for one of large maggots.

I was on a bus in Iran when out of the blue George Harrison's song "My Sweet Lord" unexpectedly came on the driver's radio. For some reason, all songs sound twice as good when unexpected, but "My Sweet Lord" sounded fifty times as good. It was the first time I'd heard any Western music since the Pudding Shop, and the lyrics, in praise of the Hindu god Krishna, felt oddly meaningful. Listening to them choked me up. At the same time—and probably by no coincidence—my heart rate slowed to its normal rhythm. And luckily, it's stayed that way.

By the time I reached Istanbul, I was close to broke. Unable to stomach the idea of hitchhiking, I spent most of my remaining forty dollars on a third-class train ticket to Munich. Arriving in München Hauptbahnhof, the city's main train station, two days later, I went to its bookstore and, intending to visit Monique, bought a map of Holland. Behind the counter was an attractive older woman (all of twenty-six) with a sympathetic manner. I couldn't bear the thought of sleeping next to those basement boilers again, so I took the plunge and asked the woman if she knew a place where I could stay the night. She gave me a serious look, then wrote the name of a bar on a scrap of paper, saying: "Meet me here at eight."

With little else to do, I arrived at the bar three hours early. The place was quite bohemian and full of young, intellectual-looking Germans. The bookseller arrived and generously bought me dinner. Her name was Gisela.

Gisela spoke English well but chose her words carefully. She possessed an innate sadness that, combined with her accent, reminded me of Harry Lime's melancholy girlfriend Anna Schmidt in *The Third Man*. Even so, I wasn't attracted to her. But as the night wore on, this changed considerably. (As it often does.)

Once assured that I wasn't a psychopath, Gisela offered me a bed for the night at her apartment. I followed her back there, imagining she had a spare room. As I had not been in a Western home for so long, her simple book-lined apartment felt like a luxury penthouse. (And in my state, even the sofa looked sensual.) But the apartment had no spare room.

Although we had a four-day affair, I didn't fall in love with Gisela. Mainly because I couldn't stop thinking about Monique. Nevertheless, I had a wonderful time with this serious *buchhändler*.

By day Gisela took me to art galleries, and at night cooked dinner for the two of us. One day she bought us tickets to see a Moody Blues concert. If I hadn't noticed the bookshop in the station, I would have been sleeping on a basement floor inhaling noxious fumes. So much of life is chance.

Before I left to hitchhike to Holland, Gisela made me an elaborate German sandwich for the road, putting it in a paper bag and giving me strict instructions not to open it until I got my first ride. Getting into the first car of the day, I opened the paper bag and discovered that as well as the sandwich there was a roll of twenty-mark bills.

From Munich, it took three days to hitchhike to the small Dutch town where Monique lived. After nine months of exchanging intimate letters, we were finally going to see each other again. Like most highly anticipated events, the rendezvous with Monique turned out to be quite different from the one I'd imagined.

We met on a park bench an hour after sunrise one damp morning in May. Unlike the fluency of our weekly letters, the conversation was forced and stilted. Words were so hard to find, I felt like a pilot unable to reach liftoff. After forty minutes, Monique said, "I have to be honest . . . you're not the person I thought you were, so there's really no reason to continue."

I wanted to say, "I *am* that person, I promise," but was so stunned I couldn't speak. I tried looking into her eyes, but they were cast at the gravel beneath her feet. After saying something like "So that's it, is it?" and getting no response, I knew the plane would never be airborne. After a few minutes of intense nothingness, I stood up and, exaggerating the struggle to put on my backpack, mumbled, "I'm going then." Monique's eyes never left the floor. I walked slowly away, hoping—like in films—she'd call me back. She didn't. I kept going to the main road and from there hitchhiked toward Amsterdam.

It seems ironic that in the space of a week I'd hit it off really well with someone I met casually for just two hours and disastrously with someone I'd corresponded with intimately for nine months.

I wonder what happened to Monique. As with the Indian who left the train in the middle of the night, I guess I'll never know. Ultimately, we all leave the train in the middle of the night. It's just that Monique left it at daybreak.

10.

I returned to London from Kathmandu in the late spring of 1971. Although eager to see Alan Bennett again, I wanted our relationship to be purely platonic. At the same time, I knew he remained in love with me and would be devastated if I broke things off. I wasn't sure what to do. Ultimately, I took the coward's way out and resumed our relationship. ("The coward does it with a kiss. The brave man with a sword!")

Not long after I returned to England, I began dating a girl from my own background, Christine Baker. I was living with my parents and Chris would often drop by our flat in Hackney. She once came over while I was out and asked my dad to let me know she'd dropped by. Unlike my mother, my longshoreman father was never good with words, and when I returned there was a note on the mantelpiece from him saying, "Christ was here today looking for you, and will return later."

For months I managed to conceal my relationship with Alan from Chris. I was back to leading a double—or rather triple—life. I would stay the night at Alan's house twice a week without Chris catching on, which I realize was some feat. Although I'd become accustomed to dividing my life, this was more stress than I was comfortable with.

After my trip to Nepal, I'd decided to give up my fledgling career onstage. Besides being a mediocre actor, I now found the profession itself frivolous. I might not have discovered universal meaning on my travels, but I did discover what was meaningful *to me*. And it wasn't acting.

No longer wanting to work in a world I now viewed as hollow, I took a job in London's Smithfield meat market instead. I would soon lose my eagerness for manual work, but having just returned from some of the world's poorest countries, I viewed all blue-collar jobs as being virtuous. (*Feeling* virtuous, I would later discover, is the polar opposite to *being* virtuous.)

Work at the meat market began at 5:30 a.m. When my thirty-minute break came a couple of hours later, I'd go to a small workingman's café and, exhausted from being up before sunrise, order a steamed coffee and a toasted sandwich of roast beef with Branston pickle. The first taste was absolutely out of this world. In forty years of dining out, nothing has rivaled this sublime sandwich. Enjoyment of food is more situational than people admit. I'm sure if I ate that exact same sandwich today in a top Manhattan restaurant, it would never match my memory of eating it in a run-down café at 7:30 in the morning.

Where food is concerned, the past is a four-star country.

My younger son, George, was named after George Orwell, whose essays I've been drawn to for fifty years. There are other writers I may prefer, but none whose character I admire more.

Though part of England's "lower-upper-middle class," Orwell hated privilege. It was probably this contradiction that fueled his interest in England's class system and led him to write so perceptively about it. Steeped in guilt for being upper class, Orwell tried to escape his origins by burrowing into society's underbelly. The books *Down and Out in Paris and London* and *The Road to Wigan Pier* both stemmed from Orwell's self-disgust at having served in Britain's colonial police force in Burma.

In June 1973, I had a bout of self-disgust of my own. At twenty-two, I spent a month in the South of France with some rich bisexual friends. It was the most dissolute month of my life. Seeking atonement, I moved to the dreariest city in England: Wigan. A year earlier I'd read *The Road to Wigan Pier*, in which Orwell describes the city in 1937 as a "landscape of slag-heaps and belching chimneys." Though belching chimneys no longer existed, Wigan—in the early seventies—was so determinedly bleak and void of character that it felt more like a city one *left* at twenty-two rather than *arrived in*, as I did in the summer of 1973.

I found a job as a laborer in an industrial paint-spraying factory. Being from London gave me a clean slate. I've spent half my life longing for a clean slate and can't comprehend why more people don't feel the same way. To live is to err, surely? I believe a life without regrets would be a nightmare and certainly not one I'd like to live.

Perhaps it was the monotony of the job, but I found working in the paint-spraying factory oddly satisfying. I particularly liked the camaraderie that came from working with a group of people all pulling in a similar direction. I'd felt the same way as an actor when rehearsing *The Winslow Boy*—and would feel that way again several years later when building and opening restaurants.

Although I enjoyed my inconspicuousness in Wigan, I did make one friend there. I became close to—in a purely friendly way—a man ten years older than me. Vernon was intelligent and easygoing and had worked in the factory since he was sixteen, with no desire to do anything else. Surprisingly, he seemed fulfilled by the job, and unlike me, didn't hanker after anything else. Though I admired this, I couldn't understand how someone with so much potential could be satisfied staying in one place all his life. A few years later, after reading something written by the painter Giorgio Morandi, I had an inkling: "One can travel this world and see nothing. To achieve understanding it's necessary not to see many things, but to look hard at what you do see."

I grew up believing that travel broadens the mind; nowadays I'm not too sure. Perhaps it depends on the mind. There's a character in a short story by Somerset Maugham who says: "The wise traveler travels only in imagination." Reading this post-stroke, when my traveling days were numbered, cheered me up because it fit neatly into my narrative. But after reading that Maugham was the most widely traveled writer of his generation, it no longer fit so well. Socrates—the philosopher, not the Brazilian footballer—never once traveled outside Athens. He argued that it was possible to learn more about the world by reading than by traveling. Being exiled in my own body these days, I'm eager to believe this, but I'm not convinced I do.

In 1790, the French writer Xavier de Maistre wrote a travel book set entirely in his bedroom: *Journey Around My Room*. In 1825, he published a sequel, *A Nocturnal Expedition Around My Room*, in which he really pushed the envelope by traveling as far as the window ledge. De Maistre believed it was better to know one thing well instead of many things superficially. Since my stroke I've thought the same thing.

I remained working at the paint-spraying factory in Wigan throughout the summer and returned to London in early September 1973. Through a friend I found a job operating a spotlight on the original stage production of *The Rocky Horror Show* at the King's Road Theatre. It was the first time I'd worked back of house and much preferred it to being onstage. Nevertheless, I had a brief affair with one of the show's cast: Nell Campbell, who played Columbia, the tap-dancing cohort of the transvestite Frank N. Furter. (She also played the same role two years later in the film version.) Nell was funny, interesting and eccentric, but I had no idea that our passing fling would lead to her investing in my first restaurant, the Odeon, let alone that we'd open a nightclub together in New York in 1986.

Within six months of operating a spotlight, I was promoted to the show's main lighting board. Besides teaching me more about lighting, operating the main lights also gave me a modicum of power over the actors. However much I appreciated their performances, the actors irritated me by milking the audience's applause at the curtain call. Having control of the lighting, I'd often counter their indulgence by "accidentally" cutting the lights on their endless bowing. This gave me more satisfaction than it should have.

These days, I'm more irritated by the reverse: the audience's self-indulgence, notably when it gives a standing ovation to a less than brilliant performance. Most of the time, those rising to their feet and clapping maniacally are applauding themselves and in the process giving a performance of their own. A standing ovation used to be rare and conceded only to the exceptional. Today, it's commonplace. The drawback to giving a standing ovation to the unremarkable is that we have nothing left to give to the *truly* remarkable.

Standing ovations began to increase in the 1970s, which, by coincidence, was the same decade in which the use of the exclamation point increased. It wasn't until the 1970s that the key for the exclamation point—which in some ways is the standing ovation of correspondence—was added to a typewriter's keyboard. The exclamation point has no grammatical purpose except to turn up the volume to eleven.

Language is diminished by inflation, and the drawback to exclamation points and standing ovations is that they box language into a corner with nowhere to go. The exclamation point is now used with such frequency that, like standing ovations, its absence conveys more meaning than its presence.

My stroke left me unable to use my right hand, which makes it impossible for me to clap the way I would like to at the theater. No matter how much I dislike a play, I find it impolite not to clap for the actors at the curtain call. And with shows I enjoy I'm terrified that those sitting around me—or the actors—may interpret my non-clapping as disapproval. No matter what Buddhists say, clapping with one hand cannot be heard by anyone.

Working fewer than three hours a night on *The Rocky Horror Show* left me with plenty of free time. Never a great reader, I read more during that period than ever before. Or since. As well as plowing my way through all but one of Dickens's novels, I read most of Graham Greene, E. M. Forster, Orwell (preferring the essays to his novels), Evelyn Waugh, Maugham and D. H. Lawrence. I read tons of Hemingway, Scott Fitzgerald, Steinbeck and Theodore Dreiser (I was mad about *An American Tragedy* and *Sister Carrie*—and still am). I also read a boatload of plays, everything by Pinter, Chekhov, Stoppard, Joe Orton, Shaw, Arthur Miller, Noël Coward and John Osborne. Although I lapped up Edward Bond, Tennessee Williams and Arnold Wesker, I'm afraid Shakespeare, Virginia Woolf and Thomas

Hardy were still a bridge too far. Woolf still is, but Hardy has become one of my favorite novelists. I also like his poetry. But just as I feel with most poetry, there's an awful lot within the poems that I don't understand. (Oddly enough, Hardy called himself a poet and not a novelist.)

In those days I rented a room in Notting Hill that cost five pounds a week. It was around the corner from Powis Square, the street made famous by housing the weird den of vice in one of the most riveting movies of the seventies: *Performance*. Starring Mick Jagger and James Fox, *Performance* is also the most interesting film I've ever seen about identity.

I rented my Notting Hill bedsit in 1973, two decades before the area became unbearably smug. In those days, Notting Hill had an exhilarating energy that, just like New York's SoHo around that time, was on the brink of change, with a glorious mix of working artists, laymen and layabouts as its residents. The brink of change is always more thrilling than the change itself.

I had always loved films, and observing the mechanics of theater while operating the lights on *The Rocky Horror Show* sparked an interest in directing them. The trouble was I had no idea how to get into the film business. Having neither a college education nor experience in filmmaking, I felt I couldn't enter the industry legitimately. And coming from the wrong side of the tracks, it seemed like all professions in England were clubs that I could never gain entrance to.

Despite having an increasing number of middle-class friends, I remained achingly conscious of my poor background. My better-off friends had an air of assuredness about them that I badly lacked. The only time I truly felt confident about myself was when I was abroad. I began to think of emigrating to America, a country with a more-than-thriving film industry. After going back and forth on the idea, I decided to go to New York. After all, I had nothing to lose—the basis from which I make most of my decisions.

To save money to go to America, I took a second job. Five nights a week after the curtain came down on *The Rocky Horror Show*, I rode the number 19 bus from King's Road to Shaftesbury Avenue. From there I walked three blocks to a seedy alleyway in Soho, where from midnight till four thirty in the morning I worked in a strip club. Not as a stripper (surprisingly) but as a manager, responsible for the music and lighting. The job also included catching the strippers' discarded clothes as they tossed them to me in the wings. I remember someone in the audience once shouting, "Oh, lucky man!" when he saw a lone hand extending onto the stage to catch a pair of pink underwear.

The name of the club was The Nell Gwynne. According to its owner—or *proprietor* as he insisted on calling himself—it was the most elegant strip joint in Soho. The slippery owner would come in once a night to collect his take and to tell the strippers not to chew gum while they worked. The strippers hated him.

After leaving the club, sleepy-eyed, at 4:30 a.m., I'd pass wide-eyed office cleaners on their way to work. The harmony of opposites.

On the rare occasions I had extra money, I'd take a minicab home. Otherwise I'd trudge wearily to the bus stop and have a forty-minute wait for the night bus. The night bus often didn't arrive until the sun was rising, which sort of made it a day bus. (Funny how a night bus doesn't *feel* like a night bus in the daytime.)

The strippers were several years older than me, except one, Chloe, who was my age: twenty-three. Chloe was quieter and more studious than the rest and, when not taking her clothes off for strangers, was studying part-time to be a chemist. Her French parents had moved to the north of England when she was five, she told me, but shortly afterward her father left for another woman. Raised by her single mother, Chloe excelled at school and went on to study science at Leeds University, with a promising future as a chemist. For whatever reason, she dropped out in her final year and hitchhiked to London. This was three years before I met her.

Chloe wasn't conventionally attractive, but one night I caught a glimpse of her in the dressing room, reading a chemistry textbook and smoking. I was transfixed. Rarely had I seen someone so absorbed in a book. The intensity of it seemed to inform the way she smoked. She took long unselfconscious drags from her cigarette as if nothing else in the world mattered. I've never desired anybody, before or since, as much as I desired Chloe that night.

In spite of everything, the atmosphere at the strip club was far from sexual. If anything, it was asexual, which is probably why, when I eventually asked Chloe out for dinner, I felt like I was crossing a picket line. The following Sunday we went to a pizza parlor on Fulham Road. Over dinner, I noticed a few of Chloe's words bore traces of a soft French accent that were at odds with her hard northern tones. It was like some rare flower struggling for light between the cracks of a sidewalk.

Chloe and I began seeing each other every week. Whenever we met, I longed to touch her, but I never did; we just talked. Yet Chloe had no interest in small talk and hated mentioning anything about herself. It took three dates before I managed to wrench out the bare minimum of her past. She once surprised me by saying her father had been right to walk out on her mother: "He did the right thing. When it's over, it's over. There's no point after that." I asked if she missed him, and after a slight pause she said, "I don't want to talk about it." Trying to have a conversation with Chloe was no easy task. There were so many subjects she refused to discuss. When I once left her a note in the dressing room, it infuriated her. Not because of the note's content but because I wrote "Chloé"—the spelling she had been christened with—instead of "Chloe." However, this didn't make me desire Chloe any less.

On nights when we weren't eating pizza together, I was forced to watch the woman I was falling in love with take off her clothes in front of other men. After several dates, I nervously invited Chloe back to my bedsit in Notting Hill. She agreed, and once there, we sat on the edge of the bed talking and drinking red wine from plastic cups. During a pause in the conversation, I tentatively touched Chloe's arm. She suddenly let out an almighty scream: "Don't touch me! Don't touch me! How dare you!" Terrified, I pulled away and started apologizing furiously. She shot me a disgusted look and without another word collected her things and fled.

A month later I moved to New York and never saw Chloe again. Afterward, whenever I touched a woman for the first time, I half expected the same response.

Noli me tangere.

Even though my physical relationship with Alan Bennett came to an end when I moved to America in 1975, we remained good friends and he'd regularly visit me in New York. Alan adored my first wife, Lynn. After Lynn and I divorced, the two of them became even closer.

When I moved back to London in 2011, Alan and I didn't see each other as much as I would have liked, mostly because his long-term boyfriend, the editor Rupert Thomas, felt awkward around me. Alan and I would chat on the phone once or twice a week and often made each other laugh. Hearing Alan laugh reminded me of all the times— some forty-five years earlier—when I'd delight in listening to him and Jonathan Miller laughing uncontrollably together in Miller's basement kitchen.

Late one afternoon in November 2016, I called Alan on my mobile phone to talk about a new play called *The Red Barn*, which I was planning to see with George the following night. Living in London, I tried to take my son to the theater as often as possible. I'm sure it wasn't lost on Alan that I was attempting to pass on to George what he—far less heavy-handedly—had passed on to me many years earlier.

Before speaking to Alan, I'd just bought tickets at the National Gallery for a Caravaggio exhibition I planned to see with my kids the next day. We talked and laughed for thirty minutes or so as I walked from Trafalgar Square across St. James's Park to Victoria train station, where I had to pick up George, who was returning from boarding school for the weekend.

With London on high alert for a terrorist attack, its stations were thought to be prime targets, and while waiting for George I had, in my mind's eye, a terrifying image of an unexploded bomb ticking away in a garbage can. After collecting him in the arrivals hall, I left the station as fast as I could.

I was right to be concerned about a ticking bomb. Only I was wrong about its location. Within twenty hours of picking up George, I would have a massive stroke.

11.

Five weeks after my stroke I was still sifting through the rubble. My speech was shot to pieces and my entire right side paralyzed. But the worst thing about my condition wasn't the condition itself—it was having my children see me this way. For the first time since my stroke, I had thoughts of suicide. There had to be another way out.

After a month of rehab, I found a possibility. One of the therapists at my West London clinic mentioned a post-stroke program in which a patient with a similar condition as mine had made a full recovery. But there was a drawback. The program was in New York, and there was a yearlong wait to get in. Luckily, a friend of Sophie's knew someone on the board of New York-Presbyterian Hospital and promised to have a word.

Ten days later I was accepted into the program.

Enrolling in this program meant I'd be living in New York for three to five months. Alina and I thought about her and the children moving back with me, but for George and Alice's sake we decided against it. After going through the trauma of my stroke, we didn't want to give them additional stress by uprooting them from a country and education system they had so recently adapted to. I decided I'd go to New York alone.

Alina balked at the idea of me leaving. She couldn't bear me being away for so long, she said. Though I believed her, it did cross my mind that part of her reason might be that living in New York, I'd regularly be seeing my former wife and older children.

Since moving to London, I'd spent long stretches of time in New York building the restaurant Augustine, and though I'd missed Alina and our children, I'd also enjoyed the freedom these trips gave me. The allure of sitting in a café alone with a book, or taking a long, contemplative train ride to search for French café tables, epitomized an independence that, quite selfishly, I hadn't been eager to give up as a married man. That I required periods of time on my own—with its obvious temptations— must have been hard for Alina to accept. But I believe that ultimately all marriages live or die by the way both partners deal with the other's occasional need to be alone.

Six weeks after my stroke, I was all set to leave my London clinic for America. I was hoping that several months of intensive rehab in New York would bring about my return to health.

A week before I left, a nurse with sharp features prepared me for an issue I might face on the long flight: urinating in the plane's cramped bathroom. In order to practice this, she led me to the clinic's smallest bathroom and had me take down my pants and feign peeing in front of her. Not once, but ten times. I was convinced she took some kind of callous enjoyment from it. Like most people who've seen *One Flew Over the Cuckoo's Nest*, I regarded all sullen-looking nurses as sadists. However, before I left for New York, this sharp-featured nurse came by on her day off to present me with a Parker fountain pen and to wish me a smooth journey. Two days later I received an email from her saying she hoped I'd arrived safely. I guess you don't have to look like an angel to be Florence Nightingale.

Saying goodbye to George and Alice was agonizing. The night before I left, they came to visit me at the clinic and I broke the news. Holding them close, I said I was leaving for New York for several months but when they next saw me, I'd be a new man.

Saying goodbye to Alina was different. Her role in my recovery was being taken away from her. Worse, it was being given to those she felt most competitive with—my ex-wife and older children. She felt betrayed.

To me, there was no choice. I felt New York was the only place where I had a chance of a full recovery. Maybe if I'd known then how badly

Alina had been hit by my stroke I would have stayed. Perhaps I should have stayed regardless.

Selfless to the core, Harry volunteered to accompany me on the plane journey back to New York. The two of us left St. John's Hospital for Heathrow at four o'clock on an icy January morning. I was fastened to a wheelchair and pushed to a waiting taxi. This was no ordinary taxi, but one with a hydraulically operated metal ramp specially designed for the handicapped. So began the complicated procedure of transportation that I was to be wedded to for the next few months. Possibly forever.

Harry sat next to me in silence. It was still dark outside. The hushed drive to the airport reminded me of our early-morning journeys to ice hockey rinks many years ago. Mamaroneck, Long Beach, Hackensack. How much more appealing suburbia now sounded.

Once we arrived at the airport, the disembarking process was as cumbersome as the boarding and equally demeaning. Unfortunately, the special requirements dictated by my new condition only accentuated its indignity. At Heathrow I was jolted into the real world. After six weeks in the hospital and rehab, the frenzied terminal was an assault on my nerves. It was a snake pit of manic confusion. Faces strained and contorted. Couples arguing. Kids being screamed at. Is any vacation worth the anxiety that precedes it? When did travel become such a torment?

When I was a boy, leaving from Waterloo train station to go on holiday with my parents had been the happiest—and calmest—day of the year. No passports. No airport security. No body searches. We simply bought a ticket and breezed onto the platform. The joys of unhurried travel.

During the long flight I thought about the first time I had taken this same journey forty-two years earlier. I wondered if I'd known then how my future would play out—that I'd have a loving wife, five beautiful children and seven successful restaurants, but I'd also end up half paralyzed and semi-incoherent—would I have continued on? Or would I have bought the first ticket back to London and remained there? Why does success—no matter how small—always come at a price?

I didn't want the eight-hour flight to end. Being a passenger and not a patient made me feel normal again. Before my stroke I'd been eager, in my convoluted way, to stand out. But now that I did, I craved anonymity.

As we flew over Greenland, I began to wonder if there were any French restaurants on the island, and if so did they ever run out of ice? I also wondered if Greenland had a restaurant critic with the power to close down restaurants by writing a bad review.

As the plane prepared to land and the seat belt sign came on, my frivolous mood vanished. Deplaning meant the return of my patient status and it also meant having to face the music with my Pastis lease. If I couldn't extricate myself from the lease, I'd be forced to cough up the guarantee of a million dollars. This and the thought of my draining finances made me dread getting off the plane. I wished I could have circled the globe indefinitely.

We touched down at JFK Airport on a blindingly sunny day. That was the first thing that shocked me when landing there for the first time: how dazzlingly blue the sky could be in winter. English winters were gray and dull. Like one endless Sunday.

Strapped to a wheelchair again, I was maneuvered into a handicapped-accessible cab and we drove to New York-Presbyterian Hospital on Sixty-Eighth and York. The following day I was due to start its famous post-stroke program. I hoped that on completing it I'd no longer belong to what I saw as the wretched world of wheelchairs and steel ramps. I viewed this new program the way one imagines a holiday while leafing through glossy images of palm trees and sandy beaches. Though part of me knew that things never live up to expectation, the other part insisted that this would be the exception.

Why does one never learn from experience? The new program would turn out to do absolutely nothing for me. It was even less advanced than the one I'd just left in London. By my fourth day I realized my recovery depended less on the quality of the therapy than on the severity of my stroke. Mine had been pretty severe. Barring a miracle, I was going to be tied to this contorted body forever. Recognizing this was one of the most depressing moments of my life.

But if my mood veered toward self-pity, the feeling disappeared at the sight of some of the other patients. One in particular: Ralph was a ruddy-cheeked man in his late twenties who'd recently lost both his hands in an industrial fire. In their place were gruesome-looking raw stumps. Something I heard this young man once say to the doctor was unbearably sad: "My dad's saving up to buy me this place far in the woods. The good thing is you can walk for ten miles in any direction and not see another person." Whether Ralph's tendency to reclusiveness was a direct result of this horrific accident I didn't know, but I couldn't stop thinking about him afterward. How can anyone believe in God after witnessing the brutally raw stumps this gentle young man was left with?

Unfortunately, knowing someone is far worse off than you doesn't reduce the pain of your own suffering.

Knowing how close to despair I was, Alina made a surprise visit in the second week. On a freezing January day, she walked into my room bundled up and looking like some beautiful Alaskan Eskimo. That night, after we had worked out the times of the nurse's inspections, the Eskimo slipped off her clothes and snuck into my narrow hospital bed. There was just enough room—and time—for us to have sex without being interrupted.

During this passionate encounter, I was reminded how much love-making is intensified when clandestine. (But I wouldn't suggest having a stroke in order to experience it.) This was the best of Alina: the insouciant, spontaneous and loving side.

It was on this trip that Alina stopped talking to my older children altogether. She refused to visit the hospital when they were there. As Harry and Sophie were now playing a vital role in the running of my restaurants, having to juggle their hospital visits caused unnecessary stress. At times I felt that Alina's feud with my children was taking precedence over her concern for my recovery. However, having her next to me at the hospital was so reassuring, it made me again wonder if I'd made the right choice in seeking treatment in New York. Sometimes there *is* no right choice.

Alina returned to London four days later and my spirits fell to an all-time low.

At no time after my stroke did I ever hear the word "convalescence." This somewhat outdated word seems to have been usurped by the more assertive "rehabilitation." One implies passive recovery, the other, active. While rehabilitation is vital for recovery, I believe convalescence—the passive and gradual restoration of one's health—is equally important.

Despite sticking to the rigorous therapy, I saw no improvement in the paralysis of my right side and so quit the program in the fourth week. In hindsight, I would attribute what little progress I've made since not to any grand medical treatment, but rather to the ceaseless repetition of small actions. This is probably true of most things in life.

During my stay, I was often subjected to fleeting visits from the hospital's chief neurologist. On the heels of this esteemed doctor there followed, like a king's pages, a posse of obsequious trainees. The neurologist's name was Dr. Leifer, pronounced "lifer," which was ironic as he had the disposition of an undertaker. Lugubrious Dr. Leifer made no effort to conceal from his trainees that my only role was as a human guinea pig and he presided over my bed, discussing "the patient's" condition as if the patient himself weren't in the bed but in the cafeteria having lunch.

I dreaded Dr. Leifer's visits. Mainly because he'd ask me to repeat the phrase "No ifs, ands or buts" when he knew the difficulty I had saying it was increased tenfold by having to repeat it in front of his fifteen trainees. The only other neurologist with whom I'd had any contact before my stroke was the writer Oliver Sacks. But there was no comparing the deeply compassionate Dr. Sacks to the cold, businesslike Dr. Leifer. To do so would be like comparing a Shakespeare sonnet to an instruction manual.

The day before I was set to leave, the hospital's psychiatrist sat me down and, in a *concerned* tone, asked if I'd ever contemplated suicide. I replied, "Yes, often, but only before my stroke." As always, faced with something uncomfortable, I'd resorted to humor. It wasn't the mention of suicide that unnerved me so much as the presence of a shrink. No matter how much I approved of treating other people by psychological means, they weren't for me. Being the son of a working-class long-shoreman is how I justified my aversion to psychology. But that wasn't the truth. The real reason would come to light eighteen months later when I'd try to take my own life.

12.

After being hospitalized with barely a day's interruption for nine weeks, I left New York-Presbyterian in late January accompanied by Harry and Lynn. The sheer thrill of being in a taxi racing downtown reminded me of my first cab ride in the city forty-two years earlier.

It was October 1975. I was twenty-four and had arrived in New York with vague plans of making films. Running out of money in my second week, I ditched the film idea and found a job as a busboy at an ice cream parlor called Serendipity on East Sixtieth Street.

While I was stacking chairs onto tables after my shift one night, a group of the waiters offered to take me to a place they called the Village. It was after midnight when five of us squeezed into a Checker Cab. The taxi sped down Fifth Avenue more than fifty blocks to Washington Square without stopping at a single red light. Each time we approached a red stoplight it effortlessly gave way to green, which seemed to symbolize a world of blissful unencumberedness I'd never before experienced.

Stepping out of the cab into the Village, I was shocked by the number of people still on the streets. At this hour in London the streets would be deserted. As Bette Midler once said: "When it's three o'clock in New York, it's still 1938 in London."

Like many immigrants, my desire to live in New York came from watching films. One in particular: *Klute*. In the film, there's a terrific scene in which the two leads, Jane Fonda and Donald Sutherland, are out past midnight buying fruit from a sidewalk produce stand. As Sutherland reaches for some luscious-looking peaches, Fonda's sexual desire for him explodes onto the screen. This was the exact moment when I longed to live in New York. But it wasn't the scene's eroticism that triggered the longing. It was the idea that you could buy fresh fruit in Manhattan after midnight.

The odd thing about experiencing New York for the first time was that it seemed more like the films than the films themselves. Places rarely live up to expectations, but New York did—particularly its element of availability. Unlike London in 1975, subways ran all night, bars served until 4 a.m., taxis were available twenty-four/seven and diners never closed. Not that I needed to have an egg sandwich and a coffee at three in the morning, but *knowing* I could helped me sleep better. It still does.

Knowing I can do something, without necessarily doing it, is vital for me. There's a scene in the film *Pennies From Heaven* in which an unhappily married man who's fallen in love with a schoolteacher asks if she'd ever consider having sex with him on an elevator floor. He doesn't want to have sex on the elevator floor, he just wants to know it's a *possibility*. I feel that way about most things. (She says yes, by the way.)

I was working illegally and living in Queens with a couple of guys I'd met at a kibbutz three years earlier. New York was dangerous in the seventies, and after leaving work at night I'd stuff whatever tips I'd made into my socks and ride the 7 subway to the last stop, Flushing–Main Street.

Needing extra money to rent an apartment in Manhattan, I found a second job as an oyster shucker at a downtown place called One Fifth. This stylish restaurant had recently opened on the ground floor of a 1920s skyscraper at number one Fifth Avenue in Greenwich Village. With its art deco design, attractive floor staff and artistic customers, One Fifth opened up a whole new world to me.

After shucking oysters for a month, I was promoted to waiter. Having a poor short-term memory, I was hopeless at the job. I'd often wake in the middle of the night remembering the two cappuccinos that table 12 had ordered nine hours earlier.

On my second shift a busboy called Po Ming was assigned to me. Before the service began I jokingly gave him an oversize cup for the supposed abundance of tips we were going to earn that night. Extending the joke he silently exchanged the oversize cup for a large wine bucket. That was the moment when Po Ming and I became friends. Humor and integrity are two qualities I value above all others, and one rarely finds them in the same person. But this busboy from communist China possessed both. Thirty-year-old Po Ming would soon become my closest friend.

Undeterred by my ineptness, customers could be surprisingly forgiving once they heard my English accent, and after six weeks of waiting tables, I got promoted to maître d'. I then realized that charm played a more important role than competence in America. Or could do, if you bought into it. And I bought into it big-time.

Soon after I began working at One Fifth, I went into a Sixth Avenue diner for coffee and noticed a blackboard on the wall with the sign COFFEE ONE DOLLAR. REFILL 50 CENTS. Because I was low on money I asked the waitress (in my English accent) if I could *start* with a refill. She told me to fuck off. Three days later we began an affair.

One Fifth's owner was a radiologist called George Schwarz. Schwarz was so passionate about food and wine that in the early seventies he began building his own restaurants. Although he had no experience in the business, Schwarz trusted his own taste and each restaurant he built succeeded beyond expectation, One Fifth most of all.

If only Schwarz had trusted his staff as much as his taste, One Fifth would still be around today. But he was so convinced his employees were stealing or plotting against him that Schwarz would fire one of them every other week. Consequently, five months after being hired at One Fifth, I became its most senior employee working in the dining room.

For some reason, Schwarz took a liking to me. Born in Germany, he had a quirky sense of humor and seemed to appreciate mine. All the same, when he asked one night to have a word with me at the end of my shift, I felt sure I was getting the chop. Like an Academy Award nominee in reverse, I worked for hours on some disparaging last words. Yet instead of firing me, Dr. Schwarz promoted me to general manager.

I was twenty-four and working illegally but suddenly found myself being shot out of a circus cannon into this swanky Manhattan restaurant and being paid handsomely to manage it. On top of this, Schwarz promised to sponsor me for a green card. I couldn't believe my luck. I still can't. Which is why not a day goes by when I don't fear an authority figure tapping me on the shoulder and saying, "McNally, you're a fraud. We're putting you on the next plane back to London." Even after my stroke I still feel this.

I got to know George Schwarz and his wife, the painter Kiki Kogelnik, quite well. It's not often one likes both partners of a married couple to the same degree. Half the married couples I'm friends with I dread seeing together. But I liked Kiki as much as I did George. In some ways, more so. Every other month, as a sort of field trip, they'd take me and a few other employees to dinner at a three-star restaurant. George analyzed every ingredient on his plate as if he was examining an X-ray. I learned more about food and wine from him than anyone else in the business.

In the precarious world of New York restaurants, One Fifth was something of a game-changer. Its large, bustling dining room combined uptown glamour with downtown cool and was a forerunner to many future Manhattan restaurants, including many of my own. Though I'm loath to attribute changes in character to one pivotal moment—and am suspicious of people who do—I often wonder what turn my life might have taken if I hadn't been hired at One Fifth. I think most events that have a significant effect on us are impossible to detect until years later. It's only now, forty-odd years after working at One Fifth, that I realize what a huge influence it had on me. Especially in terms of design.

Professional designers like to say that good design "is all about the details." This isn't true. Good design is all about the *right* details. Good design is also about what you *don't* do, what you refrain from doing. Unfortunately, I don't always take my own advice.

Good design, like good cinematography, should never strain to be noticed. It should appear as natural and effortless as if it had fallen into place. The moment a designer's hand becomes conspicuous, the game's up.

Restaurant design begins and ends with lighting. Working at One Fifth, I discovered that the less overhead lighting and the more side lighting one uses, the more attractive the dining room becomes. Having many different light sources at low wattage often gives a room a special glow.

But of course, seductive lighting doesn't compensate for tasteless food or inept service. Likewise, extraordinary food, design and service never guarantee a successful restaurant. Nothing does except that strange indefinable: *the right feel*. At its best, the right feel can transport a customer like nothing else. Without it, you might as well pack your bags.

For its first two years, One Fifth was the most fashionable restaurant in Manhattan. It opened around the same time that *Saturday Night Live* first aired on NBC, and the cast held their original after-show parties at the restaurant. After my promotion I was responsible for organizing these charismatic events, and many would last until four in the morning (particularly if John Belushi was present). It was at one of these parties that I met *SNL* producer Lorne Michaels, whom I've remained surprisingly close to ever since. My son Harry was the ring bearer at Lorne's wedding in 1992, and my daughter Alice was named after Lorne's wife.

In the mid-seventies, singer Patti Smith and her ex-boyfriend, the photographer Robert Mapplethorpe, were regulars at One Fifth. Mapplethorpe's benefactor and at one point lover, Sam Wagstaff, lived in an apartment above the restaurant, and all three of them would eat at One Fifth together a few times a week. They made an intriguing-looking threesome. While Smith and Mapplethorpe had the surly appearance of young, rebellious artists (which they were), the quietly understated Wagstaff, who was a former museum curator and exceptionally handsome, seemed to embody the patrician values of an earlier period. At the time I found Wagstaff to be the most interesting of the three. I still do today.

On nights when Wagstaff wasn't at the table, Smith and Mapplethorpe could be very difficult to wait on. Smith, unfortunately, was incredibly rude to the servers. It's impossible for me to listen to a Patti Smith song today without remembering her reducing a waitress to tears because she forgot to put bread on the table.

Although Mapplethorpe, with his tough-boy leather jacket image, could be terse with the servers, he never tried to belittle them the way

Smith did. The only time I saw Mapplethorpe without his leather jacket—when the restaurant's air-conditioning broke down—he seemed strangely reduced and, like a policeman out of uniform, surprisingly ordinary-looking. Maybe it was a coincidence, but without the leather jacket he was also friendlier to the staff. Regardless of what he was wearing, Mapplethorpe was a brilliant photographer. However, I believe that without Wagstaff's patronage, his photographs would not be as celebrated as they are today.

The last time I saw the urbane Wagstaff was on the New York subway. We rode ten blocks together on the Lexington Avenue line one evening rush hour. Our car was so full that we stood all the way. Though sixty-three, he was still remarkably good-looking. It seemed incongruous to see someone this wealthy and refined riding the subway.

And although he didn't know me well, Wagstaff graciously chatted with me throughout the journey. It was only after we parted that I realized he hadn't said a word about himself. This was 1985. Within two years he would die of AIDS.

There are only two or three people in life that I wish I'd known better. Sam Wagstaff was one of them.

Not long after being promoted to general manager, I noticed something vaguely interesting about a young English woman who came for brunch every Sunday. She was often accompanied by several writers and always ordered the same dish: eggs Benedict. One Sunday she came in alone a few minutes after the kitchen had closed. Knowing she was a regular, I asked the brunch chef, Chang, to reopen the kitchen and make her eggs Benedict. Like most restaurant chefs at the time, Chang refused to cook the order because it was given to him minutes after closing time. I told him the customer came every week and besides, she was quite pretty. Once he heard she was pretty, the chef went bananas and threw his sauté pan at me. His aim was as bad as his cooking and he missed by a mile. I picked the pan up off the floor and for the first and last time went behind the kitchen line and cooked a customer's order.

Although I made a hash of the eggs Benedict, the incident itself had rich consequences: The young woman was future *Vogue* editor in chief Anna Wintour, and despite coming from opposite ends of the English class system, we became friends. Nothing romantic happened between us, yet we'd often watch movies together in the afternoon, which, outside of the bedroom, is the most intimate thing two people can do at that time of day.

Despite my English accent and passing charm, not all of One Fifth's customers liked me. A few days after being promoted from waiter to maître d', a fashion designer who was one of the restaurant's regulars summoned me to his table. Wearing a fancy tuxedo (which I wouldn't be seen *dead* in now), I went to the table expecting a question about the wine list. In front of his boyfriend, the fashion designer eyed me and sneered: "The worst thing this restaurant has ever done is to make you its maître d'."

Oddly enough, the restaurant's owner, George Schwarz, would eventually think the same.

As One Fifth's general manager, I now had the responsibility of hiring the restaurant floor staff, which was absurd, seeing as I was illegal and had been working in restaurants for just five months. I was also hiring people whose jobs I knew next to nothing about. Only in America is it possible to get to the top of the heap without knowing anything about the job. (Some even become president.)

Two of the people I hired would play an integral—and often complicated—role in my New York life. One was my brother Brian and the other was my future wife, Lynn Wagenknecht.

Brian arrived in New York on Thanksgiving Day 1976. Since I was working that afternoon, he came directly from Midtown's Port Authority Bus Terminal to One Fifth to meet me. It was my twenty-eight-year-old brother's first time in New York and also his first time in a restaurant this glamorous. He was stunned. He'd never experienced anything as sophisticated as downtown New York and was in awe that, in managing

93

this stylish restaurant, I seemed to have my foot in the door of Manhattan's high life. Though well-read (far more than I am) and well-traveled, Brian resented the fact that he was working class and longed to escape it. Superficially, New York gave him the chance to break free.

Over the next few weeks I found Brian an apartment on Bleecker Street and gave him a job as a bartender at One Fifth. My brother was a terrific bartender and it wasn't long before he had an impressive following of downtown's artists and intellectuals.

After a few months tending bar, Brian—like me—now had one foot in the door of the city's smart life. The only trouble was that at times the opening wasn't wide enough for both of us.

One day, while interviewing floor staff, I found myself sitting across from a twenty-four-year-old woman applying for a waitress job. Her name was Lynn Wagenknecht. It was clear from her complete lack of guile that she must have been new to Manhattan. She was. Lynn had arrived in the city six weeks earlier from the Midwest. She had long blond hair and eyes bluer than robin's eggs. After five minutes I hired her. After five years I married her.

During the interview I discovered that after graduating from Stanford, Lynn had attended the University of Iowa, where she received her MA in fine arts. She'd come to New York with aspirations to paint and perhaps eventually teach drawing at a university, but meanwhile needed a job to pay the rent. Being hired by me led the educated Ms. Wagenknecht to exchange a noble life in academia for a lowbrow one in restaurants.

Apart from being the restaurant's general manager, I was also its maître d' three nights a week. This meant seating customers in the dining room, where Lynn was one of eight servers waiting tables.

Lynn was a brilliant waitress—she was also completely herself when waiting tables. I was so mesmerized watching this Midwestern woman work that I quickly fell in love with her. (People become strangely appealing when performing a job with skill.) The only problem was Lynn wasn't in love with me. Even so, she agreed to see me outside of work.

In the early days of our dating, there was such an imbalance of affection between us that, consumed with jealousy, I often refused to seat attractive men in Lynn's section. Even unattractive ones. (When you're eaten with jealousy, all men become potential suitors.) One night, I remember scanning the room and seeing only women seated in Lynn's section. What excuse I gave the men for refusing them tables, I've no idea. But as maître d' of this hip restaurant, I had many difficult exchanges with customers. One busy night I told a pushy New Yorker—a John Gotti look-alike—that there wasn't a table for him.

"Do you know who I am?" he snarled.

"No, but I can find out for you," I quickly replied.

After he threatened to break my legs, I found him a table *tout de suite*.

My worst mistake as maître d' was failing to recognize Ingrid Bergman. One night, a middle-aged couple graciously asked me for a table. Because the dining room was full at the time, I asked them to wait at the bar and explained that I'd give them the next one available. The man took me aside: "You *do* know that the woman I'm with is Ingrid Bergman, don't you?" Having no idea who Ingrid Bergman was (I somehow got her confused with Ingmar Bergman), I looked at the tall, sophisticated woman standing several feet from me and just repeated my spiel about waiting at the bar. The man looked me in the eye, turned around and left. A week later, I watched the film *Casablanca* for the first time and saw the most beautifully dreamy actress imaginable. I felt like disappearing down the closest manhole.

Since the eggs Benedict incident, Anna Wintour and I saw each other regularly. In 1978 she moved to Paris to live with her boyfriend, Michel Esteban, a French entrepreneur who'd made a fortune in the T-shirt business. After a few months—perhaps out of loneliness—she invited me and Lynn to join her for a week. Knowing that we were penniless, Anna paid for our airfare and hotel.

Anna and Michel took us for dinner every night, usually to some of the best brasseries and bistros in Paris—La Coupole, Allard, Chez René, Vaudeville, Au Pied de Cochon, Balzar. My favorite was a place called Chez Georges. I loved the smell of escargots drenched in butter and garlic, the look of the red banquettes, the scored mirrors, the handwritten menu, the waiters with starched white, ankle-length aprons. Everything about the place stimulated me. Even the jug of pickled cornichons on the table. I ate ris de veau (veal sweetbreads) for the first time at Chez Georges, which for someone who'd grown up on a diet of boiled vegetables and tinned salmon was like manna from heaven.

Although the aesthetically pleasing world of French bistros was a million miles away from my Bethnal Green prefab, something about the experience at Chez Georges that night struck a chord.

By taking me to these incredible restaurants, Anna's plan was to seduce me into remaining in France to work alongside her boyfriend. By the end of a long week having been treated to such terrific bistros and brasseries, I was thoroughly seduced: not by the idea of moving to Paris, however, but by the thought of returning to New York and building my own version of a Parisian brasserie.

13.

The mid-to-late seventies were my happiest years in New York. In the spring of 1977, I moved downtown from East Ninety-First Street to SoHo, a neighborhood of cobbled streets, fire escapes and cast-iron buildings. There was a tremendous sense of exhilaration in the air, and the whole neighborhood seemed to be boiling over with ideas. Everyone appeared to be carrying slabs of Sheetrock and in the process of renovation. The area pulsed with the spirit of approaching change.

Unknowingly, I caught the wave of that change, and for the next few years would experience the most stimulating and open-minded period of my life.

My apartment was a three-room walk-up on Thompson Street. It had a bathtub in the kitchen that ran rusty brown water for the first thirty seconds, and at night, when you switched on the light, a dozen or so cockroaches scattered every which way. But at $250 a month I wasn't complaining.

The apartment wasn't in terrible shape, but it still needed work, and fixing it up was my first stab at renovation. Since I didn't know how to use a saw or an electric drill (I still don't), I stuck to the one task that required no skill whatsoever: stripping sixty years' worth of paint off old pine doors and baseboards. In the process, I discovered that over time pine oxidizes when coated with oil paint and the longer the paint stays on, the richer the wood looks when exposed. Stripped of sixty years of paint, the wood in my apartment turned the most beautiful shade of honey.

Even though stripping wood didn't require any skill, it was surprising how much satisfaction it gave me. When you're as impractical as I am, just picking up a hammer makes you feel invincible. However, for the real work, I relied on the skill of one man in particular: Po Ming, the Chinese busboy from One Fifth. Leaning on people who knew better than me would become a lifelong habit and the key to whatever restaurant success I would later have.

Po Ming was the most honorable friend I've ever had. Without accepting a dime, he helped me renovate my apartment for five hours every other day for three months. He knew how to plaster walls, build cabinets and sand floors. Though he spoke English well, Po Ming never talked when working. He had such a stoic character that during the ten years I knew him I never once heard him complain.

When Lynn, my brother Brian and I opened our first restaurant, the Odeon, Po Ming came with us and was a huge help. We sponsored him for a green card that he received three years later, and he immediately brought his wife and two children to New York from communist China. Several years after this, Po Ming died from stomach cancer. Typically, he never told me he was sick, and as a consequence I never got to say goodbye to him.

Po Ming was an exceptional man with a kind face and rare integrity. I once read that great people never regret anything. I regret almost everything. But most of all I regret not saying goodbye to Po Ming.

I first heard of SoHo eighteen months before moving there, when an attractive woman invited me to a party on Mercer Street. I was an oyster shucker at the time, and the woman, who resembled Mrs. Robinson from *The Graduate*, was sitting at my zinc bar sipping champagne and eating oysters. It was the first time I'd seen someone eat an oyster without a fork. She simply picked up the shell and slid the oyster into her mouth. It was deeply provocative.

Before leaving, she wrote on the inside of the restaurant's matchbook the address of a "sixties" party she was going to and asked me to join her after work (even her handwriting was suggestive). Although out of my league in terms of sophistication, this woman had such a seductive manner that when my shift ended, I quickly changed and headed to Mercer Street.

SoHo is no more than a ten-minute walk from Greenwich Village, but to reach it one has to navigate the major thoroughfare of Houston Street. In the mid-seventies, crossing Houston into SoHo felt like defecting to a dimly lit European city. The streets were so dark that it took me some time to find the address. On a bleak cobblestone side street, I pressed the buzzer several times before the door suddenly opened of its own accord.

The party was in a "loft" on the top floor of a converted factory. I had to climb four flights of steep wooden stairs to reach it, and the higher I climbed, the louder the stairs creaked. The door to the party was wide open and the music was booming. The loft was packed with about two hundred arty types, many of them splashed with psychedelic images that were being projected onto the walls and ceiling. I felt desperately out of place but so anxious to see Mrs. Robinson that I wasn't going to leave until I found her. After twenty minutes I spotted her in conversation with an underground film director whose face I recognized but whose name I couldn't remember. I introduced myself but she looked right through me. I explained that I was the person who'd served her Wellfleet oysters an hour before, but the more detail I went into, the more blank her face became. After two minutes, she turned her back on me and renewed her conversation with the filmmaker. I hovered nearby like an untipped waiter and then embarrassingly made my way to the door. Before leaving I looked back. The two of them were standing even closer together and were enveloped in bold, psychedelic images.

It often happens that when in pursuit of a particular goal one accidentally stumbles upon another of greater significance. Making my way home, while trying to remember the name of the director, I passed a factory building that fascinated me. Unable to resist touching it, I ran my fingers along its iron façade. It was hard to believe that such intricate details were made of a metal as undistinguished as iron. I couldn't stop touching it. This was the first cast-iron building I'd ever seen and today I'm just as obsessed with these buildings as I was that night.

SoHo has more cast-iron buildings concentrated in its twenty-six blocks than anywhere else in the world. Most were cast in the late nineteenth century when a wave of large-scale manufacturers moved into the district. SoHo soon turned into the textile center of New York. After World War II the industry moved out of the area, leaving most of the factories unoccupied. What used to be one of the manufacturing hubs of New York was, by the 1950s, an industrial wasteland.

Ten years later came a kind of reawakening.

Attracted by the huge windows and cheap rents of SoHo's buildings, artists first began to drift into this "wasteland" in the late sixties. They rented whole floors of these former factories and began converting them into homes and workspaces. From this transformation emerged a bohemian counterculture that characterized the SoHo I knew in the late seventies.

Ten years before I moved into the neighborhood, SoHo came within a whisker of being destroyed.

In the late 1950s, New York City's planning commissioner, Robert Moses, proposed constructing an expressway through the heart of SoHo. This would have meant destroying four hundred buildings—many of which were nineteenth-century cast-iron—in Little Italy and SoHo.

Between 1924 and 1968, Moses was the most powerful man in New York and responsible for—among other projects—the Cross Bronx Expressway, the West Side Highway, the Verrazzano Bridge and Lincoln Center. For over forty years, no building, bridge or highway of significance could be constructed in the city without the approval of the man known as the "master builder" of New York. Astonishingly, this man who was obsessed with automobiles didn't drive himself.

In 1967, Moses's plan to destroy SoHo was supported by the city's mayor, John Lindsay, the *New York Times* and, inexcusably, the American Institute of Architects. Opposing Moses were the neighborhood's residents, downtown artists and intellectuals, and the writer turned activist Jane Jacobs. A year later, after storming the stage during a public hearing, Jacobs and other protesters were imprisoned and charged with criminal mischief. Jacobs's arrest made the papers, drawing national attention to the controversy, which led Mayor Lindsay to drop his support of the project. In 1969, the New York City Board of Estimate formally abandoned plans for the highway. The neighborhood's survival foreshadowed the decline of Moses's power and the rise of Jacobs's reputation. In August 1973, SoHo was officially designated a historic district.

I moved to SoHo four years later, in the summer of 1977. This was the summer when Elvis died. The summer of the Son of Sam. And also the summer of New York's famous blackout. On July 13, all of New York's clocks suddenly stopped and remained frozen at 9:36 for twenty-four hours.

In those days, I was obsessed with films—both American and European—and New York in the seventies was a great place to watch them. The only way to see Truffaut's *The 400 Blows* or Antonioni's *L'Avventura* in the seventies was on the big screen at a handful of revival house cinemas dotted around the city: the Thalia, the Bleecker Street, the Beekman or the stunning Carnegie Hall Cinema on Fifty-Seventh Street. (Lynn and I had our first date there—we saw Hitchcock's *The 39 Steps* in 1978.)

These arthouses were owned by dedicated cinephiles who were far more passionate about films than they were about turning a profit. The moviegoers they attracted were equally passionate about films, and as a result, arthouse cinemas were often filled with like-minded people. You could be watching Fellini's *La Dolce Vita* at the Thalia on a Monday night and then see the same people at the Bleecker the next night watching Godard's *Contempt*. A true affection for films brought about a sense of community back then that I'm not convinced Netflix provides today.

It's incredible how many great American movies came out in the seventies: *Taxi Driver, Chinatown, One Flew Over the Cuckoo's Nest, Klute, Network, Marathon Man, The French Connection, Don't Look Now, Mean Streets, Young Frankenstein, Deliverance, Annie Hall, Barry*

Lyndon, *Three Days of the Condor*, *Shampoo*, *The Conversation*, *Five Easy Pieces*, *The Godfather* parts 1 and 2, *Paper Moon* and my favorite film of the period, *Dog Day Afternoon*. By coincidence or not, each of these films came out before the blockbuster *Star Wars* had its theatrical release in the summer of '77.

Before *Star Wars*, the press seldom wrote about a film's first "weekend gross." Afterward, they never stopped. Perhaps *Star Wars* is a phenomenal film. I wouldn't know. I've never seen it.

My landlord at 68 Thompson Street was a tightly wound ex–police detective named Sam Bress. Bress was intimidating enough without a gun, but for good measure kept a loaded one in his breast pocket. Although he often threatened to use it, I never believed he would. I was wrong. One day a would-be mugger put a knife to the sixty-five-year-old's throat, demanding cash. Bress pretended to reach for his wallet, but pulled out his gun instead and shot the thug. Luckily for Sam, the thug survived. (Lucky for the thug too.)

Unable to work out why I plowed so much money into fixing up a rented apartment, Bress at least recognized that my efforts increased its value. Expecting friends of mine to do the same, he offered me every apartment that became vacant. Pretty soon, nine of the thirty apartments at 68 Thompson Street were rented by people I worked with. Though I never went to college, the camaraderie of sharing the same building and stairway was, I imagine, similar to the feeling of living in a college dormitory. It also made life safer. In all the time I lived in SoHo my apartment was never robbed. Mind you, with its abundance of deadbolts, window gates and floor-mounted police locks, my apartment wasn't exactly child's play to break into.

Sam Bress was intrigued by the young tenants I brought in, particularly its women. Despite giving the impression of being stonehearted, Sam would occasionally waive a month's rent if someone was strapped for cash. But if he discovered they were lying, he'd clip them around the ear and kick them out. I liked Sam a lot, and I'd stop and chat with him and his wife whenever I was close to his office on East Thirteenth Street. Directly behind the office was the famous German restaurant Lüchow's, whose motto was "In a changing world, nothing changes at Lüchow's." Lüchow's closed in 1983.

When I made my first film, *End of the Night*, in 1989, I gave Sam a role as a diner's short-tempered counterman. In the film, a fellow worker describes Sam's character with the dreadful line, written by me, "He probably fucks like someone with a taxi waiting." To be fair, this woeful dialogue is not altogether representative of my film, but it may help explain why it took me thirty-three years to watch it after its original screening at the Cannes Film Festival. I haven't seen my second film, *Far From Berlin* (which was far from a success), since the editing room a month before its theatrical release. I'd rather be waterboarded than watch it again.

Sam Bress sold 68 Thompson Street in the late eighties, but I kept my rent-stabilized apartment until 2003, when I passed it on to my son Harry. After Sam died in the mid-nineties, the building was sold to an anonymous property company whose owner was never seen by the tenants.

In 2007, the building suffered a serious fire, which suspiciously began in the basement in the early hours of the morning. Luckily, none of the tenants were injured, but the fire caused so much damage—including by firemen breaking into apartments—that the landlord closed down the building for five years, forcing the tenants, including Harry, to find other homes. Apartment 25 at 68 Thompson Street, which had been in my family for thirty years, was gone forever.

(Ironically, I would move back to Thompson Street forty-five years later. In 2022, I moved into an apartment on the exact same block as 68 Thompson Street.)

Downtown New York in the seventies was an extraordinary period for me. It was a pre-AIDS time when freedom took precedence over responsibility and commerce. It was the world of the *Village Voice*, CBGB, Spring Street Books, the Mudd Club, the Bleecker Street Cinema, the bars of Mickey Ruskin and the films of Amos Poe. It was a world populated by those whose downtown fame would later take off stratospherically, like David Byrne, Spalding Grey, Patti Smith, Philip Glass and Deborah Harry. It was also populated by those whose downtown fame would remain on the runway, like Eric Mitchell, Lizzy Mercier Descloux, Rene Ricard, James Chance and Taylor Mead. It's those who stayed on the runway who now symbolize this remarkable period for me.

One of life's cruelties is that we only recognize special times in hindsight. Although my happiest years in New York were spent living downtown in the seventies, I wasn't aware of it until decades later. For the very briefest of moments there was a kind of convergence between my life and the spirit of the times. But every generation has its own convergence, its own version of SoHo in the seventies. This was mine.

14.

In February 1979, I received my green card from the US Immigration Service. After working at One Fifth for three years I was now legal and free to do the one thing I came to New York to do: write and direct films. Except I didn't have the balls and so I remained in the restaurant business. Besides, One Fifth's owner, George Schwarz, had sponsored me for my green card, and while Schwarz was difficult to work for, it didn't seem right to leave him the second I became legal. Like many mentor-pupil relationships, ours was destined to end badly. A month after I got my green card, we had a fight over the bartenders' schedule and I walked out. I hoped that was the last I'd see of him. I was wrong.

Lynn and I decided to open our own restaurant. We were fed up slogging away for other people and were anyway bursting with restaurant ideas of our own. In the spring of 1980, we hit the streets looking for a space. The only area downtown we could afford was Tribeca, a neighborhood between SoHo and the Twin Towers unknown to most people living above Fourteenth Street.

The real estate broker gave us a list of three available spaces. The first two were lemons, but approaching the third, I noticed a red neon sign that shone so brightly it could be seen from Kansas. This was Towers Cafeteria. The second we pressed our faces against one of its three enormous windows, Lynn and I knew we'd struck oil.

Within the month, we'd signed a fifteen-year lease and roped my brother Brian into being our third partner. It was Brian who came up with the idea of calling it the Odeon—growing up, our local cinema was the Mile End Odeon.

The hardest part of building a restaurant is finding an investor. Especially if you hate the person you become when asking for money. The ease with which I cede integrity and turn into the most awful, groveling Uriah Heep–type figure makes me wonder if building a restaurant is worth the degradation. Before I left One Fifth, two of its regulars took me aside and whispered conspiratorially that if I ever built a restaurant of my own, they'd invest without hesitation. When push came to shove, both rejected me. I learned the hard way the difference between promising to invest and writing out the check. The Odeon cost $150,000 to build. After endless brush-offs, Lynn and I raised the money from our parents and our friends Alan Bennett and Nell Campbell.

The Odeon is the only restaurant I've built, or co-built, where I didn't go over budget. This wasn't due to being disciplined with money; there was simply no money to go over budget with. After paying for equipment and furniture, we had so little left that the three of us had to do most of the physical work ourselves. Oddly enough, a shortage of cash was a good thing because it forced us to solve problems creatively. Or at least accept compromises. I never liked the existing terrazzo floor but couldn't afford to replace it. After we opened, I thought the terrazzo floor was one of the best things about the restaurant. Having a miniscule budget probably accounts for the Odeon being the most original place I've built. Even though I have an aversion to physical work, I believe that, generally, the dirtier the restaurateur's hands get during construction, the more compelling the restaurant.

No matter how hard we worked putting the Odeon together, opening a large restaurant in an obscure neighborhood was a risky undertaking. By day, Tribeca was busy with mid-level office workers, but at night there was absolutely no one on the streets. It was a desolate neighborhood eerily dominated by the Twin Towers. How on earth were we going to fill our 130-seat restaurant?

Between signing the lease for the restaurant and fixing it up, Lynn and I spent a week in New Orleans. While walking around a shady area outside the French Quarter we saw a large thirties-style neon clock in the window of a junk shop that looked perfect for our unbuilt restaurant. The only problem was there was a NOT FOR SALE sign in front of it. The eternally shy Lynn persuaded me to go in alone and make an offer. "Offer a hundred dollars but *no more*," she advised.

Entering the shop, I faced an angry-looking man behind the counter. "I know the neon clock's not for sale," I began hesitantly, "but I'd like to make an offer of . . ." Before I could say "a hundred dollars," he blurted out, "I won't take a penny less than *twenty-five dollars*!"

That twenty-five-dollar neon clock was our first purchase for the Odeon and has been hanging in the same position on the wall next to the bar since October 1980.

During renovations, Alan Bennett came over from England to pitch in. One stiflingly hot day, Alan and I drove to the far reaches of New Jersey to pick up three large pink-tinted mirrors. These eighty-year-old mirrors were so fragile that Alan had to drive back to Manhattan at the speed of a hearse, with a line of frustrated drivers behind, honking at him the entire way. At the time I wondered if their honking would have been half as loud if they'd known that the tentative driver ahead was one of England's most distinguished playwrights. In hindsight, I think they would have honked twice as loud.

The pink-tinted mirrors survived the journey and were later installed on the wall opposite the Odeon's entrance where, forty-odd years on, they remain.

Midway through renovations I heard about a phenomenal chef called Patrick Clark who was working at the Pear Tree restaurant in Midtown. After eating at the restaurant, Lynn and I were so stunned by his food that we called Clark at 9 a.m. the next day and offered him the position of head chef at the Odeon. At twenty-five years old, Clark already had a reputation within the industry as one of New York's best exponents of nouvelle cuisine and would, several years later, become the first Black chef to receive a James Beard Award. Clark was one of the best chefs I've ever worked with. But also the most difficult.

In 1980 the Mafia still had a stranglehold on New York's restaurants. A month before the Odeon opened, I was visited by a heavyset man. He asked if I had a contract with a carting company to pick up the restaurant's garbage. After I said no, he replied, "You do now." With his New Jersey accent, he welcomed me to the neighborhood, saying he hoped I'd be a "good client." Placing his large, fleshy fingers on my shoulder, he lowered his voice and whispered, "If you got any problem wid anything, anything at all, you call me and I'll sort it out."

We paid our garbage bills extra promptly and never heard from this mafioso figure again. But over the years, there were a few times when I considered calling him. Inexplicably, the day after my stroke was one of them.

A week before we opened, seven servers from One Fifth jumped ship and joined the Odeon. A bold move on their part considering the Odeon's future was so uncertain. Working alongside waiters I'd worked with before greatly contributed to the Odeon's success and made my job easier and far more enjoyable. In retrospect, I'm amazed at how young the floor staff were when the Odeon opened. Ninety percent of us, including the chef, were in our twenties. This added the kind of energy that only young people can provide. Like a rock band's first performance, we were unpolished but brimming with potential. Plus we had the one thing that no amount of experience can give you: generosity of spirit. And we had it in bucketfuls.

The Odeon opened its doors on October 14, 1980. The first night wasn't a disaster, but the first customer was. She entered the second the doors opened at 6 p.m., without a clue she was the Odeon's very first guest. Alone in the dining room, she waited ninety minutes for a green bean salad before being told we had no green beans. Fuming, she ordered a coffee and nothing else. She got nothing else rather quickly, but the coffee never arrived. No one knew how to operate the coffee grinder.

The second night went slightly better. The dining room was never full, but at least we knew how to use the coffee grinder. The third night was a restaurant owner's dream. The kitchen was perfect, and the dining room was full most of the night, with an interesting, mixed crowd. Luckily, it has continued that way ever since.

The Odeon's success was mostly due to happenstance: being in the right place at the right time. It was a sort of success that defies logic and defines its time. Through no intention of our own, the Odeon quickly became the epicenter of the downtown art scene with Andy Warhol, Jean-Michel Basquiat and Julian Schnabel mixing with the likes of Anna Wintour, Lorne Michaels and the cast of *Saturday Night Live*. Harold Pinter, as well as the writers Joseph Heller and Edward Albee, ate at the Odeon that first year.

The Odeon combined the spirit and unfussiness of a downtown restaurant with food that rivaled some of the best French restaurants uptown. Though we served lobster à la nage and oysters in a champagne sauce, we also served hamburgers and French fries. Customers could arrive in jeans and sneakers and be seated next to someone in a tuxedo and both parties would feel comfortable.

On the Odeon's fourth night my former boss George Schwarz turned up for dinner. Seeing a restaurant owned by his ex-manager (and former protégé) packed to the rafters and being run by many of his old employees drove him insane. After he'd finished his meal, he walked over to the maître d's desk and took a swing at me. My brother Brian leaped over the bar and, with one punch, floored my ex-boss.

As Schwarz lay on the terrazzo floor, his nose oozing blood, I felt disgusted with myself. Schwarz wasn't perfect, but he'd taught me everything I knew about restaurants and had even sponsored me for a green card. And this was his reward. In one way or another, perhaps it's the reward for mentors the world over. Humiliated, the esteemed doctor had to be helped to his feet. Holding a handkerchief to his nose to stem the flow of blood, Schwarz looked me in the eye and walked out. I never saw him again.

As a child, I never ate in a proper restaurant. But I came close. On holiday one summer, my parents stood outside a smart restaurant staring at the prices on an exterior menu, unsure what to do. They lingered by the door, with me and my young sister close by, struggling to summon the courage to enter. After ten minutes or so, they decided against it and turned around. Whether it was the expense, or the fear—common to many working-class people—of restaurant protocol, I don't know, but they never managed to cross the threshold that day or any other day. For people like my parents, entering a white-tablecloth restaurant was like being pushed on stage without knowing their lines. They were crippled with embarrassment.

The first time I ate in a "real" restaurant, I was seventeen. In 1968, after the curtain came down on the play *Forty Years On*, Alan Bennett regularly took some of us to a restaurant called Bianchi's. The place was run by a petite Italian woman called Elena Salvoni. A year earlier, she'd become famous in theatrical circles for discovering the dead bodies of playwright Joe Orton and his lover, Kenneth Halliwell, in their Islington flat.

For most of the young cast, going to this semi-formal restaurant with the play's author was a thrilling experience. For me, it was an agonizing one. Staring at the battery of silverware petrified me. I was particularly mystified by the curved shape of the butter knife. Whenever a course was served, I'd wait for everyone else at the table to begin and then try to imitate them.

I'd never eaten cantaloupe before and after finishing the soft interior I started digging my way through its hard rind. It wasn't until Elena whispered to me that it wasn't necessary to eat the whole melon that I stopped my jackhammering. Eating in a formal restaurant after the play was the most frightening aspect of my life in the theater.

After such miserable experiences, it might seem perverse that I should end up in the culinary trade. Just as many children with serious health issues end up being doctors, I believe my early restaurant traumas gave me a leg up in the business. If nothing else, they made me hypersensitive to the couple standing timidly by the maître d's desk who are unsure of procedure.

When I arrived in New York in 1975, the snobbishness of the maître d' often signaled a restaurant's excellence. Opening the Odeon five years later, I was determined to avoid anything that reeked of affectation: no menus written solely in French, no arrogant maître d's, no wine lists the size of the Bible. Lynn, Brian and I wanted the Odeon to be a great restaurant without the absurdly pretentious features of great restaurants in the past.

Today, I'm forever drumming into my maître d's to be acutely aware of the shy and unconfident customer. The savvy New Yorker will always find a way to get a table. But the shy and unassertive will not. I cringe as I write this, but at the end of the day, it's the customers lacking in confidence I care about most.

One service custom I insist on is that waiters always tell the guests the price of the specials not listed on the menu. This is essential. There used to be a famously hip restaurant in Greenwich Village called Da Silvano whose Italian waiters would stand at the head of the table and reel off about a dozen specials. Silvano himself would instruct his servers never to mention the price. Some of the "specials" were unconscionably expensive. Particularly during truffle season. Which, at Da Silvano, was twelve months a year. The first time I ate there was in 1977, and almost choked when I got the bill. I had to borrow money from my date to pay it. Da Silvano closed in 2016.

I often wonder where I found the confidence at twenty-nine to open a 130-seat restaurant in Manhattan after arriving in America only five years earlier. Considering how little Lynn, Brian and I really knew about the restaurant business, the confidence we possessed to open the Odeon was one born of ignorance. Sometimes in life, experience is a fucking hindrance. Opening the Odeon was one of those times.

Unlike at many restaurants that become fashionable, the original servers at the Odeon were never full of themselves. Quite the opposite: they took the work seriously but not themselves while doing it. In my fifty years working and owning restaurants, my happiest times were at the Odeon, sitting down with the waiters and waitresses at three in the morning, listening to them joke about the night as they smoked, drank beer and counted their tips. Nothing since has ever matched that feeling.

* * *

During the Odeon's early days, the actor John Belushi was our most regular customer. An original cast member of *Saturday Night Live*, he'd recently starred in the blockbuster film *Animal House*. Looking like someone who'd perpetually slept through his alarm, Belushi would swagger in just before closing and sit down with the staff as they gossiped about the night's customers. One time, he came in after the cooks had left and volunteered to make the few remaining staff hamburgers. I somehow felt he was eager to show them that he could do something other than make people laugh. Watching him alone in the kitchen, cooking, was the only time I felt that Belushi was truly himself. The rest of the time I felt he was acting. But he had such a boyish charm that one couldn't help but like him. The staff adored him.

One weekend he came in around four. He'd been partying all night and was scared to return home to his wife. Given the situation, he offered me some advice: "When you're married and return home at four a.m., go into the house really depressed and tell your wife that everything went wrong that night. She'll instantly forgive you." I've since tried it. It doesn't work.

Belushi owned a private bar with the actor Dan Aykroyd. It was several blocks south of the Odeon, and not long after it opened, they sent a limousine for Lynn and me to come and watch them perform their Blues Brothers routine. The invitation came with a condition: we had to arrive with two medium-rare cheeseburgers.

Cheeseburgers on our laps, we sat in the limousine as it delivered us to an anonymous bar in the middle of nowhere. Anonymous, that is, until we opened the door: two hundred of Belushi's friends and hangers-on were crowded into the tiny bar. After wolfing down the burgers, Belushi and Aykroyd jumped onto a makeshift stage and began belting out a well-known Motown song. Predictably, the crowd went berserk, and the place became too frenzied for me. Aside from a chronic inability to enjoy rock concerts—even small ones like this—I had my own bar to run. Unnoticed by Belushi and Aykroyd, Lynn and I meekly left midway through James Brown's "I Feel Good" and returned to work.

* * *

No matter how vibrant the Odeon was, without Patrick Clark's stupendous talent it wouldn't have become the success it was. But that success came at a cost.

Outside the kitchen Patrick was intelligent, kind and wholly rational. Inside he was a screaming bully who intimidated Lynn and me and terrorized the staff. How would I have behaved under the crushing pressure of having to cook more than two hundred meals a night in hundred-degree heat? Probably a lot worse than Clark.

During very busy nights, Chef Clark often threatened to walk out if the Odeon served more than two hundred dinners. Considering that on weekend nights we usually had reservations for three hundred, this made my life—as the restaurant's maître d'—nerve-racking. I was the only restaurateur in New York who regularly prayed for no-shows.

Most business owners claim the consequences for breaking the rules are the same for every employee. That's not true. Like gifted sportsmen, talented chefs can be difficult to control. They can break the rules with an impunity seldom afforded to other, less brilliant staff. Whether a tendency to rebel is inherent in exceptionally talented people, or whether public recognition makes talented people more difficult, I couldn't say. But the sports figures I'm inclined to admire—like John McEnroe and Diego Maradona—often defied the rules.

Patrick Clark was in a different category altogether. He got away with breaking the rules because Lynn and I were scared shitless of him. On some nights he would scream so loudly he could be heard in the dining room. A cook called Rex was nicknamed "Nervous Rex" because he shook with fear every time Clark entered the kitchen. Nervous Rex quit after a month. Every weekend at least one server would cry during their shift as a result of Patrick's temper. Eventually, his tyranny became insupportable. Regardless of the consequences, Lynn and I decided to fire him.

When D-Day arrived, I nervously explained to Clark that we couldn't accept his bullying anymore and, taking a step back—just beyond punching range—explained that we were "letting him go." (Although I hate euphemisms, I wasn't brave enough to say the word "fire" when facing Clark.) I fully expected him to hit me, but instead he burst into tears. Lynn and I didn't know what to do. It's unnerving watching a bully cry. Despite his volatility, we both felt close to Patrick and were infinitely grateful to him for having launched the Odeon's kitchen. But we had to draw the line. We had to. Yet the more Patrick cried, the fainter that line became. After it disappeared for good, I offered him his job back. He stopped crying, blew his nose and vowed never to bully anyone ever again.

That night he was back in the kitchen, screaming at the staff.

I'm glad I rehired Clark. Having often screwed up myself, I'm a firm believer in giving people second chances. In my experience, those who don't fuck up a second time frequently become great employees. Unfortunately, that didn't happen with Patrick.

In 1984, an unknown author called Jay McInerney showed up at the Odeon and asked if he could use an image of the place for the cover of his first book, *Bright Lights, Big City*. He offered to pay generously for the image and gave me a copy of his manuscript. I began reading it but couldn't get further than the first chapter. My instinct told me the book was going to be a turkey. Feeling sorry for the unknown McInerney, I let him use the image for free. Seven months later the book came out to worldwide success. So much for my instinct.

During the Odeon's second year, I began arguing with my brother Brian, who, as well as being a partner, was the restaurant's bar manager. Our arguments stemmed from his habit of leaving the bar during service to chat with customers in the dining room. At least that's what I told Brian the reason was. The real reason was complicated and went back to our childhood.

As a boy I attended the same elementary and high school as my two older brothers. Though I looked up to them, I also found them intimidating. Leaving school, I was determined to carve my own path and became an actor. After giving up the theater, I lived on a kibbutz, which I liked enough to return to twice in three years. But when Peter and Brian moved to the same kibbutz, I left and never went back.

After Brian landed in New York, besides giving him a job and an apartment, I introduced him to all my friends. And though I wanted him to thrive, churlishly I didn't want him to thrive *quite* to the extent he did. Despite enjoying his company more than anyone else's, I also felt tailgated. But what grieved me the most was that Brian possessed a far greater social ease than I did. Especially with women.

Rivalry between brothers should never be underestimated.

One night I pushed Brian too far and during a bitter argument on the sidewalk outside the restaurant he punched me so hard he broke my cheekbone. After spending two days in St. Vincent's Hospital, I dissolved our business partnership and we stopped speaking for nearly a decade. Unfortunately, it wasn't to be the last time.

New Yorkers relish family feuds, and our very public one was the source of gleeful speculation in the press, which compared our volatile relationship to that of Dave and Ray Davies of the English pop group the Kinks. (These days it would be Liam and Noel Gallagher of Oasis.) It made my life very uncomfortable. We moved in similar circles and whenever I left the house I dreaded running into Brian. It felt like I was nine years old again: terrified of being bullied by my two older brothers, and spending half my days trying to avoid them.

By chance, Brian and I ended up seated next to each other at a Paul Simon concert. It was agonizing. Since then, whenever I hear a Paul Simon song my jaw hurts.

Not long after selling his Odeon shares to Lynn and me, Brian built a downtown Vietnamese restaurant, Indochine, which quickly became New York's hippest restaurant and one of its most successful. I was livid, of course. A few years after opening Indochine, Brian ran into trouble with the IRS and ended up selling the restaurant to one of his busboys.

Indochine is still open today and still making a truckload of profit.

As so often with siblings, our relationship is a mass of contradictions. We're very close but never touch. The idea of hugging is out of the question. We share similar views on films, soccer, books, politics (of which I know little), plays and the English language, yet could have a huge argument over a single misspelling. We're equally repulsed by clichés, emojis and exclamation points yet are always one wrong word away from blows. Or worse, another estrangement. To his credit, Brian has never been jealous of my restaurant successes.

Though he and I infuriate each other constantly, he's the first person I turn to in an emergency. Life without him is difficult to imagine. In many ways, Brian is the sort of man I wish I'd been.

The year of our opening, the titan of restaurant critics, Mimi Sheraton (whom I greatly admired), reviewed the Odeon for the *New York Times*. She gave it an average write-up. That same year she reviewed seventy-one restaurants, the majority of which received better ratings than ours did. Of the seventy-one Sheraton reviewed in 1980, sixty-three had closed by 2024, including one four-star and three three-star restaurants. Thanks to Lynn, who has been its sole owner since 1992, the one-star Odeon is one of eight that remain open today.

Though cobbled together by three amateurs with little money, the Odeon has been packed solid every night for almost half a century.

15.

If there was a single person most responsible for helping me cope with my stroke, it was Lynn Wagenknecht.

As well as organizing my rehabilitation at NewYork-Presbyterian, Lynn found me an apartment to rent, which was waiting for me the day I left the hospital. She also hired and scheduled all my therapists, visited me at least four days a week and often made me lunch while helping with my speech. She did this almost every day for five months while operating the three restaurants she owned in Manhattan.

Lynn's ancestors were Lutherans from northern Europe who'd settled in the Chicago area in the first half of the nineteenth century. My ex-wife may have inherited her integrity and formidable work ethic from them, but not her liberalism and kindness. Those were entirely her own.

After she helped me move into an apartment on West Seventeenth Street, Lynn arranged for me to see a new GP, a jocular doctor in his late sixties by the name of Cohen. Strangely, at our initial consultation, the very first question Dr. Cohen asked me was how many restaurants I owned. When I said seven, he exclaimed, "No wonder you've got gray hair!" Coming from someone who was bald as a coot, this was rich indeed.

Of the many physical therapists I've worked with since my stroke, none was more intelligent than Martin Spollen. With his precise diction and no-nonsense manner, Spollen may have had the appearance of a New England headmaster, but he was a brilliant therapist.

Besides having me do calf and hip stretches, Spollen also had me practice stepping up and down high curbs on Seventeenth Street.

After six months of working with Spollen, I was able to "hobble" about a quarter of a mile with the aid of a cane. When tempted to brag about this, I quickly reminded myself that such progress wasn't anything a three-year-old couldn't master in half the time.

Shunning taxis and public transport, Spollen cycled everywhere. No matter how lousy the weather or where in Manhattan his patients lived, he always arrived by bicycle and precisely on time. A creature of habit, Spollen never began a single session without first washing his hands, which, like the lawyer Jaggers in *Great Expectations*, he did obsessively throughout our ninety minutes together.

Spollen was a Shakespeare buff and would often recite one of the playwright's soliloquies during our twice-weekly sessions. As I lay on the massage table practicing my stretches, he'd be standing over me reeling off Portia's "quality of mercy" speech from *The Merchant of Venice*. Spollen had such a phenomenal memory that if I happened to mention a Shakespeare passage unfamiliar to him, he'd memorize it and by our next session recite it verbatim. Afterward, as I was practicing the dorsiflexion of my right foot, we'd analyze the passage for a full twenty minutes.

Although it seemed incidental to the therapy itself, Spollen's acting out of Shakespeare provided a kind of healing in itself. It also taught me that learning can sometimes unwittingly produce striking results—and that eccentrics like Spollen often make the best teachers.

While physical therapists devote their efforts to the patient's lower body, occupational therapists concentrate on the upper body—in my case, a paralyzed right hand and arm. The occupational therapist Lynn found for me was an ex-marine. In contrast to Spollen's somewhat bookish school of therapy, this ex-marine came from the General Patton school and would bark orders at me to raise my right arm. After three months of being bawled at, my arm was even more obstinate than when we started. As soon as Lynn and I fired the ex-marine, my arm mysteriously became less rigid.

* * *

One unintended benefit of my stroke, at least initially, was the improvement of my relationship with Harry, Sophie and Isabelle. Our relationship had been quite rough since I'd remarried and had a second family. In moving back to New York, I wanted to make up for past mistakes.

I stayed at Seventeenth Street for five months and spent most nights talking to Lynn and our three children. The five of us hadn't spent this much time together in over twenty years. Evenings began with us ordering dinner, which, given that between us Lynn and I owned ten of Manhattan's most popular restaurants, was not a problem. So as not to appear biased, our children felt compelled to alternate between their parents' places. One night they'd order in from Lynn's Café Cluny, the next from my restaurant Schiller's. Lynn and I couldn't have cared less. If anything, we preferred eating from each other's restaurants.

It was during one of these dinners that I discovered my taste buds had vanished. Having ordered fried artichokes from Morandi, I took one bite and was convinced I was eating fried calamari. Not wanting to alarm the kids or spoil the dinner, I didn't mention it, but over the next few days it got worse. Suddenly, I couldn't tell the difference between chicken and fish. Or even between red and white wine. I was terrified. Having a decent palate was fundamental to my work. I didn't know what to do. I couldn't tell a doctor in case it got leaked to the press. Luckily, after nine months it would improve a little—but it wouldn't come back completely until after my suicide attempt, when it returned with such a vengeance that over the course of five weeks I gained thirty-six pounds.

After dinner, the five of us would sit in the living room and reminisce. Like all children of divorce, our kids received endless enjoyment from watching their parents get along. No doubt, subconsciously, they wanted us to get back together. But that was never going to happen—I was still very much in love with Alina.

I called and emailed Alina incessantly. She was still angry with me for going to New York, and perhaps she was right to be.

I wrote an email to George and Alice every day we were apart. Mostly just gossip and a little about the pitfalls of clichés and euphemisms. I also sent them YouTube clips of early Woody Allen or Nichols and May.

Every day for seven months I sent them the definition of a "difficult" word with examples:

March 5, 2017

> *JEOPARDIZE (a good word to use):*
> *To jeopardize a situation means to do something that may destroy it*
>   *or cause it to fail.*
> *"By turning up drunk at school, George's teacher, Mr. Savage, has*
>   *jeopardized his career."*
> *"George is going to jeopardize his relationship with Jago if he does*
>   *not stop stealing money from him."*
> *"Alice will jeopardize her reputation as a lover of animals if she*
>   *continues to pull the legs off chickens."*

Although a terrifically loving mother, Alina was less concerned about our children's education than I was. Before my stroke, I regularly took George and Alice to the theater and museums, especially the National Gallery, which, when we were living in London, we'd visit once a month. But never for longer than twenty minutes. We'd pop in just to look at three or four specific paintings and then leave. I've never understood why people think they have to see every single painting in a museum. It's like eating every dish on a menu. Alan Bennett once wrote that art galleries should have a sign by the entrance: YOU DON'T HAVE TO LIKE EVERYTHING. He could have added: YOU DON'T HAVE TO LOOK AT EVERYTHING.

Taking an overnight train is, for me, one of the two or three things that make life worth living and, once we'd moved to London, I took George and Alice on as many train journeys as I could: one time to go fishing in the Scottish Highlands, and another to Venice to feed pigeons in a waterlogged St. Mark's Square. During one school holiday, George and I took a train to Belgium to visit the battlefields of the First World War and afterward traveled to Normandy to see the beaches of the Allied landings. Alina never joined us on any of these trips abroad and seldom participated in cultural family outings. This seemed to be my role with our children. At the time, I never questioned her reluctance to join us, but while convalescing in New York, I spent half my days worrying whether she'd taken on this responsibility. I spent the other half worrying about my finances. The D-Day invasion force of personal assistants, specialist doctors, reflexologists, acupuncturists, masseurs, physical therapists and a driver now needed to keep me afloat was staggeringly expensive.

On top of these expenses, I was under pressure from landlord Bobby Cayre to begin building Pastis, which in my condition was unimaginable. But if I didn't build it, I'd have to cough up my million-dollar guarantee, which, with my draining resources, I couldn't afford.

The only thing that could make me more financially secure would be if my latest restaurant, Augustine, received two stars or more from the *New York Times*. It had been open for almost four months and was full every night. Yet we still hadn't been reviewed by the *Times*, and as every New York restaurateur knows, you never celebrate a restaurant's success before it's been reviewed by the *New York Times*.

The night before I left London for New York in January 2017, I told George and Alice that when they next saw me I'd be a new man. Five weeks later, they asked to visit me. Alina agreed to bring them to New York during their school's half-term. On a cold February day, she texted me from JFK when their plane touched down.

Opening the door to my apartment two hours later, I was still the same half-paralyzed cripple who couldn't string a coherent sentence together. Physically, I hadn't changed one bit. Eleven-year-old Alice appeared—on the surface, at least—untroubled. But when thirteen-year-old George saw me, he started shaking uncontrollably and burst into tears. I quietly explained that no matter how I looked and sounded, I was still the same person inside. We stood rooted to the spot, in the apartment's narrow hallway, clutching each other, sobbing.

Nine months earlier I had taken George hiking in England's Lake District. We stayed overnight in Ambleside, a town in Cumbria where Wordsworth once worked as a stamp distributor. At dawn, we dressed in silence, cramming our small backpacks with sandwiches, maps and water-resistant clothing. George was annoyed at being woken so early to do something that plainly wasn't his idea, and radiated a sullenness that I bent over backwards to appease. When did we all become terrified of our kids' bad moods? For donkey's years it was the opposite. When on earth did this change?

Finding one's way out of town is often the most difficult part of a hike, and Ambleside proved no exception. I had to stop every five minutes to consult a map. Of course, I could have asked a local to show me the way, but I would have felt silly asking some dentist in the middle of Ambleside High Street for directions, especially when dressed to the nines like a professional hiker.

Eventually, we found our way out, and as we began the steep ascent of Loughrigg Fell, George's surliness increased. Staggering up this craggy mountain for almost four hours, he didn't speak, just glanced in my direction occasionally and grimaced. Once we were in sight of the summit his mood lightened, and thirty feet from the top, George looked up at me and smiled. As we reached the peak, he broke into an enormous grin. Giddy from exhaustion, we both collapsed to the ground and started laughing our heads off. It was the best day of his life, he told me. (Perhaps mine too.)

Six months later I had a stroke.

Throughout her weeklong visit to New York that February 2017, Alina and I argued a lot. She was confused and angry that I was living in New

York and being cared for by my ex-wife and older children. She wanted me home in London, where she thought I belonged with her, Alice and George. I could see her point.

Attempting to bury the hatchet, Lynn cooked an elaborate meal for both families. It was gratifying to see my five children getting along so well. After all, they were brothers and sisters. Sadly, Alina chose not to join the dinner.

Before we had children of our own, Alina got on incredibly well with my older children. The five of us traveled to Hawaii one winter, Saint Bart's the next and spent summers together at my house on Martha's Vineyard. But soon after Alina and I married, the relationship became tense, and once we had children of our own it began to deteriorate.

It all came to a head one summer. I was on Martha's Vineyard with Alina and my five children. With everybody under one roof, I tried to divide my time between George and Alice—who were both under two—and my three older kids. At one point, Alina thought there was an imbalance, that the attention I was giving my older children was attention taken away from her and the babies. Harry, Sophie and Isabelle thought the opposite. Whether they were unconsciously jealous of the care I was giving the new babies, or Alina was right, I couldn't say, but it left everyone angry and in tears.

After that, Alina's relationship with my older kids was never the same. It wasn't long before Harry, Sophie and Isabelle stopped staying with us on Martha's Vineyard. In retrospect, I should have been more assertive and organized group therapy for everybody. Stupidly, I had no faith in family therapy then and, as usual, just stood lamely to one side in the hope that things would sort themselves out. They never did, and as a result, everybody suffered—and continues to do so today.

Looking back, I realize how brave Alina was to become involved with someone who had three children from a previous marriage. It must have been like missing the first hour of a film, in that she was probably never certain what had gone on beforehand. Stepchildren never consider this. When things go haywire with second families, the cards are unfairly stacked against stepparents. Stepmothers especially. I wish this wasn't the case.

The day we got married, I was surprised that Alina took my name. In spite of her cumbersome surname, my first wife, Lynn, never changed Wagenknecht to McNally. The thought of making love to someone called Mrs. McNally would have disturbed me beyond. Luckily, Alina was always so loving toward me in bed that I clean forgot she was Mrs. McNally. Thank God.

16.

For as long as I can remember, I've hated weddings. The dressing up, the enforced conviviality, the best man's unfunny jokes and the sheer interminability of them. In the last twenty-five years, I've attended only three weddings, one of which was my own.

When Lynn and I married in 1983, I didn't tell a soul. Not even my own family. To avoid the hoopla of a big event I dragged Lynn three thousand miles to get married in Los Angeles. Though we stayed at the Beverly Hills Hotel, we had a decidedly spartan wedding and invited only three people to the party. (*Some* party.) Lynn never forgave me.

SNL producer Lorne Michaels somehow got wind of what we were doing and generously sent a case of Dom Pérignon to our hotel. Noticing that the champagne was produced in 1975, I suddenly realized what an extravagant gift an entire case was. A single bottle in 1983 cost $1,000.

As our wedding consisted of just five people—one of whom was on the wagon—we drank fewer than two bottles. Afterward, I put the remaining ten bottles back in our hotel room. The next morning I received a frantic phone call from the manager of the store who'd delivered the champagne saying he'd made a dreadful mistake. Lorne had ordered, and paid for, just one bottle of 1975 Dom Pérignon, not a whole case. The manager was desperate to know if there were any unconsumed bottles. I told him there were, but after hanging up I hid three in a drawer. He arrived twenty minutes later and was so relieved that seven bottles of Dom Pérignon remained, he offered me a $100 tip. Under the circumstances, I couldn't possibly have accepted it. (But I did think about it.)

* * *

The previous year, Lynn and I took a night off from running the Odeon to see Jean Renoir's classic film *The Rules of the Game*. It was showing at the Thalia, an art house theater on the Upper West Side. I'd seen the film before but was eager for Lynn to watch it, mainly because it contains my favorite line in all of cinema: "The awful thing about life is this: everyone has their reasons."

Leaving the cinema, Lynn suggested we have dinner at a restaurant close by called L'Elysée. The only problem was the restaurant hadn't been open long, and I feared it'd be full and we wouldn't get a table. But it was worse than that. The place was stark empty and we got one much too easily. Lynn felt embarrassed because she had worked with L'Elysée's co-owner, who happened to be there that night and recognized her. Mortified to have fellow restaurateurs bear witness to such a deadly night, the poor man used a line I've used a hundred times: "You should have been here last night. It was packed."

"Are you doing well, then?" Lynn asked sympathetically.

"Not bad. We're getting a mention in the *Post* this week."

There was an awkward pause.

"You wouldn't like to buy the place, would you?"

"Perhaps."

Two months later the space was ours. After nine months of renovation, we opened our second restaurant. We called it Café Luxembourg.

Café Luxembourg is the only restaurant I didn't struggle to name. Which is ironic as it's the only restaurant I spelled incorrectly. It was supposed to be named after revolutionary socialist Rosa Luxemburg, not Luxembourg, the blandest country in the world.

With every restaurant I have a hand in designing, I can't start the project until I have one specific detail in mind. It doesn't have to be significant, but without this detail, I'm stuck. Like a writer who can't begin a book until he has the perfect first sentence, I'm frozen until I find the first building block. With Café Luxembourg, it was a cream-and-blue wall tile.

A week before renovation started, I went alone to see an Australian film called *Starstruck*. I didn't like the film much but was interested by something in the background of one of the scenes: an insignificant wall that was lined with sensational tiles, each one of cream and blue. I thought they would look terrific in Café Luxembourg. I mentioned the tiles to Lynn, and the next day we went to see the movie together. Armed with a Polaroid camera, Lynn waited until the scene with the tiles appeared, then fired away. The photographs made such a racket spewing out from the Polaroid that someone a few rows behind shouted out: "Why the fuck are you taking photos?" I wanted to shout back "Everyone has their reasons," but was too scared.

Although we couldn't find the exact cream-and-blue tile, Lynn, the far more practical one in our partnership, found two different tiles—a cream one and a deep blue one—and laid them in alternate rows on the walls and columns. The rest of the moderately art deco design came easily. Apart from some terrible venting issues, Café Luxembourg was the most painless restaurant build I've been involved in. Whatever great expectations I start a project with usually begin to disintegrate at around the halfway point, and six weeks from opening what began in my head as a masterpiece has now turned into a salvage job. However, Café Luxembourg was the opposite, and the only time the end result has matched the picture I had of the place before I started. It being only my second restaurant, I had no idea what a rare occurrence this was and fully expected it to happen again. Forty years later I'm still waiting.

Café Luxembourg opened in the summer of 1983 and received good reviews all around, including two stars from the *New York Times*. Lynn and I couldn't do any wrong in the eyes of restaurant reviewers. But that would soon change—and then some.

There used to be a tiny shop in SoHo that sold nothing but postcards. This hole-in-the-wall was called Untitled. Living around the corner from the place, I often spent hours there sifting through thousands of postcards of well-known—and some not-so-well-known—paintings and photographs. Each one cost eighty-five cents. By the end of the seventies, I must have bought five hundred of these postcards, one of which was a riveting

Brassaï photo of three naked prostitutes shot from behind. What made the Brassaï work for me wasn't the fact that the women were naked, but that they were totally unselfconscious of being photographed naked.

Not long after Café Luxembourg opened, Lynn suggested we take a photo of the restaurant's interior and turn it into a postcard to present to the customers with their check. Instead of a conventional photograph, I thought it'd be more interesting to take one like the Brassaï. But for the photo to have an impact, the three women should be working women standing naked at Luxembourg's zinc bar in a guileless, unaffected manner. Any hint of the photo being tongue-in-cheek and the effect I was looking for would be lost. I conveyed this to the restaurant's general manager and left him to hire the models and photographer and oversee the shoot. One thing I've learned from directing a couple of movies myself is the near impossibility of reproducing on film something seen in real life or a photograph. Even something as simple as three naked women standing at a restaurant bar.

I had to miss most of the shoot due to a servers' meeting at the Odeon, but as soon as the meeting was over I took the subway uptown to Café Luxembourg. I made it just as the photographer was taking the last shot. What I saw appalled me. The entire shoot looked *designed*. And worse, the three women the manager had hired looked like *Vogue* models, not like regular women at all. I was furious with him for getting my idea so wrong—but it wasn't his fault. As usually happens when things go wrong in my restaurants, I was completely to blame for not explaining my idea more clearly.

I called the model agency to specify the exact type of women I wanted: Women with kids. Women who have trouble making ends meet. Women who've never heard of Diane von fucking Furstenberg. *Real* women. And that's precisely who I got. And probably why the photo works so well. It's worth visiting Café Luxembourg just to see this photograph.

Even though I sold my shares in Café Luxembourg to Lynn when we divorced in 1992, I still eat there. And in a way I enjoy the place more. It's a bit like going from being a parent to being a grandparent—I get all the fun without any of the responsibility.

* * *

Three years after opening Café Luxembourg, Lynn and I—with considerable help from our friend Nell Campbell—built a nightclub on Fourteenth Street. We called it Nell's.

When Nell had moved to New York in the early eighties, I introduced her to Lynn, and the two of them became close friends. One night while having dinner I was joking about Nell's struggling acting career, and casually suggested she should open her own nightclub. I felt that given her witty, flamboyant manner, Nell would be very much at home running a club. In fact, the place should feel like an extension of her home, which is why I suggested we call it Nell's. Two weeks later the three of us signed a ten-year lease on a six-thousand-square-foot raw space on West Fourteenth Street.

Living directly next door at 242 Fourteenth Street was the former girlfriend of the painters Jackson Pollock and Willem de Kooning, Ruth Kligman. Kligman was in the car Pollock was driving when it crashed and killed him. Her apartment and studio at 242 Fourteenth previously belonged to the abstract expressionist Franz Kline. While we were building Nell's, Kligman would regularly drop by and chat. (She'd proposed to Jasper Johns, she once told me.) Kligman knew all of 1950s New York's abstract expressionists. Even those she hadn't slept with.

At the time, abstract expressionism didn't interest me, so I never really listened to Kligman's stories on the subject. What an idiot I was.

Lynn, Nell and I began building Nell's in the fall of 1985. Because I don't dance, I called it a nightclub for people who don't like nightclubs.

Nell's had two levels. The ground floor had comfortable sofas, a live jazz band, red leather booths for dining and a thirty-foot mahogany bar we bought in Harlem. The floor below—where the lights were much lower—had a lounge, two bars and a small, funky dance floor. We also put in two sets of staircases from ground floor to basement, creating constant movement between the two contrasting areas. I believe these two sets of staircases played a crucial role in Nell's success.

Unusually for a downtown club, Nell's had a fair-size kitchen and a dining area for fifty people. Although I wanted the food to be special, I didn't want the kind of faux-elegant menu usually served in nightclubs. I wanted the food to be the best thing about the club, but didn't want to announce it—I wanted people to discover it. Ideally, the couple who'd spent three hours dancing in the basement would surface upstairs in need of a snack and end up having a three-course meal. But what type of meal, I had no idea.

A month before we opened, Nell recommended an English friend of hers, a brilliant home cook, she said, but someone who'd never worked in a restaurant kitchen. While being skeptical of hiring a nonprofessional, I was intrigued enough to fly to London to meet this woman. Her name was Rose Gray.

Gray lived in a cozy, ramshackle house in Paddington with her artist partner and four children. The meeting started awkwardly because we both knew I was there to discuss food but we consciously avoided the subject. For the first hour we talked about anything but food. Eventually, Rose asked me if I fancied "a bite" to eat. Her "bite" was a grilled marinated lamb sandwich. It was one of the most delicious sandwiches I'd eaten in my life. I hired her on the spot.

Rose planned to stay for two months but it ended up being four. She couldn't continue any longer, she said, because she was planning on opening an amateur-sounding place in London with her friend Ruthie Rogers. After she described her "café by the Thames," I told her it probably wouldn't work and that she was better off remaining with me at Nell's.

On Rose's return to London, she and Rogers opened the River Cafe, the success of which would change Italian cooking in England forever. A year after it opened, the River Cafe was awarded a Michelin star, and in 2010 this "home cook" of whom I had initially been so doubtful received an MBE from the Queen. After the monumental success of the River Cafe, I stopped giving opinions about my employees' future projects. I also threw away my voodoo doll.

Nell's opened in the fall of 1986. We had no PR—I hate public relations and, in forty-five years, have rarely used it—but nevertheless, most

New Yorkers seemed to be aware of Nell's opening. The first night we turned away five hundred people. Within weeks, celebrities like Sting, Susan Sontag and Andy Warhol were mixing in the same club with rappers, homegirls and restaurant waiters and waitresses. On some nights the atmosphere was so charged Nell's felt like the epicenter of the universe. The best of these nights was when Prince gave a two-hour concert for free. It was electrifying. Unsuspecting customers were stunned to see this megastar giving an unannounced performance on a tiny stage on Fourteenth Street.

Although I spent most of my time on the ground floor, overseeing the jazz and the crowd outside, a few times a night I'd make forays downstairs to check on the dance floor. Never having danced *once* in my life, I'd often stand silently on the edge of the dance floor, spellbound by the dancers and envious of the ease with which they abandoned themselves.

To gain admittance to Nell's, customers were asked to pay a nominal five-dollar entrance fee. This rule applied to everybody. In those days, it was unimaginable for a celebrity to pay to enter any club. Mick Jagger, Bob Dylan and other stars took this eccentric policy in good humor and paid the five dollars. Madonna, however, was so incensed to be asked to pay that she demanded I let her in for free. When I said no, she called me a "fucking bastard" and left in a huff. As she was leaving, I wondered if the real Madonna ever called a Nazareth nightclub owner a fucking bastard.

I've no wish to kick a man when he's down, but in the case of Bill Cosby, I will. During Nell's heyday, I took a phone call from Cosby's assistant announcing that the comedian was coming into the club alone the following Sunday. He planned to listen to live jazz but didn't want any favorable treatment. His assistant was adamant that Cosby wanted to be treated like everybody else. I passed her instructions on to my staff.

The following Sunday Cosby arrived alone, stood at the bar, ordered a drink or two, listened to the band and left without incident. My staff treated him no differently from anybody else. Three days later, I received an incredibly nasty letter from the funnyman complaining about the rude service he'd been subjected to at Nell's. His parting shot was a vow never to return. Thank God. I'd never found Cosby funny before, but after this I found him repugnant—as I do all narcissistic, self-obsessed men who allegedly drug women in order to have sex with them.

Though Lynn and I spent six nights a week at Nell's, neither of us smoked or took a single drug, which meant we rarely let go. Me even less than Lynn. For a place where I never let myself go, I made an awful lot of money. (Perhaps I shouldn't let go more often.)

In the eighties, financial and social success came so easily I tended not to place much value on it. As usual, I only respected the things that came with effort. I wasn't comfortable in my own skin and it showed on my face. One night a customer at Nell's told me I had the look of a man on a plane who hates flying.

After a great deal of angst, I decided to take time off and do what I'd planned to do since arriving in the city fourteen years earlier: make a film. The script I wrote and directed six months later was called *End of the Night*. It revolved around a married man whose life spirals out of control after his wife becomes pregnant. Considering I'd had nothing but success since I landed in New York, this now seems like an odd subject for me to choose. Or perhaps not. Perhaps I somehow sensed that my stream of successes would soon run dry.

In the ten years that Lynn and I worked together, each of the four places we built ended up being phenomenally successful. We have different strengths but shared an ability to recognize honesty in our staff. The only time we disagreed about an employee was when we opened our final restaurant together.

The smallest and last place Lynn and I ever built, Lucky Strike, opened in the fall of 1989. A late-night, forty-seat bistro in SoHo with young servers, hip music and menus scribbled on mirrors, it was the perfect place for steak frites and a glass of red wine at two in the morning. The *New York Times* described it as having "the congenially grungy feeling of an ancient haunt in Les Halles in Paris."

Essentially a neighborhood place where employees of other restaurants would hang out after work, Lucky Strike also attracted its share of non-locals. In the early nineties, I witnessed Madonna cozying up to Warren Beatty over a cheeseburger there at three in the morning. A few hours earlier, I saw a diminutive Tom Cruise waiting at the bar for a table. Lucky Strike was fiercely egalitarian—we didn't take reservations—and when it was full customers had to wait at the bar for a table. Even Lynn and me.

None of the floor staff at Lucky Strike wore uniforms. This put them on a more equal footing with customers, but it also made me feel closer to them, especially to Lucky Strike's general manager, Fabio Ambesi (not his real name). An Italian set designer, he'd arrived in America in 1979, intending to work in films, but, like half of New York, had stumbled into the restaurant business and remained there.

Between leaving One Fifth and opening the Odeon, I waited tables at Mr. Chow on East Fifty-Seventh Street, and this is where I met Ambesi; he was my manager (or "captain," as the position used to be called.) Mr. Chow was my worst ever experience working in a restaurant.

There are two kinds of restaurateurs: those who identify with the staff and those who identify with the customers. Michael Chow (or "M," as he pretentiously calls himself nowadays) definitely identified with the latter. Ever the manipulative egotist, "M" created a cutthroat atmosphere among his staff. Apart from Ambesi and myself, everybody hated each other. Friendships formed under adversity either last forever or flounder in calmer seas. Ours did neither.

Ambesi and I left Mr. Chow at the same time. After such a toxic atmosphere, Ambesi—who was a lot more sensitive than most men—had had enough of restaurants and returned to Italy to work as a carpenter. I stumbled on in the catering trade.

While building Lucky Strike in 1989, I bumped into Ambesi in a hardware store on the Bowery. He'd just come back to New York and was in need of a job. As Lucky Strike was opening the following month, I offered him the general manager position. This was a huge mistake.

After the stress of operating a New York nightclub almost every night for three years, I imagined running a forty-seat bistro would be a breeze. Due to my hiring Ambesi, it ended up being the opposite.

Despite Lucky Strike taking in more money than we had anticipated, Lynn, who oversaw the finances, felt that someone was stealing money from the place. Besides ourselves, only two people had access to the office: the bookkeeper, who had worked with us since the Odeon, and Fabio Ambesi. Lynn had never really taken to Ambesi and felt it was probably him. I knew the man much better than she did and was certain he wasn't the embezzling type. We argued about it constantly.

Although she had no solid proof he was stealing, Lynn wanted to fire him. It's way too easy to pin a crime on someone you don't like, and that's what I felt Lynn was doing.

Things came to a head one morning after more money went missing from the previous night's takings. Lynn gave me an ultimatum: either we get rid of Ambesi or she was going to quit overseeing Lucky Strike's finances. Despite being certain that my former coworker wasn't stealing from us, the next day Lynn and I sat opposite Ambesi and fired him. I felt thoroughly ashamed of myself for firing someone I knew to be innocent. It was one of the worst things I've ever done and it stayed with me for the next decade. The incident didn't lead directly to our divorce, but it undoubtedly rocked the boat.

Ten years after the firing, Lynn and I each received a certified letter from Ambesi. In the letter, he confessed to having stolen from Lucky Strike and now wanted to pay back the money. Never trust certainty.

17.

I own more than two hundred paintings. My obsession began when I was waiting tables in New York. Flush with the kind of money I could only dream about in London, I'd scour the flea markets on my days off, searching for cheap paintings that no one else wanted. Once I owned restaurants, the goalposts widened. As did my ego. Like some nouveau riche big shot, I started bidding for paintings at auction houses. At least I didn't have the gall to call myself a "collector." I'd shoot myself before using that word.

I tend to buy a lot of twentieth-century art—mostly paintings from the Fauvist and the English Bloomsbury movements. I'm quite keen on Cubism and modernism, but until recently my favorite painters were a group of German Expressionists known as Die Brücke ("The Bridge"). Given the choice between spending money on a good school for my children or an oil painting by Max Pechstein, I'd spring for the Pechstein every time.

For the last ten years I've been gripped by a movement of working-class realist painters called the East London Group. These largely uneducated artists of the late 1920s and early '30s lived and worked in the neighborhood where I grew up. After years of following the highbrow Bloomsbury and German Expressionist painters, I've ended up in my own backyard.

When I was doing well financially—after opening Balthazar but before my second divorce—I splurged on an expensive painting by French Fauvist Maurice de Vlaminck. I hung it next to my more modest pictures, but the Vlaminck looked out of place, like some rich upstart who'd bribed his way onto my wall. This wasn't far from the truth, as I'd bought

it solely to impress people. Myself, most of all. Straining to like this toff
as much as I did my more unassuming paintings, I ended up resenting
it—as you always do with things (and people) you force yourself to like.

W. H. Auden said, "All that we are not stares back at what we are,"
and I felt exactly this way whenever I looked at the Vlaminck. Which
wasn't often, on account of what stared back at me. Eventually, I sold the
painting back to the auction house and in the process took a gigantic loss.
Serves me fucking right.

I hate the word "art." It's strange, because I've spent almost fifty years
buying paintings. Stranger still is how little I truly know about a subject
I've been pursuing for close to five decades. To make amends, I spent ten
days in 2006 touring Germany and Switzerland, visiting up to four museums a day. To cram in as many places as possible, I broke the bank and
rented a limousine and driver. That's where the trouble began.

I spent two days in Hamburg alone before my "chauffeur" arrived to
drive me to Berlin, the second stop of my fourteen-city tour.

His name was Max and he enjoyed speaking English but didn't get
much practice because most of his customers were German. Or English,
but too busy to talk. I wish I'd been too busy to talk. I *was* too busy to
talk, but didn't have the guts to say it. Sensing that Max knew this, I
wanted to prove to him it wasn't true: that just because I could afford
to pay for a driver and limousine to swan around German art galleries
for ten days didn't mean I was above talking to him. I *was* above talking
to him but I wanted it both ways. I wanted distance between Max and
myself but at the same time was desperate to be liked by him. That's why
I broke the cardinal rule between driver and passenger: I slid open the
glass partition that divides the two worlds. And once I did that I couldn't
close the partition again without causing offense. I then found myself
trapped in the usual dilemma: whether to close the partition as I wanted
to do, or leave it open and risk offending the driver. I left it open.

Toward the end of the three-hour drive, the closer the car got to Berlin, the more Max's babble receded and the more consumed I became by
memories of a city that had been a turning point in a life full of regrets.

I had been here before. I knew all about it. . . .

* * *

I'd arrived in Berlin fifteen years earlier to direct my second film. It was 1991.

I'd made my first film two years before in New York. At that point, I had a beautiful wife, three wonderful children, two phenomenally successful restaurants and a nightclub that was the toast of Manhattan. I had all the ingredients of a happy life and yet . . . a part of me was deeply dissatisfied. I'd come to New York to make films but had taken a wrong turn and become steeped in the restaurant trade. And although restaurants made me wealthy, working in them hadn't made me happy. In June 1989, I thought of changing this by trying to make a film.

For six weeks, I did nothing but write a screenplay. It was a psychological thriller influenced by a mix of Antonioni and film noir. After finishing the script, I sent it off to a producer I knew. A month later he still hadn't read it. Accustomed to building restaurants where I'd find an empty space one day and begin construction two months later, I wasn't prepared to wait around for ten years for the film to be made.

On the pretext of building another restaurant, I borrowed $500,000 from my bank and used the money to make the film myself. At least, that's how I like to tell it. The truth is, in making both my first and second films, I relied on other people no less than I did when building a restaurant. Maybe more so. Two of those I leaned on most to make *End of the Night* were cinematographer Tom DiCillo (who'd shot Jim Jarmusch's *Stranger Than Paradise* six years earlier) and actor Eric Mitchell. I made the film in black and white and shot it in Brooklyn and Manhattan. Filming took seven weeks and editing three months. Before it was fully complete, I had the chutzpah to enter the film in the Cannes Film Festival.

While waiting for the selectors' decision, I tried to find someone to compose the music. I'd always liked the score of Wim Wenders's *The American Friend*, which I felt had a similar tone to *End of the Night*. The film's composer, Jürgen Knieper, lived in Berlin. I wrote to Knieper out of the blue, and surprisingly he wrote back. Ten days later, I went to visit him.

This was February 1990. The Berlin Wall had fallen four months earlier. Even though it was no longer divided, the Berlin I experienced seemed strangely at odds with itself. Nevertheless, there was an intoxicating energy in the air. With its jarring architecture and clashing cultures, Berlin felt like the most dynamic city in Europe. I had a tremendous urge to film there. While working with Knieper, I started writing a second screenplay, which I set in Berlin.

The day after I got back to New York, I received a fax from the Cannes Film Festival. My film had been selected. *End of the Night*, a movie I'd begun writing only nine months earlier, was going to be shown at the world's most prestigious film festival in seven weeks' time. I found it hard to believe. Buoyed by the news, I suggested to Lynn that we move to Paris. Like me, Lynn was ambivalent about her restaurant success. She'd arrived in New York twelve years earlier with the intention of painting but had been sidelined out of it by me to build and run restaurants. I promised to find her a studio in Paris where she could paint all day if she agreed. "You forget we have three children under seven," she replied. "Who's going to take care of them?" We agreed to talk about it later.

The day after the selections for Cannes were announced, film producer Harvey Weinstein called, asking to see my film. Although I'd never met Weinstein, I'd heard of him because he'd produced the previous year's winner, *Sex, Lies, and Videotape*. Having been advised not to show the film before Cannes, I nervously told Weinstein he couldn't see it. He wouldn't take no for an answer (a trait that would eventually lead to his downfall) and called me four or five times before the festival, asking to see the film. Each time I said no. Weinstein's persistence was too lighthearted to be called harassment, and to be honest, I was flattered by it. He took my final rejection well and before hanging up kindly wished me good luck.

Lynn and I arrived in Cannes three days after the festival had started. We brought with us our two leading actors, our cameraman Tom DiCillo plus Don Palladino, our maître d' and partner at Café Luxembourg, and Nell Campbell. We didn't know how the film would be received, but with our combined experience in New York's nightlife, we were pretty sure the after-party would be a hit.

End of the Night had its first screening at Cannes's main cinema, the Palais des Festivals, in front of two thousand people, including Harvey Weinstein. It was torture. The film seemed agonizingly slow, and the dialogue stilted and inauthentic. I hated my film so much that night I wouldn't be able to watch it again for over thirty years. As the credits rolled, everyone clapped enthusiastically, but what they really thought I didn't know. In the presence of the director, the more I dislike a film, the louder I clap.

I'd agreed to meet Weinstein afterward on the steps of the Palais. If he liked the film, there'd be a good chance he'd distribute it in the States. As Weinstein approached, I recognized his pugnacious look from photos I'd seen of him. Up close, he had a large pockmarked face, small suspicious eyes and the early stages of a double chin. But he also had an admirable directness.

"I didn't like your film and I'm not going to buy it," he calmly stated. "But I'd still like to come to the after-party." I was too stunned to give a coherent reply and mumbled, "Of course." He turned and bounded confidently down the rest of the steps.

Oddly enough, Weinstein's rejection didn't upset me. I appreciated his frankness and I respected his ability to cut to the chase. Other, less direct reactions would be more frustrating to take, indifference being the worst of all. But Weinstein had seen the film as promised and then sought me out and told me exactly what he thought of it. I valued that.

Or maybe I'm wrong. Maybe he was just desperate to go to my after-party.

The film wasn't bought by an American distributor, but it gained a theatrical release in France, Italy and Spain. *End of the Night* broke no records but did sufficiently well that a producer called and asked if I had another script. I sent him the one I'd set in Berlin. He bought it for $100,000 and offered me another $100,000 to direct. Hoping this would be the start of a new career in Europe, I finally convinced Lynn to make a comprehensive move to Paris.

* * *

I first went to Paris in the fall of 1967. I was sixteen and flew there for the weekend to watch a horse race, the Prix de l'Arc de Triomphe. I'd put a year's savings on a horse called Ribocco.

My interest in horse racing began when I was twelve years old. By fourteen I could reel off all the English Derby and Grand National winners of the previous fifty years. Every penny earned from my early-morning paper route would be gambled on horses on the weekend, and every month, without my parents' knowledge, I'd travel with friends to racecourses around England: Ascot, Newbury, Goodwood, Kempton, Alexandra Park and Sandown Park. Weekdays, I'd be up past midnight studying the form of English racehorses. Fortunately, my schoolwork only interfered minimally with my gambling habit. Against the odds, the majority of the horses I backed won, which made giving up this golden goose next to impossible. Until I went to Paris, that is. Nothing lasts forever, and Ribocco came in third in a photo finish. It wouldn't be the last time I lost my life's savings.

Only chronic gamblers know the feeling that comes from losing more money than you can afford. It's a harrowing mix of panic, distress and absolute dread of facing the world.

After leaving Paris, 1967's Prix de l'Arc de Triomphe horse race was stamped indelibly on my mind. But as often happens with memory, these "indelible" images have been slowly usurped by sensations that I was to-tally unaware of at the time: specifically the smells of Pernod and Gauloise cigarettes. Over fifty years these two smells have infiltrated my mind and worked overtime eradicating all memory of the horse race. The only thing they didn't eradicate was the memory of my horse losing. Unfortunately, that gets clearer every day.

I hadn't returned to Paris for eleven years when in 1978 Anna Wintour invited (and paid for) Lynn and me to visit her there. While staying close to Boulevard Saint-Germain, we spent many hours sitting in Café de Flore nursing a café crème and, like many tourists, fantasized about making a permanent move to Paris. And by Paris, we really meant Café de Flore and everything it represented. With its red banquettes, art deco mirrors and irresistible French allure, Café de Flore is the quintessential French café and the most comfortable place on earth to sip a coffee and read a newspaper.

In the summer of 1990, Lynn and I and our three children moved into a late nineteenth-century apartment six blocks from Café de Flore. Soon after the kids were settled at a school on Rue Madame, I began the slow process of putting a crew together for my next film, and in the first month, the majority of our production meetings were held over coffee at the café. I must have had coffee or a late breakfast there at least four times a week. It became both my office and second home. I loved the place.

Not long after we'd moved to Paris, a friend from New York, Susan Forristal (the former wife of Lorne Michaels), was visiting the city and invited Lynn and me out for dinner. I forget where we ate, but we ended up at Café de Flore afterward for a quick nightcap. Two hours later we were still there. As the waiters began putting chairs on the tables, Susan asked a waiter for another drink. He refused. She asked again and he just scoffed and turned his Gallic back on her. Incensed by the waiter's rudeness, Susan threw one of the café's ashtrays at him. It struck him hard on the back of the head and he immediately turned to hit her. Instinctively, I stood up to prevent him, but as I did so, another waiter jumped onto my back. Although no blows were exchanged, the two waiters and I had a nasty scuffle on the floor in which my shirt was torn to pieces and my chin badly bruised. After a few minutes, we were separated by the café's manager, who announced that I was banned from the place. Being banned from the very café in Paris that had prompted me to move there was hard to take. Perhaps even harder than losing a year's savings on a horse. Perhaps, but I wouldn't put money on it.

Nine months after being banned from Café de Flore, I left Lynn and our three children in Paris and selfishly flew to Germany to direct *Far From Berlin*. I would be gone for ten weeks. A more disastrous ten weeks would be hard to imagine.

Halfway through the shoot, I knew the film I was making was a dud. Set just after the wall came down, *Far From Berlin* was about a young father from East Berlin manipulated into committing murder by a wealthy architect from West Berlin. Real writers write stories they have a connection to. Fake writers write stories about Berlin. What did I know about manipulative German architects? Less than nothing. The film was a catastrophe and deserved to be. But worse was to come. When I returned to Paris, Lynn asked for a divorce. Although devastated, I couldn't blame her. I'd coaxed Lynn to leave New York and then abandoned her and our three children in Paris in order to wallow in the glory of making a film. Some glory. I learned the hard way that filmmaking isn't all it's cracked up to be. And certainly not worth breaking up a good marriage for.

My Berlin film lost the producer $4 million. And now, on my museum tour of Germany, I was back in the same city. I thought about how uncomfortable Michael Cimino would have felt returning to Hollywood after the failure of *Heaven's Gate*. I felt that way and more.

My driver, Max, pulled up at the hotel, still babbling away. He'd talked continuously for the past few hours. Decent though he was, I was going to have to replace him. I wondered if there was any limousine service in Germany that specialized in mute drivers. He opened the trunk and offered to carry my bag into the hotel. I said no thank you. He did it anyway.

We were in Charlottenburg, a block away from the legendary Paris Bar, which was—and still is—my favorite restaurant in the world. Fifteen years before, after spending the day shooting a film I didn't believe in, I'd sought refuge in the restaurant by eating there alone.

On the surface, the Paris Bar looked no different from hundreds of other bistros: subdued lighting, starched white tablecloths, red leather banquettes. What distinguished it from other bistros were its walls, which were covered from floor to ceiling with paintings, drawings, photographs, installations and sculptures: an avant-garde mix of the fashionable, the provocative and the brilliant. Although I didn't care for any one piece individually, the effect of seeing them as a collective, hung salon style, was extraordinary—and was an artwork in itself. The man responsible for this, and for the restaurant's longevity, was its charismatic owner, Michel Würthle.

Seeing Würthle for the first time in 1991, I was struck by his total command of the dining room. Something about his bearing and aristocratic good looks gave him significant presence, and on nights when there were famous artists and actors in the place—which was often—it was always Würthle you looked at first. "For a shy man, I'm a very social person," he once told an interviewer.

In his late forties, Würthle conveyed old-world elegance and bohemian spontaneity, and though he always wore a suit, he was far more of an artist than businessman. Never without a cigarette in hand, Würthle had the look of a man who knew things others didn't. He lived with his girlfriend, but you felt sure he had at least one lover on the side.

Artists flocked to the Paris Bar, yet Würthle disliked the term "artists' bar," and treated people according to their attitude, not their fame or status. He was polite to customers but never obsequious. Although he didn't talk much, it was clear Würthle had the confidence of a man used to being listened to. This came more from dignity than arrogance. Everything I saw Würthle do, he did with conviction and enormous self-respect. Even when emptying an ashtray—which he wasn't above doing—he did so unapologetically.

I longed to talk to Würthle but never did. Once or twice I came close, but something stopped me. I don't know what. I wish I had. In 2023, he passed away.

I was desperate to make movies because I considered filmmaking to be a more dignified profession than operating restaurants. Watching Würthle operate the Paris Bar made me realize that it's not the job that gives a man dignity, it's the man doing the job.

Seeing Würthle work so seamlessly while my own world of filmmaking was falling apart had a significant impact on me.

After making *Far From Berlin*, I lost all desire to direct another film.

Shortly after I returned from Berlin, Lynn and I separated. Our children Isabelle, Sophie and Harry were three, six and seven. Although Lynn had asked for the divorce, I had provoked it. A couple of years after the split, we would become friends again, partly for the sake of our children but mostly out of admiration. There's nobody in the world I admire more than Lynn. And the fact that she has the good sense not to feel the same way about me makes me admire her even more.

18.

In the winter of 1992, as Lynn proceeded with the divorce, I began dismantling the assets of our marriage: the brownstone on Eleventh Street, the Odeon restaurant in Tribeca, Café Luxembourg on the Upper West Side and Nell's, the Fourteenth Street nightclub—each signed away late one morning in a lawyer's office in midtown Manhattan. The untangling of a life Lynn and I had built together.

A month later, I drove to Martha's Vineyard to look for a house. I was starting over. I've screwed up so many times that I'm constantly starting over. And always for the last time.

In those days, the feeling on Martha's Vineyard was closer to the unhurried world of the 1950s than to the busy world of private planes and text messaging it's since become. Houses were far less expensive then. For $525,000—around half the proceeds from selling my share of the restaurants to Lynn—I managed to buy a run-down clapboard house in Chilmark, which, with its open skies and hidden beaches, is the island's most seductive area. It wasn't until two days before the closing that the agent told me the house came with a private beach. Things were different back then.

Chilmark's town planning department granted me permission to double the size of the two-thousand-square-foot house. Although I'd renovated places in the past, I'd never built anything from scratch. After hiring a local architect and figuring out the design, I rented a vast U-Haul truck and drove around New England for three weeks in search of doors, floorboards, window frames—anything that had been made within forty years of the Civil War.

In those pre-Internet days, all the salvage yards and antique shops I visited I heard about through word of mouth. This might have made the search less convenient, but it was infinitely more satisfying. The drawback to buying online—which I do all the time now—is the microscopic experiences one misses by not leaving the house. It's ironic that I buy all my books online today because by no longer walking to the bookshop, I miss out on any number of seemingly trivial incidents that, if properly observed, would enrich my life as much as or more than any book might do.

My road trip took me through Massachusetts, Maine, New Hampshire and Vermont. Having never driven a truck before, I felt uncharacteristically masculine behind the wheel of this giant U-Haul. Car drivers seemed so scared of crossing my path that I was soon reveling in the power this enormous truck gave me. The feeling of manly superiority increased tenfold every time a fellow truck driver honked at me in solidarity. It was like being saluted by Mussolini. Given the proper uniform, even a pacifist can become a bully.

After a week of searching for nineteenth-century fixtures, I began to recognize a similar disposition in the owners of salvage yards. When I entered the yard, the owner—always a man—would be occupied with some strenuous physical job and would instantly dismiss me as if I were some city slicker who hadn't done a *real* day's work in his life (which wasn't far from the truth). It wasn't until I asked about an obscure object for sale that he'd become less guarded. As he revealed more of himself, I found it hard not to be intrigued by someone who could unload a truck full of heavy radiators one minute and talk knowledgeably about eighteenth-century strap hinges the next.

The owners of antique stores were quite different. They were immediately friendly and seemingly more refined, and in striving to give the impression of class they became slightly pretentious. Salvage yard owners were the opposite: suspicious, taciturn and assertively working class. Though my own personality is, regrettably, closer to the owners of antique stores, I wish it were closer to the owners of salvage yards.

Returning to Martha's Vineyard with a truck full of fixtures and fittings, I realized it was the people I met, more than the wares I'd gone in search of, that gave the trip meaning. The journey of my stroke has been similar. I believe I've benefited more from the people I've encountered on the margins of my rehab than from the rehab itself.

The work involved in extending the house was substantial and scheduled to begin in July 1993. During the last week of June, I'd wake up early and walk my land. Growing up poor, I'd never owned land before and I now felt quite smug about it. Until, that is, I began thinking about all the creatures living below the surface whose lives would be forever altered by my construction. The only visible casualty would be two fifty-foot trees, which were so nondescript I had no qualms about chopping them down. But during the first week of July, clusters of white flowers burst onto the branches, making them the most stunning trees I'd ever seen. (Whether the trees were *truly* stunning or whether looking at them close-up for the first time made me think they were, I couldn't say.) No longer keen to demolish the trees, I amended my building plans to ensure their survival. This was a pattern with me: I only appreciate things when they're about to be taken away. My two ex-wives are a testament to this.

I later discovered these trees were called northern catalpas. Today, more than thirty years later, they stand sixty feet high and eighteen inches from my porch. I've become so attached to these trees that no matter where I am in the world, I rush to Martha's Vineyard on the first day of July each year to witness their blossoming. Just as they governed the building of my house, the two "nondescript" catalpas now determine the dates of my annual summer vacation.

My new house was going to have a large country kitchen and six bedrooms. During the year it took to build, I stayed in a tiny rented cottage fifteen miles away. Initially, the cottage felt pokey and cramped, but the closer my six-bedroom house got to completion, the more comfortable the cottage became. In general, I dislike large houses and prefer small apartments. Smallness is underrated. The last summerhouse the architect Le Corbusier lived in measured 160 square feet. He was blissfully happy there.

* * *

My house on the Vineyard is half a mile from the oldest farm on the island: the Allen Farm. This ninety-acre sheep farm has been in the same family since 1762 and its ninth-generation owners, Clarissa Allen and Mitchell Posin, are among the most conscientious farmers on the island. Forever drawn to those more principled than myself, I became great friends with these farmers, and knowing them inspired me to become something of a farmer myself.

Over several years, the Allens patiently taught me the fundamentals of organic gardening and animal husbandry, and in 2007 I knocked together my own farm. With a platoon of help, I built a large vegetable garden and started growing carrots, cucumbers, eggplants, potatoes, beets, green beans, squash and tomatoes. It was a shock, however, to discover how much maintenance vegetables require to survive. I thought one simply sowed, watered and a few months later plucked big, juicy tomatoes from obliging vines. I didn't know about sap-sucking insects called aphids. Or wireworms, cutworms, whiteflies, cucumber beetles, spider mites, squash bugs or the vicious European earwig. It's easy to sermonize on the virtues of organic farming if you haven't spent three hours prizing hundreds of Japanese beetles off your well-tended bed of green beans. The temptation to spray my uncontaminated carrots with a giant can of Raid was huge. But of course I didn't. I used OFF! instead.

The more enjoyable part of farming was rearing chickens, sheep, pigs and goats. Unfortunately, ninety percent of that enjoyment came not from the raising of animals but from boasting about it to friends. It embarrasses me to say I was more interested in being known as a farmer than in farming itself. However, there was one aspect of the animal business that gave me genuine pleasure: hand-milking a goat called Tatiana.

Milking Tatiana was a double blessing: being relieved of her swelling udder was a blessing for Tatiana, and being able to make mouthwatering cheese from her frothy milk was a blessing for me. Because the process was moderately physical, and because it was done by me alone, I found milking Tatiana and transforming her milk into cheese unusually satisfying. It made me feel authentic in ways that building and operating restaurants did not. It seemed that everybody else did the real work in my restaurants and I simply made a few decisions. It was only after my stroke that I realized how misguided that feeling was.

I first visited Martha's Vineyard in the summer of 1976. Gerald Ford was president, and the country was celebrating its bicentennial. I was staying with a friend in Boston who mentioned an island off Cape Cod he thought might really suit me. It was called Nantucket. I bought a secondhand bicycle and cycled to Hyannis where, in those days, you could take a large ferry to the islands of Nantucket and Martha's Vineyard.

Arriving in Hyannis, I bought a ticket to Nantucket. Five minutes after the ferry docked, another ferry arrived. Watching the Nantucket passengers saunter ashore, I was put off by how white and preppy they all looked, and much preferred the look of the passengers coming off the second boat: a mixed bag of farmers, dropouts and long-haired academics. I was told that this ferry was from Martha's Vineyard. I quickly switched tickets and boarded the ferry for the two-hour journey to a place I hadn't heard of until five minutes earlier.

Cycling around the island that first day, I was immediately struck by the absence of commercialism. No roadside billboards, no chain stores— just a coastline of sandy beaches and a lush green interior dotted with farms and old stone walls. The Vineyard had an understated charm that appealed to me. Without knowing a thing about its past, I sensed something of a connection. Only later would I read about the island's unique history of liberalism.

In the 1930s, Martha's Vineyard was one of the only East Coast summer resorts to accept Jews. In the mid-nineteenth century, the island accepted runaway slaves, and for the last hundred years it has been a popular summer resort for African Americans. It also created the first truly successful deaf community in America.

Between the eighteenth and twentieth centuries, Martha's Vineyard had an extraordinarily high rate of hereditary deafness, predominantly on the western half of the island. In the mid-nineteenth century, one person in four in Chilmark's Squibnocket district was deaf. Residents compensated for this by inventing their own sign language, used by almost everyone, hearing and deaf alike. Embraced by the residents, deaf people on the Vineyard quickly assimilated, and as a result, deafness was never considered a handicap. In fact, acquiring sign language gained islanders a similar status to learning another language, like French or Italian—it was something to be envied.

Spending longer hours at school, deaf children attained a higher literacy rate than children with perfect hearing. In those days, Martha's Vineyard was known as a deaf utopia. To me, cycling along its country roads with unexpected views of a dazzling blue ocean, the island, if not quite utopia, seemed the next best thing.

I only had enough money to stay for one night. Two, if I slept at the island's youth hostel the first night and went without dinner the next. I chose two. Planning to cycle around the island's fifty miles, I woke early and slipped out of the hostel while the other backpackers were still sleeping. Although the grass was heavy with dew, I sensed the day was going to be a scorcher.

The only thing I like about terrifically hot days is the soothing balminess one feels an hour or two beforehand, when there's still a semblance of a breeze and you take extra notice of shopkeepers unfurling their awnings. There haven't been many times in my life when I've been conscious of being happy, but cycling along the Vineyard's empty roads that early July morning in '76 was one of them.

The first inhabitants of Martha's Vineyard were a tribe of Native Americans called the Wampanoags. They named the island Noepe ("in the midst of the sea"). In 1602, the year after *Hamlet*'s first performance, English explorer Bartholomew Gosnold became the first European to set foot on the island. Unimpressed, he left three days later. Before he set sail, Gosnold thought about his recently deceased daughter Martha and named the island Martha's Vineyard.

In 1642 another Englishman, Thomas Mayhew, bought the title to the island and, with the help of his missionary son, founded a settlement.

Left to right: Brian, Peter, me and our mother, circa 1954. From the way my mother's bundled up, it must be the height of an English summer.

Bottom row, second from left: me, aged nine, at Olga Street School, circa 1959. Mrs. O'Keefe was a terrific teacher.

1959. Sunshine Holiday Camp in Hampshire. Sulking in the sun.

1963. Me at twelve. To my right is a school friend, Freddy Collins. My mother wouldn't allow me to wear long pants until I was fourteen. "It's good to get air to your legs," she would say.

My beautiful younger sister, Josephine, whom I adored, circa 1959.

Paris, 1967. My first trip abroad. Sixteen years old, looking all of twelve.

My brother Peter in Denmark, 1972.

Alan Bennett's 1968 play, *Forty Years On*. Alan is second from right. I'm to the immediate left of the play's star, John Gielgud, center.

Fake student ID card, 1972.

1976. The last time I smiled.

1976. On the roof of my first Manhattan apartment, on Ninety-First Street between First and Second Avenues.

My best friend in New York, Po Ming, helping me renovate my fourth-floor walk-up in SoHo, 1976. *Les Gillings*

1977. Outside my apartment on Thompson Street. I now live across the road.

1977. Illegal in America.

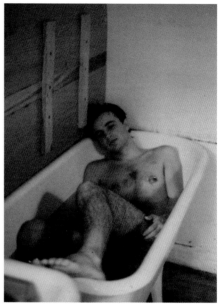

1977. My *Never Mind the Bollocks* phase. It lasted two minutes.

Dreaming of buying a smaller bathtub, circa 1977.

One Fifth restaurant, 1978, celebrating my twenty-seventh birthday with Lynn Wagenknecht. *Lynn Wagenknecht*

Not sure what's worse: my white bow tie or my repulsively smug look. Taken in the kitchen of One Fifth, 1976.

Brothers Grimm. With Brian in 1977. *Les Gillings*

With Po Ming in 1977. *Les Gillings*

With Tim Curry and Nell Campbell at the stylish all-night Empire Diner in 1978.

With Brian in 1978. We never tire of each other's company.
Les Gillings

ABOVE: Reservoir Dogs. Walking between my parents in Chinatown, 1978. *Les Gillings*
LEFT: San Juan airport in 1978, returning from St. John.

My sister, Josephine, in New York, 1978.

With Lynn in Scotland in 1978 while staying at Jonathan Miller's house in Archiestown. *Tom Miller*

One Fifth's dishwasher didn't show up, so I roped Nell Campbell into helping me wash dishes that night. We lasted five minutes. 1977.

With Lynn at my 68 Thompson Street apartment in 1979.

The Odeon's staff, taken three days after we opened. Front row, left to right: Me, Lynn, Chef Patrick Clark and Brian. Po Ming is behind Lynn, to the immediate left of Chef Clark. Behind him is Jonathan Miller's son, Tom. *Larry Williams*

Left to right: Journalist Anthony Haden-Guest, Brian, Lynn and me standing in front of the Odeon the week it opened, 1980. *Dennis Pantzer*

A New York icon. Standing in front of the icon is artist Andy Warhol in 1985.
Paige Powell/Paige Powell Archive

Playful end-of-the-night behavior between the bosses and the servers at the Odeon in 1981. HR would not allow this to happen today.

The Odeon's first New Year's Eve party. Left to right: Lynn; me; my sister, Josephine; and my oldest brother, Peter.

ABOVE: New Year's Eve 1982 at the Odeon. Alan Bennett is on the right, and Kay Wagenknecht, Lynn's beautiful sister, is on the left. *Lynn Wagenknecht*

LEFT: From left: Erwan Illien, me, Geraldine Bartlett and Po Ming at the Odeon. *Lynn Wagenknecht*

Café Luxembourg postcard.
Postcard photo by Cheryl Koralik

With Lynn and Jonathan
Miller at Nell's nightclub, 1987.
Lynn Wagenknecht

Lucky Strike, 1989–2020.
Victoria Dearing

1984. The year Harry was born.

1985. My grandmother, Lillian Woodroof, my mother, Harry and my dad.

With my dad and son Harry in Ménerbes, France, 1985.

With Lynn, Harry and Sophie on
St. Barts, 1987.

With Harry in Provence, 1985.

One of the few times I'm on my hands
and knees and not asking for money.

ABOVE: With Sophie, Isabelle and Harry in Provence in 1990.

LEFT: Paris 1991. Me, Harry, Sophie, Lynn and Lorne Michaels at Lorne's wedding to Alice Barry.

With Harry on Martha's Vineyard in 1991.
Claudia Weishaupt

I cast my Thompson Street landlord, Sam Bress, in my first film, *End of the Night*. This was taken on the set in 1989.

LEFT: Herr Director on the set of *End of the Night*.

BELOW: A poster for *End of the Night*; ads for the film's Spanish release.

At the time, there were about three thousand Wampanoags living peacefully in coastal villages. Mayhew and his son established a policy of respect and fair dealing with the native people unequaled anywhere else in the colonies. Perhaps it was Mayhew's willingness to negotiate and work with the Wampanoags—people from a vastly different background and culture to his own—that laid the tracks for the island's future liberalism.

I don't know if it was a strain of Mayhew's acceptance of strangers that unknowingly lured me to the Vineyard that summer, but I've seldom felt such a sense of belonging to a place as I did cycling around the island in July of '76.

I made my way toward Edgartown, the most picturesque of the island's towns. With its narrow, tree-lined streets and white clapboard houses, Edgartown was way too precious for me. But twenty minutes later I was cycling along the most sensational strip of land, which seemed to be floating between two vast bodies of water. This sliver of land was Beach Road, and it was wedged between Nantucket Sound and a lagoon called Sengekontacket Pond.

Cycling around the back roads of the free-spirited town of Oak Bluffs, I started to get hungry. Someone at the youth hostel had mentioned a place called Humphreys Bakery in West Tisbury, which I was keen to try. It took me forty-five minutes to reach the bakery from Oak Bluffs but was well worth it.

Humphreys was a shingle building with a handwritten sign above its entrance—HUMPHREY'S BAKED GOODS & SANDWICHES. Even before I opened its screen door, the unmistakable smell of bread baking wafted outside. Is there any better smell on earth? I bought a roast turkey sandwich and two jelly doughnuts and ate them at a low trestle table outdoors. Though it was barely noon, my money was so low that this sandwich had to be my last meal of the day. I savored every bite.

The farther west I cycled, the more attractive the island became. The white picket fences of West Tisbury gave way to the rolling green farmland of Chilmark, which gradually turned into the wild, windswept beauty of Gay Head (now called Aquinnah).

Pedaling along a dreamy stretch of coastal road called Moshup Trail, I saw so little evidence of contemporary life that it could have been 1923. Why are past epochs so appealing? I wonder if the Native Americans of 1642 longed for the Martha's Vineyard of 1602.

Toward the end of Moshup Trail I saw a number of bicycles leaning by a sign for Moshup Beach. I dismounted and propped my bike next to five or six others and followed a narrow sandy path that opened up onto public beach. It was full of people. After eight hours cycling I needed a nap. I took off my backpack and lay on the beach. I only needed ten minutes.

It's strange how the miscellaneous sounds heard at a beach—a baby crying, a couple playing paddle ball, the waves crashing—are, in normal circumstances, hindrances to sleep, but, lying on a beach under the hot sun, they become conducive to sleep.

I woke up shivering. The beach was near empty. I felt disoriented. Where was the crying baby, the couple playing paddle ball? I'd slept for almost three hours. I got up and made my way sluggishly to the road. My bike stood alone by the sign. Part of me wished it'd been stolen. The last thing I was in the mood for was more cycling. I got back on and resumed my journey.

Though my joints ached, I began to once again take intense pleasure from cycling alone. As the light dimmed, the scent of honeysuckle seemed to hang in the air, and out of nowhere a deer leaped across the road. It was spectacular. Like other things in life, the best sightings of animals happen when you least expect them. I've never understood the appeal of African safaris. Searching for a wild animal seems to be an oxymoron—or is an oxymoron some sort of wild animal? I've never known the difference.

Ten minutes before sunset, I bicycled into the small fishing village of Menemsha. After my long nap, I was starving. What I really wanted was a juicy steak and French fries. Except I couldn't afford it. What little money I had was needed for a hotel. Spending it on dinner would mean sleeping the night on the beach. I stood outside an inviting-looking restaurant called the Homeport, summoning all my strength not to go in. One advantage from my having grown up poor is the ability to resist eating when hungry. Ten minutes later I was devouring a two-pound boiled lobster with sweet corn slathered in butter, and to hell with the hotel. Until I was stuffed that is, when a wave of regret spread over me. It wasn't the first time—or the last—that my unchecked desire had given me a night of remorse.

There wasn't much of a moon that night, which was lucky as it's illegal to sleep on Martha's Vineyard's beaches after dark. The less visible I was, the better. Plonking my bike down and using my backpack as a pillow, I lay on the still-warm sand of Menemsha's public beach. I closed my eyes but couldn't sleep. Having had a three-hour kip less than two hours before, it was no wonder. Just then, I heard the sounds of a couple giggling in the distance. The sounds slowly increased until I saw the vague outline of a man with his arm around a woman. She was laughing at something he said. Both seemed tipsy. The man flopped to the sand, pulling his unresisting companion on top of him. As the unmistakable sounds of foreplay gave way to those of clothes being ripped off, I began to feel nervous. I was in an awkward position. If I stood up to move away, I might draw attention to myself. I sat frozen to my small patch of sand, scared to death that I might be mistaken for a peeping Tom. The soft sounds of the couple's lovemaking were at first discreet and suppressed, as if accustomed to making love with her parents in the next room. And then, perhaps remembering that the parents were two hundred miles away, the sounds became raucous and guttural. This was certainly not deaf utopia.

Due to the indistinctness of the couple's bodies and faces, I started to find this bizarre scene faintly erotic. I've never understood why the makers of pornographic films don't grasp that the suggestion of sex, the implication of intimacy, is so much more effective than seeing the whole nine yards (as it were).

Terrified of making a sound, I started thinking of the absurdity of the island's beach law that made it illegal to sleep all night on one but perfectly legal to fuck 24/7 on one. Suddenly, the woman let out a throaty, rasping yelp. This same striving for breath continued, until she eventually released a long, pleasurable sigh. I was envious. As they stood up to leave, I saw for the first time their pitiful-looking faces, and at once their future became depressingly clear. It was a future weighed down by the inescapable strains of life. She would become pregnant, and they would joylessly marry and never have this spontaneous, gloriously happy act of public sex ever again. The thought saddened me to the point where I lost all envy and quietly drifted off to sleep.

At first light I left the beach and cycled to town, where I caught an early ferry to the mainland.

I've been returning to Martha's Vineyard ever since. And, if I'd taken ten more sleeping pills in August 2018, I would have died there, too.

My dad was buried on Martha's Vineyard in 2008. At the time, I bought a "plot" for myself for the distant future. After my stroke, that future no longer seemed so distant.

19.

I was standing on shaky ground after my divorce. Besides losing three of my restaurants, I'd lost unlimited access to my children. I felt diminished and vaguely inadequate. I was also running out of money after buying and renovating my house on Martha's Vineyard. To pay the bills I needed to open another restaurant. The trouble was I'd never built a restaurant without my ex-wife and wasn't sure I was capable of it. While I was the one receiving the applause, it was Lynn in the background carrying out the unglamorous jobs that truly made the restaurants function. This included the one area of the restaurant business that had always terrified me: the finances.

My ignorance of financial matters is shocking. For forty years I've owned businesses that have grossed between $20 million and $80 million a year, yet it wasn't until I reached fifty that I knew the difference between gross and net. I still don't really know what a balance sheet is. Invoices scare me and I rarely check them. When handed a restaurant or hotel bill, I imitate a man checking his bill. As my eyes glaze over the numbers, I'm imagining the appropriate amount of time Bill Gates would take to scrutinize a check, before offering my AmEx card. Scratch the surface and I'm nothing but a card sharp, a wheeling, dealing con man, and launching a restaurant without Lynn, I risked exposing this. It was crucial that the first place I opened alone succeeded. If not, there was a good chance that whatever I'd accomplished in the restaurant world so far would be discredited.

In 1988 I saw the classic Russian play *Too Clever by Half* at London's Old Vic Theatre. I didn't care much for the play but was blown away by the set—an extraordinary mix of the industrial and the geometric. It was my first brush with Constructivism and I was hooked.

A product of the Russian Revolution, Constructivism rejected the decorative in favor of the angular and functional. It seemed to contradict everything I was drawn to in design, yet the more I learned about this movement, the more obsessed I became with it.

Seeing *Too Clever by Half* had a pollinating effect. Like the cream-and-blue wall tiles that prompted the building of Café Luxembourg, the set of this Russian play would motivate me to build another place. In 1995, seven years after seeing the play, I began building a Constructivist bar of my own—Pravda, a gloriously sensual underground speakeasy. With bold Russian words painted on vaulted arches, attractive waitresses and a serpentine-shaped zinc bar serving strong vodka martinis, something about Pravda suggested illicit assignations—the sort of bar where affairs began and married women never took their husbands. Though inspired by communism, it epitomized everything communism deplored. And it was packed solid from the moment it opened.

The best tip I ever received from a New Yorker was: whatever the cost, always hold on to your first apartment. Taking his advice, I'd kept my $250-a-month walk-up in SoHo long after Lynn and I had bought a house in the city. Which was lucky, as it meant I had a place to live after our divorce. Even though the house we'd owned was large and beautiful, it was something of a relief for me to be living in a small apartment again. Nevertheless, the irony—after all my restaurant "success"—of returning to the same fourth-floor walk-up I'd rented sixteen years earlier wasn't lost on me.

Despite owning a house on the Vineyard, I didn't have a penny in the bank. Fortunately, the investment to build Pravda came from hotelier Ian Schrager and my friend Lorne Michaels. For the first time since arriving in New York, I was living by the skin of my teeth. All the same, it was good to be starting over, and I felt a surprising degree of happiness living in SoHo once again.

Just as great restaurants can transport and inspire, blissful walking conditions can be equally empowering. Walking through SoHo's beautifully hushed streets at 8 a.m. to Pravda's construction site in the summer of '95 gave me such a heady feeling that it seems no coincidence that it was on one of those exhilarating mornings I'd discover something that would change my life forever.

It was a particularly hot morning in June when I first caught sight of Adar Tannery. The ragged sign above the entrance gave an indication of its condition. Though I had passed this battered storefront at least fifty times, it wasn't until that June morning that I first noticed it.

Adar Tannery was an enormous leather warehouse on the corner of Spring and Crosby. The first thing that struck me about the space was its inconspicuousness. The second thing was its tremendous potential.

I wanted to enter the place there and then, but it was closed, and its hours, which were scribbled on cardboard by the door, were so bizarre they seemed to defy customers to catch it open. By standing on tiptoe and looking through one of its windows, I caught a glimpse of the inside. It was crammed from floor to ceiling with strips of brown leather. The place appeared so down-at-heel that it gave the impression of needing its half million strips of leather to patch together its declining business. I couldn't see far inside because its windows were so grimy, but I liked the location, and the fact that it was on a corner.

New York City real estate is oddly specific: while one block is considered enticing, another, fifty yards away, is deemed Siberia. Although just a block from fashionable SoHo, the corner of Spring and Crosby then felt like another borough, especially after dark, when the corner's dim lighting and hordes of squealing rats made it deeply unappealing.

Intending to contact the landlord on the off chance the store was for rent, I jotted down its address in my Filofax and continued on.

The next day I called the landlord, Rodney Propp, and a week later he showed me around Adar Tannery. It was only after seeing the whole space that I realized how immense it was. The ground floor alone was almost the size of a soccer pitch. Propp and I then descended a narrow staircase to a vast basement where, shockingly, more than a hundred immigrant women worked in conditions so cramped and airless that it reminded me of a Victorian workhouse. Each woman was hunched over a whirring sewing machine, stitching furiously as if she had a family of fifteen to feed.

On the sidewalk afterward, Propp told me the store was for rent, but he didn't want a restaurant there. When I listed the four places I'd built and operated in the last fifteen years, he said he'd heard of me and that I had a "good" reputation. He'd consider it, he said.

A month later I signed a fifteen-year lease. For someone who had no money in the bank, this was far from a wise move. Then again, most of the good things that have happened to me didn't come about through wisdom. If anything, the reverse.

Adar Tannery was just over twelve thousand square feet. I reckoned it could cost a million and a half dollars to build a restaurant in the space. (It ended up costing two and a half million.) For the next six weeks, I asked everyone I knew to invest, but nobody was interested. And then out of left field came Dick Robinson.

I first met Robinson on Martha's Vineyard in the summer of 1995. Though Robinson didn't exude wealth, something about the way that he didn't suggested he had it in abundance. Nevertheless, it still came as a surprise when I discovered he was the CEO and president of Scholastic, the world's largest publisher of children's books, which included the Harry Potter and Hunger Games series. His father, Maurice, had founded Scholastic in 1920.

Harvard-educated and in his late fifties, Robinson was a summer neighbor of mine on Martha's Vineyard. His white clapboard house was substantial but understated in the way houses on the Vineyard used to be before the millennium. Robinson personified discretion. Though I didn't see a lot of him that first summer, his worldliness and calm disposition hit home. He was everything I wasn't.

On returning to New York after Labor Day, I was surprised to find a message from Robinson waiting for me on my answering machine. His voice sounded deeper on the phone that it did in person. I called him back and he mentioned a building he owned in SoHo that he thought might make a good restaurant. I met him there the next day, but didn't care for the space. In my compulsion to please I of course said I loved the space. Luckily, I had a legitimate reason not to take it: I was simply too busy. I told Robinson that between the building of Pravda and signing a lease on the leather store space, I didn't have time for another project. He understood but was intrigued by the leather store and asked if it was possible to see it. I said of course, and after walking east for five minutes we reached the corner of Spring and Crosby.

Feeling subservient to someone so worldly, I called Dick Robinson "Mr. Robinson." On the way to Spring Street, he tried to put me at ease by asking me to call him Dick. This had the opposite effect. As with calling one's teacher by their first name, it felt unnatural to address someone who was so clearly my superior by his first name. Even though I would become really close to Robinson over the next twenty years, I was never comfortable calling him Dick. Whether this was due to excessive respect for the man or a phobia of saying the word "dick," I couldn't say.

I'd forgotten to bring keys to the space. Robinson said it was fine and just peered through one of the store's filthy windows. He must have liked what he saw because within seconds he was asking me whether I needed an investor.

Eighteen months later, Balthazar opened, with Dick Robinson supplying all of its two-and-a-half-million-dollar investment.

20.

The idea for Balthazar came about while I was living in Paris seven years before I built the place. Although it's hard for me to come up with good ideas, the few decent ones I've ever had have come about by pure accident. I was searching for vintage curtains at a Paris flea market in 1990 when I suddenly spotted an old sepia photo of a turn-of-the-century bar. Behind the bar's zinc counter were hundreds of liquor bottles stacked twenty feet high, flanked by two towering statues of semi-naked women carved in the classical Greek style. I was so mesmerized by this image that I forgot about the curtains and bought the photo instead. For years I carried it in my back pocket, thinking that if I ever found a space with a sky-high ceiling, I'd build a bar just like the magnificent one in the photo. Stepping into Adar Tannery in the summer of 1995, I'd found that space. Five months later construction began.

Before I begin building, I always have a specific idea of a restaurant's design. But as the boxer Mike Tyson once said, "Everyone has a plan until they get punched in the mouth." My watertight floor plan usually starts leaking on the first day of construction. Unable to visualize an idea until it becomes tangible, I will often build things two or three times over until I feel it's right. The artist Robert Motherwell said he painted "by correction." I do everything by correction, especially restaurant design. That's why I always go over budget. And why I'd never invest in myself.

Before construction began, the dining room had five enormous windows. For most restaurateurs, windows are sacrosanct, but at Balthazar, the first thing I did was block in two of the windows and replace them with mirrors. Like plays and films, restaurants work best when they create their own universe. To be reminded of the outside world while dining is like hearing the doorbell ring while making love.

During the first week of renovations, my codesigner, Ian McPheely, and I spent ages figuring out where the gigantic bar should go. (Assuming we could build it, that is.) It took us three days to agree on the location, but once we'd worked it out, the rest of the design fell quickly into place.

Ian and I never used architects' plans when putting Balthazar together. As ideas came, we scribbled crude drawings on whatever bits of paper were within reach. But the formidable semi-naked female statues—called caryatids—were another matter. Google had yet to be invented, and I hadn't a clue where to find six-foot statues of scantily clad women. They weren't exactly being sold at Pottery Barn. Eventually, Ian suggested that a classically trained sculptor friend, Brandt Junceau, should carve them. After working out a price, Junceau's only question was a pleasantly awkward one: Did I know a woman with a voluptuous body and firm breasts like those in the photo who'd be willing to model for him? (Classically trained sculptors have all the fun.) What I did next would be impossible today, in these politically correct times. I asked two of the waitresses from Pravda if they'd like to pose topless for the sculptor. They not only jumped at the chance, they also refused the money I offered, and in the weeks that followed, both spent several hours modeling in the sculptor's studio. The faces, bodies and breasts of the statues ended up being a mix of the two waitresses. Which parts are from whom, only the women and the classically trained sculptor know.

Halfway through building the restaurant, I still hadn't come up with a name. "Brasserie Lafayette" was a temporary one before a good friend, Claudia Weishaupt, suggested Balthazar. I took to it instantly, but most people I mentioned it to thought it was a terrible name. Until the restaurant opened, that is. Then they loved it. Places, like babies, become their names, not the other way around.

Not only am I saddled with a first name I can't stand, I chose a profession with a name I dislike even more: restaurateur. Does a plumber call himself a *plombier*? Trust the French to come up with the most pretentious word in the dictionary. And just to make it extra difficult for us to pronounce, the bastards went and took the *n* out of the word.

Since school, I've felt inferior to men who use their hands to make a living—primarily cooks and carpenters. I'm a mediocre cook and a hopeless carpenter, and yet when I build a restaurant I'm supposed to give direction to these very people—people whose jobs I could never do in a million years. The theater critic Kenneth Tynan once said, "A critic is a man who knows the way, but cannot drive a car." That's how I feel. I have such a feeling of inferiority to my cooks that I do everything imaginable to avoid going into the kitchen. Since Balthazar opened in 1997, I'm reluctant to admit that I've entered its kitchen during service fewer than twenty times. But every time I do, I come out feeling three inches shorter.

When I directed my two feature films, it surprised me how similar the role of the film's cameraman was to that of a restaurant chef. Most people think a director rules the set. They're wrong. It's the cameraman who rules the set, and just as formidably as a chef rules a kitchen. Making films, I was as intimidated by the workings of the camera as I am by the workings of a restaurant kitchen. Due to this ignorance, I used to feel as fraudulent in the kitchen as I did on a film set. It's a pity it took a stroke to make me feel otherwise.

A month before construction on Balthazar began, I drove around France looking for restaurant furniture. In a remote salvage yard in Burgundy, I found six nineteenth-century train compartment luggage racks, each one aged naturally over the past hundred and forty years. They were sensational and would fit perfectly above Balthazar's banquettes. Even though they were expensive, I splashed out and bought them. I paid in cash and asked the owner of the yard to store them while I headed south in search of bistro chairs. I'd pick them up in five days, I told him.

Between the flea markets of Béziers and Montpellier, I found all the chairs I needed and made my way back to Burgundy. As I arrived at the salvage yard, the owner told me he'd improved the luggage racks for no extra charge. I followed him inside a small wooden hut, and there on a long table were my six nineteenth-century luggage racks. Only they were no longer nineteenth century. They were twenty-first century. The owner had scraped, scoured and scrubbed a hundred and forty years of beautiful oxidation off them. He'd purged them of all character. I was distraught.

"I've had a long day," I told him. "Let me find a hotel and I'll return in the morning."

I didn't return in the morning. I didn't return at all. I drove all the way back to Paris without stopping. On the drive north I thought about all the things we can't untie. Relationships I'd messed up and people I'd let down. It's strange how a relatively trivial turn of events can set off a landslide of self-doubt. How a well-intentioned act from someone you don't know can symbolize everything you detest in life. But mostly in yourself.

Two months before Balthazar opened, I began hiring the numerous floor staff necessary to service this 180-seat restaurant for lunch and dinner seven days a week: one general manager, an assistant general manager, eight floor managers, thirty-five servers, eight food runners, ten bartenders, four barbacks, twenty-five busboys, four baristas, four maître d's and twelve hosts. Ten days before opening, I began training the servers. Every restaurant has its own waiters' manual. Here's Balthazar's original one, which I wrote a week before we opened in April 1997:

1. When describing the menu, never say "I have." Always "*we* have." Saying "I have" is affected, and an insult to the cook who made the dish.
2. Be friendly, not chummy. Always repeat the customer's order back to him. "Skate" sounds like "steak" after one martini.
3. When waiting on someone famous, direct most of your conversation to the other people at the table, especially the spouse or partner of the famous person. Spouses of famous people rarely receive attention in public. It'll make their day.
4. Never rush the guest. Good service is based on anticipation. Where possible, try to anticipate the customer's needs. This does not mean *hovering* over the table. As a customer, I can't bear to sense a server or busser lurking a few feet away.

5. Please don't clear the customer's coffee cup until after he or she leaves or drop the check before he or she asks for it.
6. When reciting the day's specials, always mention the price. When a customer pays the check in cash, never assume the change is your tip. Always return the change to the table!
7. Never offer a celebrity a free drink. Instead, offer it to a regular, or the guest least expecting it. And once the meal's served, never utter the phrase "How is everything?" It's meaningless. If you must break the flow of our customers' conversation, please let it be a simple "Do you need anything?"
8. Always replace dirty ashtrays.
9. Lastly, never, *ever* go home with a customer . . . . for less than $500.

Most of these service rules still hold true. Except in today's climate, I could never get away with the last line—clearly a joke—without risking a lawsuit.

Six weeks before Balthazar was scheduled to open, I still hadn't found a chef, but a friend mentioned Riad Nasr, a sous-chef at Daniel, a four-star restaurant uptown. It was rumored that Daniel's owner, the acclaimed chef Daniel Boulud, considered Nasr to be the best cook he'd ever worked with.

We met in Starbucks, across the road from Balthazar. With his poker face, unshaven beard and slicked-back hair, Nasr resembled more a samurai warrior than a four-star sous-chef. I thought he seemed suspicious of me, but I always feel this about people I admire. Nasr agreed to prepare a tasting for me the following week.

His food was stunning and the next day I called and offered him the job. He accepted but on one condition: that I also hire his working partner, Lee Hanson. I hesitated. If I hired his friend, I'd be paying two chefs' salaries instead of one. With Nasr sticking to his guns, I had no choice but to agree to hire his partner. It turned out to be one of the best decisions I ever made.

Over the next six weeks, the chefs and I got along surprisingly well. I admired them and they tolerated me. The only friction that occurred before opening was when I suggested adding hamburgers to the menu. Both chefs disagreed. Coming from a prestigious uptown restaurant that in those days frowned upon serving burgers, Nasr and Hanson were reluctant to put them on the menu. I wasn't pushing for hamburgers because I particularly like them or because of their relatively high profit margin. I wanted them on our menu because I didn't like the snobbery involved in not having them. The chefs eventually changed their minds. After steak frites, hamburgers would become Balthazar's best-selling dish.

Three weeks before Balthazar opened, the dining room still resembled a building site. Plumbers were installing toilets in the customers' bathrooms, electricians were running lines to the wall lights and a horde of painters were staining all the tables. Suddenly, a miracle occurred. Onto this construction site wafted the most delicious smell of food being cooked. After eighteen months of hard hats and steel beams, here was unmistakable proof that it was a restaurant we were building. For ten seconds, everybody laid down their tools and smiled. (It was as if they'd heard the first cries of a baby's birth in the next room.)

Later that day, a cook came out of the kitchen carrying an order of steak frites. It was the first dish ever cooked at Balthazar.

The final week before opening is the most exciting time of any restaurant. Everybody works late into the night, and because the invitations to the first-night party have been sent, you no longer have the luxury of delaying the opening: you *must* open by a certain date no matter how much work remains to be done.

Having an impossible task that you know you'll overcome by necessity has to be one of the most exhilarating feelings in the world. It was on one of these nights that I met the playwright Tom Stoppard. Around eleven at night, while vacuuming sawdust from the banquettes, I heard someone tapping on the window. I looked out to see Lorne Michaels standing there. He had eaten dinner at Pravda with Tom Stoppard and wanted to show the English playwright Balthazar. The two of them came in and, despite the dining room looking like bedlam, they were both very encouraging. Looking back, I like to think their late-night visit in the spring of 1997 was a good omen.

The night before we opened, I looked around Balthazar's dining room and felt sick to my stomach. Nothing had come out the way I'd imagined. Every element was, by degrees, a compromise. I took little consolation from knowing that I'd felt this exact same way with all my previous restaurants. I trudged home to my walk-up on Thompson Street dreading the next night's opening party.

Balthazar opened to the public in April 1997. The impact was staggering. It was a restaurant hurricane that caused a sensation in the city's nightlife. From day one, every seat was full. On the fourth night, we had three hundred people on Balthazar's wait list for dinner. *Vogue* editor Anna Wintour ate there five nights in a row the first week. After six weeks, *New York* magazine published a double-page spread of Balthazar's dining room with the positions and numbers of famous New Yorkers' favorite tables. (Most of these celebrities hadn't even been there.)

After several months, I decided to open Balthazar for breakfast, which the *New York Post* announced the day before. At seven thirty that first morning, we had a hundred customers waiting outside. I let them eat for free. In fact, I let all three hundred breakfast customers eat for free that first morning.

The public and press response to Balthazar was stimulating for the floor staff but a nightmare for the kitchen. Nasr and Hanson were often angry and argued that in cooking hundreds of meals every day, we were risking the food's quality. They were right, of course. But when you're driving an Aston Martin for the first time, it's difficult to think about the passengers in the back seat. Toward the end of a nine-hundred-cover brunch, I'd see Nasr scowling by the kitchen door, counting the number of customers still waiting for tables. Those were hair-raising days. I'm just thankful Nasr forced me to hire Hanson. Without a second chef, Balthazar would never have survived its first year.

The day after I opened Balthazar, someone had the gall to ask me, "So, what's next?" Curiously, the number of people asking this question doubles with each new restaurant. Why is it increasingly more difficult for people to savor the moment? I've noticed that during TV coverage of an exciting sports event, the commentator will interrupt the action with news of an even *more* exciting one in two hours' time. It's like talking about your next baby when delivering your first one. The future isn't always more exciting. Why must we always resort to hyperbole to retain people's interest? I'm going to throttle the next person who asks me, "So, what's next?"

A month after opening the restaurant, I was sitting outside Balthazar feeling quite pleased with myself, when I overheard two women talking disparagingly about the food. Crushed, I introduced myself and surprised the two women by offering them a free dinner if they'd agree to give Balthazar a second chance. They returned a week later and ordered a full meal, including wine and dessert. After they'd wiped their plates clean, I unctuously approached their table, preparing to luxuriate in their compliments, when the shorter of the two piped up: "Thank you for dinner, Mr. McNally, but to be honest, we don't like the food any more than the last time. If anything, less so."

A few years after Balthazar opened, a table of four Wall Street traders began their evening by ordering the restaurant's most expensive wine: a two-thousand-dollar bottle of Château Mouton Rothschild Premier Cru. Following procedure, the floor manager transferred the thirty-year-old Bordeaux into a decanter at a waiter's station. At the same time, a young couple on their first visit to the restaurant ordered our cheapest red wine, an eighteen-dollar bottle of pinot noir. Seeing the Mouton Rothschild being decanted at the table opposite, the couple asked if their wine could also be decanted. Though it was an odd request for such an inexpensive wine, the manager agreed, and minutes later these two radically different wines sat in identical decanters on the same shelf above the waiter's station. What happened next was every restaurateur's nightmare.

Confusing the two decanters, the manager served the cheap wine to the four traders. The table's host, who considered himself a connoisseur, sniffed and tasted the eighteen-dollar bottle of pinot noir and burst into raptures about its "balance." His three companions followed suit, praising the wine's "tannin content" to the skies. Meanwhile, the young couple who'd ordered the cheap pinot noir were inadvertently served the Château Mouton Rothschild. Taking their first sips, they jokingly pretended to be drinking a very expensive bottle and parodied the mannerisms of the wine snobs at the table opposite.

Five minutes later, the two managers realized their error. Horrified and unsure of how to proceed, they called me at home. I rushed to Balthazar.

Having never been comfortable in all-male company, I found it hard to identify with these four Wall Street traders sitting at table 62. As I watched them self-importantly drink what they imagined was a two-thousand-dollar Château Mouton Rothschild, I deplored my own profession—but who was I to criticize customers who were in the process of being deceived? Though their behavior appalled me, these four businessmen had, in good faith, bought a two-thousand-dollar bottle of wine and received an eighteen-dollar one instead. They'd been swindled.

I didn't know what to do. If I were honest and told them the wine they were eulogizing was a cheap bottle of pinot noir, I'd embarrass them to no end and expose their true knowledge of wine. The alternative was to say nothing and allow them to remain in blissful ignorance, which would also save me two thousand dollars by not having to replace the pinot noir with a second bottle of Mouton Rothschild. I ended up doing what I rarely do in this business: I told the truth.

When I explained the mix-up to the four men, the host quickly responded, "I knew this wasn't a Mouton Rothschild!" and his three comrades obsequiously agreed. I then told the young couple about the mistake, but let them keep drinking the real bottle of Mouton Rothschild. They were ecstatic, comparing it to a bank making an error in their favor. However, in this case it wasn't the bank that was down two thousand dollars, it was me. Knowing they were drinking expensive wine for real, they switched from acting out drinking expensive wine in jest to acting out in earnest. Which was a pity in ways I couldn't explain.

Both parties left Balthazar happy that night, but the younger of the two left happier.

After spending over forty years in the business, I still don't know what makes a restaurant successful. I know what makes one successful for *me* though. It's a restaurant that's conducive to engagement, where the customer can fully connect with their dinner companion. I'd rather eat mediocre food in an all-night diner and forge a connection with the person I'm with than eat in a four-star restaurant and have nothing to say to my companion.

The saddest sight in the world to me is seeing a married couple sitting opposite each other in silence. It reminds me of my parents.

A far more pleasing sight is a customer happily eating alone—preferably reading a novel between courses (or eating between pages). To help make single diners feel comfortable eating alone, I always send a glass of champagne on the house. *Always.*

When building restaurant tables, I always make them on the small side. In general, I can't bear large tables, specifically two-tops. There's nothing less intimate than sitting thirty inches or more from the person opposite. All my tables for two are twenty-six inches long by twenty-four inches wide.

During the Odeon's first year, a regular customer—film producer Bob Shaye—told me flat out that if the restaurant's gifted chef found another job, the place would close. A few years later the chef found another job, and decades on, the Odeon is still flourishing. (Thanks to Lynn.)

Every time a talented chef leaves one of my places, I remind myself of Shaye's words and the Odeon's subsequent longevity. In truth, nothing lasts forever, and Balthazar, like all restaurants, will one day fall from favor and close. I just hope I'm not around to see it.

21.

I never knew the difference between envy and jealousy until I once read that envy is wanting something that someone else has, and jealousy is fear of losing what you already have. I suffer from both.

When a carpenter friend told me in 1985 that he'd recently cycled five hundred miles alone from Paris to Saint-Tropez, I became incredibly envious. Although I'd built two restaurants of my own by this time, when compared to my friend's endeavor, it seemed like no feat at all. I had hoped that the Herculean effort I put into building Balthazar would bring me a good return on my money in terms of gratification. But any sense of accomplishment I felt when the restaurant opened disappeared shortly afterward, and once again I found myself thinking about my friend's achievement. That's when I decided to buy a bicycle and, like my friend, ride from Paris to Saint-Tropez.

I was forty-seven when I flew to Paris and, thanks to years of eating my restaurants' French fries, appallingly out of shape and in no condition to pedal five hundred miles—let alone cycle over the Prealps of Provence. I also knew next to nothing about bicycles and was so impractical that my way of dealing with a flat tire would be to buy another bike.

I arrived in France with my brand-new bike disassembled into pieces and packed into a large aluminum case. Wishing to avoid the treacherous Périphérique, I took a taxi from Charles de Gaulle Airport thirty miles southeast of Paris to the town of Fontainebleau, where I planned to start my poor man's Tour de France. I woke early the next morning in order to reassemble my bike, but due to a chronic inability to follow instructions, I couldn't put the parts together and lost a whole day searching for a mechanic who could. The mechanic turned out to be the ten-year-old son of the owner of my Fontainebleau hotel.

Finally on my bike, I took only roads with no respect for straight lines, which in France are the white and yellow *routes départementales*. Relatively free of traffic, these rural byways made my journey more charming but increased the distance by a hundred and fifty miles. I planned to cycle fifty miles a day. The first day I managed eighteen. The second I had to stop early because of raging saddle soreness. The next day my backside was so raw I took the entire day off. I was already a hundred miles behind schedule.

Between Beaune and Dijon, I got drenched in a thunderstorm. (Nothing soaks you to the bone as much as water-resistant clothing.) After the sky cleared, I changed into my only other set of dry clothes, but ten minutes later it bucketed down again. I began to miss Balthazar.

Once south of Lyon, the weather improved.

Although there are few things as pleasing to the soul as cycling along small country roads in France, pedaling up the mountains of the Alpes-de-Haute-Provence is another prospect. Some were so steep and such an agony to climb that there were many times when I wanted to stop in my tracks and take the next flight back to New York. The only reason I didn't was the fear of ridicule. I'd foolishly told most of my friends that I was going to cycle from Paris to Saint-Tropez, and to stop midway would cause me no end of embarrassment. Like many English people, I fear embarrassment more than death.

I stuck with it. Partly because no matter how hard the grind was to reach the top of the mountain, there was always the thrill of coasting down to look forward to. The trouble was, the grueling ascent took three hours, but the fun part—the freewheeling descent—took about four minutes. There was such a disparity between effort and reward that I felt I didn't get my money's worth. (But I feel this way about most things.)

After crossing the Prealps, life got easier. Yet while managing a steady pace, I was often overtaken by other cyclists. Initially, this irritated me and felt like a challenge to my manhood. But if this trip taught me anything, it was to come to terms with my physical limits. In the last few days of my journey, I actually encouraged other cyclists to overtake me by slowing down when sensing one was behind me. Of course, this didn't stop me from shouting "Fuck you!" once the overtaking cyclist was ten yards ahead.

Four weeks after leaving Fontainebleau, I reached Saint-Tropez. I'd cycled almost seven hundred miles of the back roads of France and I finally felt a sense of achievement. However, this feather in my cap would have been a lot more genuine if I hadn't felt the need to boast about it. Just as things thrive by not being observed, I believe achievements decrease in value by being talked about. The philosopher Pascal once wrote that most people wouldn't travel if they couldn't talk about it. He's probably right, but I bet the French bastard never cycled over the Alpes-de-Haute-Provence in the pouring rain.

Since my early teenage years, I've had a nagging awareness of my own limitations. This probably accounts for my exaggerated regard for those who are truly gifted. Though I'm contemptuous of my tendency to latch on to these people, it probably laid the groundwork for my success in the restaurant business, and led to a certain enrichment in terms of friendship and education.

After leaving school at sixteen, I occasionally came under the influence of exceptional older men: Alan Bennett, Jonathan Miller, neurologist Oliver Sacks, director Lindsay Anderson and, to a lesser degree, writer Christopher Hitchens and art critic Robert Hughes. Apart from Bennett, my relationship with these men was entirely platonic. (Yet is any close relationship between two men entirely platonic? Notably where there's a disparity in age and erudition?)

In befriending these writers and intellectuals, I believe that subconsciously I was seeking the same kind of moral scrupulousness I sought at nineteen when backpacking alone to Nepal. Of all of them, and others who have had an influence on me, the most remarkable was Jonathan Miller.

I remained close to Jonathan and his wife, Rachel, for fifty years.

Their three children, Tom, William and Kate, treated me like an older brother, and both sons worked briefly at the Odeon. I'd often join the whole family in their rambling house in Archiestown, a village in the north of Scotland. In the summer of 1973, after hitchhiking five hundred miles, I showed up at the house unannounced. On opening the door, Miller was so pleased to see me he spontaneously ruffled my hair. In all the time I knew him, I never saw Jonathan touch anyone besides his wife and children. His ruffling my hair made me feel part of the family.

Just before I moved to New York in 1975, Jonathan gave me the telephone number of his old school friend Oliver Sacks. He also gave me a copy of Sacks's recent book *Awakenings*, a collection of case histories of patients with sleeping sickness. Frozen into a forty-year sleep in the years after the First World War, these patients were considered incurable until 1969, when Sacks gave them a wonder drug called L-DOPA. The drug had such an explosive effect on them that they reemerged, Lazarus-like, as their former selves.

While many of the patients welcomed their brave new world, others found it terrifying. Sadly, each of the "awakened" patients gradually became immune to the effects of the drug and reverted back to their frozen self. *Awakenings* is an incredible book, and its ending is confirmation that healing from a serious malady is profoundly complex, and that it's an illusion to believe that a single pill can bring about a permanent cure.

I began reading *Awakenings* the day before I emigrated to America and finished it on the plane coming over. I was struck as much by the poetic nature of the writing as by its extraordinary case histories.

Not long after arriving in New York, I badly scalded my arm and called Dr. Sacks for advice. He immediately offered to look at the burn. Meeting Sacks prompted a forty-year friendship with the only man I would dare to call a saint. Sacks was the kindest and the most tolerant person I've ever met. He saw goodness, or the potential for goodness, in everybody. But most of all those sidelined by society.

Knowing how much I had enjoyed *Awakenings*, Sacks one day offered to take me to the Bronx hospital where some of the patients from the book still lived. Even though I knew they'd returned to their pre-L-DOPA condition, I nevertheless found it disturbing to see them in a near-vegetative state. Sacks, on the other hand, wasn't disturbed at all and spoke to them in his usual gentle and non-condescending manner. Unlike most people, Sacks was entirely unselfconscious when talking to the infirm. To me, he personified the ideal approach to medicine. He was knowledgeable, sensitive and caring. But most importantly, he listened to his patients.

During my first few years in Manhattan, Oliver and I would often meet at the cinema and discuss the film afterward over dinner. When I began waiting tables at One Fifth, he'd regularly arrive during my shift and eat alone. He'd sit down at 6 p.m. and write nonstop in one of his many notebooks for hours, oblivious to the restaurant activities taking place around him. Sacks became so absorbed in his writing that often he'd finish his main course and an hour later politely ask the waiter where his main course was. Meanwhile, he would have filled twenty pages with philosophical notes.

Although I sensed Sacks was gay, he never mentioned it. In his memoir, *On the Move*, he wrote that at eighteen he told his mother he was homosexual. Horrified, she replied, "I wish you had never been born." I often wonder whether his attempt to free people from the constraints of sickness was a subconscious struggle to liberate himself from his childhood shame at being homosexual.

Sacks loved swimming. While staying with me on Martha's Vineyard, he once mentioned that he felt more comfortable in water than on dry land. This was clear when watching him swimming effortlessly far from the shore: Sacks's movement in the water possessed a gracefulness that was noticeably missing on land. Oliver died in 2015. Besides being a wonderful doctor and writer, he was an astonishingly beautiful man.

In 2001 I was approached by the publisher Clarkson Potter to put together a book of Balthazar recipes. It wasn't something I was keen on, but knowing my chefs were excited by the idea, I agreed to it.

While the publisher pressed for an introduction by an established food critic, I pushed for the opposite: a writer with no connection to the restaurant world yet who was passionate about food. I wanted it to capture the mechanics of a place that prepared up to a thousand meals a day and wasn't sure a food critic could write this without a streak of condescension. In the upper ranks of the food world, there's an awful snobbery about large, bustling restaurants. They're tolerated, but not taken seriously. (The bustling restaurants, that is; not the food critics, unfortunately.)

With my limited knowledge of the literary world, only two writers came to mind: Christopher Hitchens and Robert Hughes. Hitchens could quote Plato all day long, but couldn't boil an egg. (And nor could Plato.) On the other hand, art critic Robert Hughes was outspoken enough to write, "Julian Schnabel's work is to painting, what Stallone's is to acting: a lurching display of oily pectorals," but could also reel off the ingredients of a barigoule sauce. Importantly, Hughes was interested in the nuts and bolts of creativity as well as its occasional beauty.

For the last thirty years of the twentieth century, Robert Hughes had been *Time* magazine's art critic. Like many Australians, Hughes was remarkably expressive, and the radiance of his language often turned criticism into literature. Hughes shunned ideology and wasn't afraid to attack artists—like Jeff Koons and Damien Hirst—whom he felt were more inspired by the trends of the art market than by their own vision. Hughes distrusted novelty in art yet was skeptical of artists who were too conservative to take risks. He was the greatest art critic of his time.

I didn't know Hughes, but seeing him alone at Balthazar one morning, I nervously asked if he'd consider writing the introduction to the restaurant's cookbook. It'd pay $40,000. "Sorry, mate, but I've more serious things to write about," he said. I then offered him free food at Balthazar for the rest of his life. "Come to think of it . . . I've always wanted to write an introduction to a cookbook."

Hughes was his own man. After the book's publisher told him to keep the piece to under ten pages and mention the decor as much as possible, Hughes wrote an introduction the length of a Russian short story and concentrated not on the restaurant's design but its underbelly. Specifically, its basement and how ingredients delivered to Balthazar's back door at 5 a.m. were uncrated, washed, diced, roasted, plated and served to a customer at 8 p.m. It was a stunning introduction. However, I was less interested in the introduction than in the man writing it, and found any excuse to accompany Hughes on his early-morning descents into the labyrinthian world of Balthazar's six-thousand-square-foot basement.

It's odd how spending time with someone as the sun rises prompts kinship, and during the course of Hughes researching the piece, we became good friends. Although we didn't see each other that often, Hughes's integrity had a profound effect on me. A genuine intellectual, he was at his best when explaining complex ideas to nonintellectuals like me. For someone who had no qualms about speaking his mind, Hughes had a rare warmth.

I kept to my end of the bargain and once the book was published, all of Bob's meals at Balthazar—and there were *many*—were on the house. In the last year of his life he would often be confined to his apartment, so one of Balthazar's waiters (Hughes hated the word "server") would deliver dinner to him. I remember walking through a deserted SoHo on a snowy night in February and seeing one of my waiters balancing a full tray of food above his head en route to Hughes's apartment. Nothing at Balthazar has ever given me such delight.

In 2005, while he was in New York directing an opera, Jonathan Miller invited me to Washington, DC, to visit the Phillips Collection. Like the Frick—Miller's favorite museum in New York—the paintings and sculptures in the Phillips reflect the discriminating taste of an individual collector and not a committee. Though the founders, Henry Clay Frick and Duncan Phillips, have long since left this world, both men had such tenacious personalities that something of their singularity remains at both museums.

On the train ride to DC, the serious book I'd brought along to impress Miller with never left my backpack, as he talked the whole way. A conversation with Jonathan Miller was less a dialogue and more a monologue, but an extraordinary one all the same. After a couple of hours at the museum, we had lunch with Christopher Hitchens, whom I knew well and adored. We'd been friends since 1978, when Anna Wintour had introduced us at One Fifth. Like Miller, Hitchens had a formidable intellect. The two of them were brilliant polemicists, but Hitchens was vastly more sociable.

Hitchens drank as much as he read, which was an unnerving amount. By his own admission, he put away enough alcohol to kill or stun the average mule. As a younger man, Hitchens was bisexual and almost expelled from school for sleeping with another boy. He explained that he became a dedicated heterosexual when his looks deteriorated to the point where no man would have him. Throughout the thirty-two years I knew him, Hitchens had a constant twinkle in his eye, as though about to unleash some devastating witticism.

In 1981, a year after Lynn and I had opened the Odeon, we bumped into Hitchens and his first wife, Eleni Meleagrou, at the Algonquin Hotel hours after they'd married. "It's good to be sleeping with a married woman again," he said with a smile.

Hitchens was an unrelenting supporter of the Palestinian cause and wrote scathingly on powerful public figures, including Bill Clinton, Henry Kissinger and the "sainted" Mother Teresa. In addition to writing a book a year and countless articles, Hitchens regularly appeared on the lecture circuit, engaging opponents in torrid debate. He had such skills that watching him, the writer Martin Amis declared, "In debate, I would back him, whatever the motion, against Cicero." The journalist Lynn Barber rated Hitchens "one of the greatest conversationalists of our age."

Another was Jonathan Miller.

Although Jewish by birth, both Hitchens and Miller were self-proclaimed atheists. Miller would say he didn't think of himself as Jewish, "except for the purpose of admitting it to antisemites." Hitchens claimed: "What can be asserted without evidence can be dismissed without evidence." If I believed in God, I would have converted to atheism the moment I heard this. As it was, I'd already become an atheist when I first met Miller in 1968.

I felt so frivolous next to these two colossuses that I didn't say a single word over lunch. I remember Miller asking Hitchens if he knew the Robert Frost poem "A Considerable Speck." Surprisingly, Hitchens didn't. Miller then recited the entire poem word for word. Even Hitchens was impressed. "A Considerable Speck" is about a writer observing a tiny insect crawling across his white page and his sudden awareness of this microscopic creature's significance.

Frost's poem struck a chord with Miller. He'd often stated that the importance of the seemingly insignificant was the basis of his work as a physician and a director: "The more you concentrate on the negligible, the more you end up with the grand."

At the time, I agreed that the insignificant is often important. But days after my stroke, I wasn't so sure. Lying half-paralyzed in a hospital bed, unable to form a coherent sentence, I wallowed in feelings of insignificance. Where was my importance now?

22.

In 2002, Woody Allen rented my restaurant Pastis for the day to shoot several scenes for his film *Melinda and Melinda*, which starred Will Ferrell.

During the editing process, Allen realized that one of the scenes he'd filmed at Pastis needed to be shot again. As the new scene had to match others already shot at Pastis, Allen had no choice but to re-rent my restaurant. Because I had him over a barrel, I could have charged the director anything I wanted for half a day's filming. Knowing this, Allen's producer braced herself when asking me the price. Since I was a huge fan of Woody Allen, I asked for a much lower fee than she expected. Upon hearing this, Allen was so shocked that a New Yorker hadn't taken advantage of a sitting duck that he wanted to thank me in person.

As often happens when face-to-face with someone you greatly admire, the meeting was vaguely dissatisfying. Allen had trouble looking me in the eye and gave the impression that it was a duty more than a pleasure to meet me. (I'd feel the same way meeting me.) All the same, I think Allen's an extraordinary filmmaker, and I was happy to undercharge him for the reshoot. And if I'd known then that he was later to be hounded by the #MeToo movement and shunned by most of the film industry for an act that no court of law ever found him guilty of, I would have charged him nothing at all.

I first saw the space where I built the original Pastis in the spring of 1998. It was eleven at night and I'd just left a friend's dinner party in the Meatpacking District. As usual, I left early. There are few feelings of relief that compare to the first gulp of night air after leaving a dinner party prematurely.

The weather was mild that night, and instead of taking a cab, I decided to walk home. I'd worked minutes from the Meatpacking area for years, but because of the stench from its butcheries and the reputation of its S&M clubs, I'd prudishly steered clear of it.

In 1900 the district's fifteen short blocks contained 250 slaughterhouses. Forty years later, after the invention of refrigerated trucks and the rise of supermarkets, many of them were forced to close.

By the 1960s the neighborhood was in decline, and when I got to know it in the 1990s, there were fewer than thirty meat purveyors and the area felt abandoned.

One of the few books I read during my first year in New York was Jane Jacobs's *The Death and Life of Great American Cities*. Published in 1961, the book argues—among other things—that instead of tearing down derelict buildings, a city should spend time and money renovating them. If restored with care and an eye for detail, Jacobs wrote, these rejects would integrate seamlessly into surroundings already familiar to them. When I read this in 1976, Jacobs's philosophy made sense, but after my stroke, with its more personal meaning, it made even greater sense.

Minutes after leaving the dinner party, I came to an intersection with so many corners it could have been an Italian piazza. Except that this intersection was desolate and my imaginary piazza would have had scores of tables and chairs spilling onto the sidewalk. I stood there taking in the wasteland. After five minutes or so, I began looking at each one of the six corners for a potential restaurant space. Luckily, the most desirable one had an empty two-story building on it. Unluckily, the building was owned by Bill Gottlieb, a landlord notorious for never renting his empty spaces.

At the time, Gottlieb owned around a hundred properties in downtown Manhattan and was known as an eccentric. Though a billionaire, he dressed like a slob and carried all his important papers in a shopping bag. Gottlieb supposedly trusted no one and in his pockets carried all the keys to his many buildings.

Over the next week, I called Gottlieb's office twice a day. The phone rang endlessly without being picked up by either a person or answering machine. This was strange because in those days all business phones had answering machines. (All except Bill Gottlieb's, apparently.) Impatient to meet him, I went to Gottlieb's second-floor office on Hudson Street and waited for him to show up. His office was in such disarray that any attempt to add to the chaos would only have made it tidier. At its epicenter sat a tiny old woman whose head was so permanently buried in the company's books I never saw her face the whole time I was there. The phone didn't stop ringing. The doddery old woman made no attempt to answer it.

After a couple of hours, I heard someone wheezing as he slowly climbed the stairs outside. The door opened, and in shuffled Gottlieb, looking every inch a homeless man. He eyed me suspiciously, then turned on the old woman: "I told you not to let anyone in!" The woman, I later discovered, was Gottlieb's sister, Mollie Bender.

Gottlieb asked me what I wanted. I told him I wanted to build a restaurant in one of his empty spaces. He didn't respond. I said I had a lot of restaurant experience; I owned Balthazar. "I don't care *what* you own!" he screamed. "Can you cook?"

"A little."

"Cook me dinner at your place next Wednesday." The homeless man turned his back on me and laid into his sister again.

Gottlieb came for dinner the following week. At the time, I'd been divorced from Lynn for six years and was renting my fourth-floor walk-up in SoHo. Fortunately, it was in the kind of run-down building Gottlieb would feel comfortable entering. He arrived wearing exactly the same clothes he'd been wearing a week earlier. I introduced him to Harry, Sophie and Isabelle, all then under fourteen and living with me that week. Bill made no concessions to their age and treated them just as suspiciously as he did everyone else.

Sensing that the last thing Gottlieb wanted was someone trying to impress him, I kept the dinner simple: penne with mozzarella, tomatoes and basil. Gottlieb devoured it like he hadn't eaten since Christmas. For dessert, I'd made a rhubarb crumble, which he asked for—or rather demanded—the moment he finished his pasta. He must have liked it, because he wolfed it down in four bites and took seconds without asking. Meanwhile, my kids were still eating their pasta.

Gottlieb never once used his napkin. His gruffness and intentional lack of refinement reminded me of Magwitch, the convict from *Great Expectations*. (Like Magwitch, Gottlieb would end up having quite a different character from the one on display that night.) Although he said nothing while eating, he opened up a little afterward, mostly about my rented apartment. He "couldn't fathom" (a phrase he often used) why I'd put so much money into a place I didn't own. This annoyed him out of all proportion. Neither of us mentioned the Meatpacking space all night.

Bill was in his early sixties, unmarried with no kids. Whenever I asked him anything personal, he'd clam up. Except once, when he let slip he had a nephew called Neil, whom he dismissed as a "waster." Besides that, I learned nothing personal about Gottlieb either then or the many times we'd later have coffee together. For someone so tight-lipped, it was odd how much he relished gossip. Knowing something salacious about someone seemed to be a form of one-upmanship for Gottlieb, a way of keeping one step ahead of the competition. Yet he was paranoid about people knowing anything about him. I believe that's why he dressed like a vagabond. It deflected from the real person, someone he was desperate to hide from people—even himself. For whatever reason, Gottlieb appeared curious about me and occasionally called out of the blue to invite me for coffee. Every time we met, the elephant in the room was his Meatpacking space, which neither of us ever referred to.

Gottlieb must have gotten bored with me, because after three months of meeting for coffee, he suddenly whipped out a sheet of paper for me to sign. It was a fifteen-year lease for the elephant in the room. Despite the absurdly low rent, I didn't sign it. I told him I wanted to show it to my lawyer first. "In that case," he said angrily, "you can pay for the coffee."

The following week I signed the lease.

While I was putting Pastis together, Bill would often visit and chastise me for spending so much money on renovations: "I can't believe you're buying chairs from France! What's so wrong with buying them on the

Bowery?" Bill's car was a beat-up old station wagon, in such bad shape its broken side windows had been replaced with cardboard. I thought this was taking Jane Jacobs's philosophy a little too far.

I liked Bill a lot. Although an oddball, he possessed a certain integrity that I admired. He hated pretension and, not surprisingly, men in suits. When the four-star chef Gray Kunz was looking to rent one of Gottlieb's empty spaces, he called and asked me if I could help set up a meeting between them. Knowing how idiosyncratic Bill was, I suggested to Kunz (somebody I also liked a lot) that he dress down and definitely come alone. Kunz arrived for the meeting in a dark suit, flanked by a lawyer and two accountants. Bill took one look at the besuited entourage and left the meeting.

A month before Pastis opened, Bill suddenly died. His passing saddened me for several reasons, the most trivial of which was that he never got to see Pastis. He rarely laughed, but I like to think its success would have given him a wry smile. A year later, Bill's buildings were assessed at $1 billion (but that didn't include his wardrobe, of course).

Gottlieb had left his entire estate to Mollie, the sister who ran his cluttered office. After Mollie died in 2007, her son, Neil Bender, inherited every penny at the expense of Mollie's daughter and grandchildren. One of Mollie's relatives accused Bender of Svengali-like control over his mother in her later years, forcing her to change her will for his benefit. The case dragged on for years, but nothing was ever proven.

Ten years later, when my landlord for the second Pastis, Bobby Cayre, told me that his mysterious third partner wouldn't free me from my lease, I didn't believe there was a third partner. It turned out I was wrong: the third man was Neil Bender, the person Bill had scornfully dismissed as a waster.

By never selling or tearing down his buildings, Bill Gottlieb, who dressed like a hobo, inadvertently became one of New York's leading preservationists. In spite of Neil Bender's spotless appearance and penchant for Armani suits, it's unlikely the same will ever be said of him.

One year after his passing, I discovered that the cause of Gottlieb's death had been a stroke.

23.

Before Alina moved into my Thompson Street apartment in 2000, our relationship was pretty turbulent. There were many times when our arguments were so heated that we'd often break up "for good," only to get back together the following month. During one of these breakups, in 1998, *Vanity Fair* published an article on my SoHo apartment that included a photo of me with my nine-year-old daughter, Isabelle. Soon after the magazine came out, a friend told me that an actress she knew in Hollywood had read the piece and wanted to get in touch. Was it okay if she gave her my number? I said yes because I was flattered, and also it was a distraction from missing Alina.

The next day the actress called me from LA. I will call her X. Despite her starring in a TV show watched by millions—especially teenagers— I'd never heard of X. We chatted for about ten minutes but failed to connect. The call ended with X promising to send a video tape of the show, and a few days later eight clunky tapes arrived. I watched one or two but didn't finish them; TV shows don't interest me and never have. Two nights later she called and asked what I thought of them. I couldn't lie. I said I loved them.

Over the next two months we called each other once or twice a week, and slowly a sort of connection was formed. And then one day she suggested we meet. She'd fly to New York the weekend after next, she said, and asked me to book her a room at the Mercer Hotel, a few blocks from my SoHo apartment. I booked the hotel, but two nights before X's arrival she asked me to cancel it. She'd stay at my fourth-floor walk-up instead. Of course I agreed, but was nonetheless surprised by her brazenness, because our conversations had never been intimate. Until then.

X's plane was landing at 11 p.m. She asked me to meet her at JFK, but fearing I'd run out of conversation during the cab ride, I lied and said I had to work late at Balthazar. Although I was excited to see X, a large part of me didn't want to see her at all. And the closer we came to meeting, the less I was looking forward to it. It's always the same with things I'm really looking forward to. Moments before they happen, I want to hide under the bedclothes. That's why, after my apartment's buzzer rang, I lingered a bit before walking down the four flights to meet her.

X was standing in the hallway. She was smaller than I'd expected and wearing a baseball cap. Although I'm not a fan of baseball caps—especially when worn backward—it wasn't the cap that put me off. It was the two huge suitcases by her side. Nothing puts me off sex more than a woman with a huge suitcase. We hugged. Sort of. I asked her to wait there while I lugged the first suitcase up four flights. Then I returned for her and the second, heavier case.

It was just after 1 a.m. when she settled in. I opened a bottle of wine and we sat in the kitchen drinking and talking. After twenty minutes, she said she was tired. I thought saying she was tired was a euphemism for wanting sex. I was wrong. Being tired meant she wanted to sleep. We got into my small double bed and within a few minutes she'd dozed off. Which was lucky, because with the image of her two suitcases on my mind, it would have been hard for me to get aroused.

I woke up five hours later. I had to pick up my son Harry from his mother's place and take him to an ice hockey match. It was around 6 a.m. when I prepared to say goodbye to X. I thought spending the night together and not having sex meant the end of the relationship. No one told me that nothing turns a woman on more than not having sex. She didn't want to stay in bed. She wanted to come with me to a freezing ice rink to watch a bunch of thirteen-year-olds play hockey.

Shivering on the bleachers, we watched Harry's team exit the changing room and make their way onto the ice. One of the boys looked up and recognized X from the TV show. Within seconds, the whole team knew. When the match started, instead of keeping their eyes on the puck, all the boys on Harry's team—except Harry—had their eyes glued on the TV star.

The NYC Cyclones were a terrific team who rarely lost. They lost badly that day.

The weekend went well. On Saturday I bought tickets to see a Broadway play called *Art* starring Alan Alda and afterward we had dinner at Balthazar. Few things impress a date more than taking her to a restaurant you happen to own. It's almost a fait accompli. The fact that I owned Balthazar and other restaurants wasn't the only reason X liked me. Just ninety percent. After dinner, we went back to my apartment on Thompson Street. Within ten minutes I was lying next to X's naked body without a single thought about her suitcases.

The next morning she woke early and surprised me by making coffee. I often think that the best thing about having sex with someone is being able to stretch your legs the full width of the mattress when the other person gets up.

Being half-asleep and hearing the faint sounds of a famous actress familiarizing herself with my kitchen made me inexpressibly happy. I wanted to freeze and bottle the moment and savor slices of it at some future date after life's inevitable backlash.

The TV star returned with two coffees. She was wearing my sweater. I don't know why, but seeing her in my sweater really excited me. I didn't tell her this for fear she'd get the wrong idea. Which was probably the right idea, which was another reason not to tell her. Besides, I was beginning to really miss Alina. Why did it take sleeping with another person to discover who I really wanted to sleep with? Do other people do the same thing? Was X sleeping with me in order to know who *she* really wanted to sleep with?

"What are you thinking?" she suddenly asked me. I couldn't be honest—that wouldn't have been fair. So I said the first thing that entered my head: "I was wondering if you ever slept with your costar?"

"Why does every man I sleep with always ask me that question?" It was the first time I heard X crack a joke. At least I think it was a joke. (In retrospect, maybe it wasn't.)

After the weekend was over, I had no intention of seeing X again. I missed Alina badly, and didn't think X and I had much of a connection. This had become clear the night before, when she said the reason she liked me was because "you tell it like it is." At that point in my life, I was the last person to "tell it like it is." Every jot of my so-called success was based on me *not* telling it like it is.

The next day, just before leaving for JFK, X handed me a first-class ticket to LA for the following weekend: "I want you to stay with me in Malibu for a few days. And while I'm working, you can drive my Porsche around LA." I wanted to say that driving a Porsche around LA was *the last thing in the world I wanted to do*, but because I never tell it like it is, I said, "I'd love that! Thanks so much!"

If I had put a tenth of the effort into making my relationships work as I'd put into extracting myself from them, I'd still be with my first girlfriend. I decided to be up front with X. A day after she left New York I called and told her point-blank that though I liked her a lot, I wanted our relationship to be simply platonic. Without missing a beat she screamed, "Fuck off!" and hung up the phone. So much for telling it like it is.

I wish I could say this was the end of my affair with X. But I can't. The morning she left New York I scrubbed my apartment from top to bottom and then called Alina. She was in a foul mood. She'd just seen a photo of me with X in the *New York Post*. Due to my habit of coming clean when cornered, I told her the truth. She was livid. Mind you, she hadn't been squeaky clean herself. During each breakup (and there were many in the early years) she'd visit her bigwig friend from Condé Nast—the one she had been seeing when we first met. (By coincidence, he drove a Porsche, too.)

With time, things became less rocky with Alina. Not exactly anchored, but stable enough that we discussed living together. In the meantime, I had built the original Pastis in the Meatpacking District. Not long after it opened, I took Alina to brunch there. It was so busy that the corner table I usually sat at was unavailable, so we took a small table between two other two-tops. As luck would have it, X was at the very next table with her new boyfriend. It was excruciating.

It had been eighteen months since X and I spent the weekend together. Despite being six inches apart at Pastis, we never spoke. But we certainly looked at each other. For the first time, I could see why people found her so attractive. The longer we sat next to each other, the more I regretted ending the relationship.

The next day I was desperate to call X but didn't. The following day I called her but hung up after one ring. I couldn't stop thinking about her. But why? What made her infinitely more attractive now than before? Was it the fact that, having a boyfriend, she was now less available? Or did the increasing stability of my relationship with Alina prompt me to look for the closest exit? Whatever it was, I could clearly see how ridiculous the situation had become. Unfortunately, knowing I was being stupid didn't help me act any less so. If anything, it made things worse.

I waited a week before calling her again. It was her answering machine in LA. The recorded voice gave a New York number. I called the number. X picked up. I hesitated, then mumbled something like I was sorry for the way things ended. Silence. Was she in New York for long? Would she be willing to meet for a coffee? "No, I don't think so," she calmly replied and hung up.

I couldn't get X off my mind. I even watched all eight video tapes she'd sent me twenty months before. Suddenly, brainless TV shows didn't seem so bad. A week after the phone call, I spent several hours putting together a long letter in which I wrote, among other things, that I'd made a huge mistake not visiting her in Malibu. In fact, nothing would make me happier. I also apologized for failing to see the connection between us when we first met, but sitting next to her at Pastis the Sunday before last, I felt it stronger than ever.

It was the most honest letter I'd ever written. It was also full of lies.

The only advice my mother ever gave me was to never send either an angry letter or a passionate one on the day you write it. I waited a week and read the letter again. I immediately tore it to shreds. Two months later I forgot all about her.

24.

I vowed never to open a restaurant in Las Vegas, but three years after opening Balthazar, I received an offer that was hard to refuse.

Over the years, I've been to Las Vegas a number of times, and no matter how thrilling it was to arrive—especially driving along the Strip the first night—by the third day I was always so sickened by its artificiality I was aching to leave.

It's absurd that someone who spends half his life creating interiors—and mostly from different periods—should feel "sickened" by artificiality. But there's a specific difference between restaurants in Las Vegas and my places in New York. At least, *most* of my places.

Food aside, Balthazar works partly by virtue of its French-looking dining room but mainly because it's an integral part of its neighborhood. The Odeon succeeded not because it resembled a 1930s cafeteria, but because it was owned and operated by three young people who were an intrinsic part of downtown. The same with Lucky Strike. That small French-looking bistro took off because it was a vital element of SoHo's late-night culture. On the other hand, Augustine didn't work because it had no connection to the neighborhood—plus, I'm ashamed to say, it was a direct copy of Brasserie Lipp in Paris. Copies of existing restaurants seldom work outside of Vegas. And if they do, they're usually soulless.

Balthazar in London is a good example. Although identical in looks to Balthazar in New York, the feel of the place is completely different. Whereas New York's Balthazar seems natural to its surroundings, Balthazar in London feels like a transplant. And that's what's wrong with ninety percent of the restaurants in Las Vegas: they're ingenious reproductions of other restaurants in other cities. And the longer you're there, the more the inauthenticity grates. At least on me it does. But that's probably because it's too close to the bone. As the novelist Hermann Hesse once wrote: "If you hate a person, you hate something in him that is part of yourself." (Hesse wrote *Siddhartha* at the Sands Hotel.)

In 2000, billionaire Steve Wynn offered me a small fortune to open Balthazar in Vegas. Besides building the $1.6 billion Bellagio hotel, the "Godfather of Vegas" had built many other hotels on the Strip. He also owned one of the most prestigious art collections in America, which included paintings by Cézanne, Van Gogh, Manet, Matisse, Picasso and Vermeer. Wynn would soon make *Time* magazine's 100 Most Influential People in the World list.

Having no interest in billionaires, this didn't impress me one bit. Besides, I'd sworn years ago that I wouldn't open a restaurant in Vegas, no matter who asked me.

However, when Wynn called and invited me to spend the weekend with him, I was secretly so giddy with excitement that he wanted to meet me that I dropped everything and booked a plane ticket to Las Vegas. In fact, I bought two. I wanted to take along my eleven-year-old daughter, Isabelle.

As the plane touched down, I felt that tingle of excitement one feels on a first date. Isabelle and I were picked up by a stretch limousine and driven to Wynn's mansion, about six miles from the Strip. Though he had an infantry of help, Wynn was overjoyed to see us and took pleasure in showing us around the house himself. He told me that Clint Eastwood was the last person who'd slept in my bed.

That night, the "Godfather of Vegas" laid out the red carpet for Isabelle and me. He took us to his hotel, the $1.6 billion Bellagio, to see a show, Cirque du Soleil's spectacular *O*, and afterward, we dined at Picasso, one of the hotel's many restaurants. Over dinner, Wynn whispered conspiratorially in my ear that Picasso made four million dollars profit a year. I'd normally despise someone so eager to brag about profits, but the way Wynn whispered the words "four million dollars profit" sounded like something worth wishing for. As we were leaving the restaurant, Wynn walked between Isabelle and me and linked arms with each of us. I'm usually embarrassed as hell when a man links arms with me, but it somehow felt okay when Wynn did it. Even pleasurable.

Wynn then gave us a tour of the hotel. All $1.6 billion of it. Every five minutes, strangers approached the "Godfather of Vegas" for his autograph. He took it in stride and obliged with the smile of a man handing a small child some candy. Wynn had an extraordinarily seductive voice, and though I loathe my name, coming from his lips—which it did every ten seconds—I began to really like it. It made me feel good about myself. As we left the hotel, we linked arms again and I felt like I was walking on air.

In bed that night, I decided that I would build Balthazar in Vegas. I wasn't selling out. I was cashing in. There's an acre of difference between the two.

Before falling asleep, I started working out how much profit a Las Vegas Balthazar could make over fifteen years. I began snoring when I reached forty million.

Although I hadn't drunk much that night, the next morning I woke up with the mother of hangovers. I felt unclean and grungy. As if I'd shared a bed with Dirty Harry and he'd touched me in the night. I detested everything about Las Vegas. I wanted to leave that second and never return.

Back in New York, I made plans to open a new restaurant. Just as some people suddenly break off a wedding engagement to marry someone with the exact opposite qualities, I wanted to build a restaurant that was the antithesis of everything that symbolized Las Vegas. I wanted to open a place that didn't cost $1.6 billion to build. A place that was fun, cheap and casual, where deadbeats, idlers and layabouts could eat well without breaking the bank. I wanted to build a place as far from the fucking Vegas Strip as possible.

After searching for a few months, I spotted a run-down pharmacy for rent on the Lower East Side. Eighteen months later, Schiller's Liquor Bar opened.

Because I went out of my way to keep the prices low, I never made any money from Schiller's. All of the restaurant's appetizers were under ten dollars and the entrées—braised lamb shoulder, grilled trout with couscous, rotisserie chicken with roast potatoes, etc.—were under twenty dollars. We had three carafes of white and red wine: cheap, decent and good. At $15, the "cheap" carafe was the least expensive, and concealed from the customers was the fact that it was often filled with the most sensational wine. One time I filled the $15 carafe with a Saint-Émilion Grand Cru and a few times with my favorite Burgundy, Gevrey-Chambertin. This meant I lost a ton of money every time someone ordered the "cheap" wine. On the other hand, the "good" carafe at $21 was filled with the worst wine imaginable and I made an absolute killing on every sale. I told the servers to suggest the cheap carafe to anyone under thirty and the good carafe to anyone over forty. The funny thing is, no one ever complained.

Largely due to the spirit of its young staff, opening Schiller's was one of the happiest times I've ever had opening and operating a restaurant.

For many years *Saturday Night Live* used shots of Schiller's in their opening credits and the writer Richard Price set part of his 2008 crime novel *Lush Life* around Schiller's. Price, whom I knew a little, based the owner of the restaurant, Harry Steele, on me, which is why I didn't read the book until sixteen years later.

Three months after my stroke, the landlord of Schiller's, Bill Gottlieb's "waster" nephew Neil Bender, wanted to raise the rent to an insane figure. In 2017 I closed its doors for the final time. Although Schiller's never turned a profit, it was fun while it lasted.

25.

In May 2007, I hiked across England from the west coast of Cumbria to the east coast of North Yorkshire, walking ten hours a day. It took two weeks and rained nonstop. Sloshing my way through the quaint villages of William Wordsworth country, I was dying to run into a Caesars Palace.

On the tenth day, while crossing the North York Moors in the rain, I saw what looked like a ghostly sailing ship in the distance. As I got closer, this *Mary Celeste* turned out to be the skeleton of an ancient monastery: Rievaulx Abbey.

Rievaulx was founded in the twelfth century and, like many monasteries at the time, soon became a thriving Catholic community answerable to the pope only. When Henry VIII broke from the Catholic Church in 1534, there were close to a thousand monasteries in the country. Two years later, he passed the Dissolution of the Monasteries act, which led to the full or partial destruction of eight hundred of these religious institutions. Rievaulx was one of them.

Stumbling across Rievaulx inspired me to visit other monasteries that had also been in a state of neglect for nearly five hundred years. To me, these ruined monasteries seemed far more beautiful—and certainly more spiritual—than cathedrals in perfect condition.

Though I dislike the bullying, misogynistic Henry, I'm glad he was ruthless enough to pass the Dissolution of the Monasteries act. England wouldn't be half as intriguing without these glorious, brooding remains dotted mysteriously around the country.

Even though I missed meeting Henry VIII by four hundred years, I did meet his modern-day equivalent, Donald Trump. Just after the millennium, I received a call from the Don asking me to look at a restaurant space in a huge building he owned in Manhattan. I arrived the next morning with my codesigner, Ian McPheely, and Trump graciously escorted us around the place. Walking through a series of overdecorated spaces, we passed one that was noticeably less gaudy than the others. I asked the Don if that restaurant space was also for rent. "No, that one's taken. I guaranteed it to someone else a month ago." There was a pause before Trump added with a smile: "But just because it's guaranteed doesn't mean it's locked in." I got the message but didn't take the space.

I regret not having a thorough understanding of one particular subject. Due to my habit of skimming the surface of things, I've picked up a passing knowledge of three or four topics, which though wafer-thin, is just about enough to help me appear more intelligent than I am. Regrettably, this is often the purpose of my learning.

I wish I'd spent some—if not all—of the last forty years concentrating on one subject rather than flitting from one to another. Not least because those who spend their years perfecting a single detail are, to my mind, more likely to lead an examined life than the rest of us. I believe that the Italian painter Giorgio Morandi exemplified this as much as, or more than, anyone.

Born in 1890, Morandi lived with his three sisters in Bologna and for forty years painted the same glasses and carafes over and over again. Each painting is a study in contemplation. In 2002, I became fascinated by Morandi's paintings. I wasn't the only one. Two of my favorite Italian filmmakers, Fellini and Antonioni, also admired Morandi. In Fellini's *La Dolce Vita* and Antonioni's *La Notte*, the same actor, Marcello Mastroianni, stands in front of a Morandi painting.

Around the time my infatuation with Morandi began, I had an urge to open an Italian restaurant. Whether one prompted the other I can't say, but I've always loved Italian cuisine. Given a choice between Italian or French, I'd choose Italian. With paintings it would be the same. With women, I'm not so sure.

Intending to research the food of the region of Emilia-Romagna, I flew to Bologna to taste its cured hams, aged cheeses and crescentine fritte. Bologna, the most underrated city in Italy, not only has the oldest university in Europe but also a wealth of sensational local produce. Unfortunately, between mouthfuls of tortellini en brodo and lasagna verde I made the mistake of visiting Bologna's Museum of Modern Art. Like the character Mr. Toad in *The Wind in the Willows*, who's constantly switching hobbies when something more interesting comes along, once I'd seen a Morandi painting in the flesh, my plan to build an Italian restaurant went out the window and was replaced by an absurd need to see as many Morandi paintings as possible.

Over the next few years, I regularly flew to Italy alone or with Alina to look at Renaissance paintings. One time, we combed Tuscany, Umbria and Emilia-Romagna looking for paintings by Piero della Francesca. In Sansepolcro, we saw what the writer Aldous Huxley considered to be the "greatest painting" in the world: *The Resurrection of Christ*. The trouble with looking at scores of paintings in a very short time is that pretty soon they merge together and often you can't distinguish one from the other. A week after looking at "the greatest painting in the world," I'd forgotten what it looked like. I still can't remember.

Although I like looking at paintings in museums, I don't like looking at them next to someone else. Just as I can't pee at a urinal if another man is standing next to me, I can't focus on a painting if the person next to me is doing the same thing. Instead of thinking about the painting, I'm thinking about the person next to me, and I'm sure they're thinking my interest in art is feigned and I'm a complete wanker. Especially if I stare at the painting for more than two minutes (which I often do). On the other hand, if I don't look at the painting at all, I'll be revealing my ignorance to the person next to me, who just happens to be a professor of art history and believes the painting is a masterpiece.

The advantage of being dead is never having to worry about these things.

No matter how obsessed I became with classical painters, I always returned to the modernist Morandi—not so much for the paintings themselves but more for the idea behind them. Morandi's paintings seemed to be exercises in restraint, and in a contemporary world impressed by swagger and novelty, it was a relief to know there's an artist who creates a ripple without making a splash. I feel even more strongly about this today.

It's fine to take a highfalutin interest in art, but it doesn't pay the bills. In 2003 and 2005, George and Alice were born, and I needed to open more restaurants and put some bread on the table. In 2006, I found an empty space in Greenwich Village and began to build an Italian restaurant.

The restaurant was supposed to take nine months to build but took a year and a half. The delay, as usual, was caused by my fixation on details. The space was to have a number of Roman arches made from hundred-year-old bricks, and the professional bricklayer—an older man from the Dominican Republic called Carlos—found it hard to follow my instructions to build the arches imperfectly. Forty years of laying bricks perfectly wouldn't allow him to lay them any other way. And the one time when he forced himself to do it, he went too far and laid them so perfectly imperfectly they looked contrived. One day, with an hour of work left, I gave Carlos four glasses of Brunello di Montalcino. The good thing was every brick he laid that afternoon was perfectly imperfect. The bad thing was when he returned home tipsy, his wife gave him absolute hell.

I called the new restaurant Morandi.

Over the years I've noticed one unvarying trait in my customers. If offered a free drink once every twenty visits, they love the restaurant. But if they receive a free drink nineteen times in a row and not on the twentieth, they become indignant.

Productive partnerships between strong individuals often end contentiously, and my relationship with original Balthazar chefs Riad Nasr and Lee Hanson was no exception. As is usually the case, things broke down over money.

Nasr and Hanson worked at Balthazar for more than fifteen years and, apart from post-9/11, the restaurant's finances increased every year (which meant their bonuses increased accordingly). An eternal pessimist, I believed Balthazar's success wouldn't continue without them. It was partly for this reason—and partly because they were remarkably talented—that I offered the pair working partnerships in my next two restaurants, Pastis and Schiller's Liquor Bar.

In 2008, the chefs asked me to build a new restaurant in which the three of us would be equal partners. Even though I had to lend them the money to invest, I agreed to the request and in 2009, the three of us opened Minetta Tavern together.

Minetta was my tenth restaurant and the only one that I didn't have to name—the name was already there. The original Minetta Tavern was built in 1937 by boxing aficionado Eddie Sieveri. Sieveri's charm and Minetta's hint of seediness attracted a mix of boxers and writers. The writers included Dylan Thomas, Eugene O'Neill and Ernest Hemingway. The boxers included Rocky Marciano, Jim Braddock and also Ernest Hemingway.

I didn't know anything of Minetta's history when, in 2008, a real estate agent showed me a filthy-looking bar with a windowless back room smelling of rotting beef. It had been on the market for six months and at least fifteen other restaurateurs had rejected the space. It was easy to see why. Minetta Tavern is located in a part of Greenwich Village long past its bohemian heyday, which now appeals to college kids who spend their weekends drinking in the neighborhood's bars and throwing up five minutes later on its sidewalks—mostly outside Minetta Tavern.

Despite the god-awful location, Minetta's history was tailor-made for me and became the inspiration I needed to take on this project. Without wanting to reproduce its history—which would be impossible—I wanted to build a restaurant with extraordinary food and a tavern-like interior based on the spirit of the original Minetta. Nasr and Hanson agreed with this, and over nine months worked on ideas for the menu. Every six weeks we had a food tasting, which was always tense and awkward. It wasn't until two weeks before opening that the two of them hit on a menu I was happy with.

Minetta Tavern was the first restaurant I'd built since the Odeon in

1980 in which I benefited from the spirit of the place I inherited. Perhaps someone will do the same with Balthazar one day. I hope so.

From the original Minetta Tavern, I saved the long mahogany bar, the tin ceiling and the beautiful faded mural in the back room. I also kept all the original boxing photographs that were framed on Minetta's walls. The only photograph I added was one of my father as an amateur boxer, taken in the ring in 1942. It still hangs on the wall above table 12. My dad never sat in a three-star restaurant in his life and he now sits in one 365 days of the year. I think he'd get a laugh from that. Especially since he's never handed a check.

A few years after Minetta opened, Nasr and Hanson surprised me by asking for equity in Balthazar. The two chefs were earning salaries, and often profits, from Balthazar, Pastis and Schiller's Liquor Bar that, when combined, was a substantial sum. Like the customer being upset when not receiving their twentieth free drink, I felt Nasr's and Hanson's behavior hinted at entitlement. For once I put my foot down and said no. Feeling aggrieved, they quit. Several years later, they opened the phenomenally successful Frenchette, and after that they went on to open two equally successful places: Le Rock and Le Veau d'Or. The three of us haven't spoken since they left Balthazar—which is a pity, as I'm especially fond of Nasr. In and out of restaurants we had some really good times together. He's also the godfather to my son George, and I miss him a lot.

Minetta had been open for five weeks when the *New York Times* restaurant reviewer came to dinner. We prayed he'd give us two stars. He gave us three. Minetta Tavern was "the best steakhouse in the city," he wrote, in an ecstatic review that triggered Minetta's success. But like all successes, it came with a sting in its tail. For the next nine years, every review I received from the *New York Times*—bar one—would be horrendous.

26.

The winter of 2008 in New York was so cold that Alina and I decided to take George, Alice and my dad—who was living with us at the time—to Guadeloupe for a week's holiday. We left in such a rush that I forgot to take a book. On the first day, I found an old paperback abandoned by the hotel pool, *Life with Picasso*, written by the artist's former girlfriend Françoise Gilot, herself a painter. I often don't get further than the second chapter with most books, but this one was so absorbing I couldn't put it down. Probably because I didn't pay for it.

Gilot met Picasso in Paris in 1943 during Germany's occupation of France. She was twenty-one and he was sixty-one. Though clearly a genius, Picasso was a monster to live with, as one might expect from someone who claimed that "there are only two kinds of women—goddesses and doormats." The couple had two children together but never married. Despite loving Picasso, Gilot was the only one of his five hundred (some say five thousand) lovers who not only refused to become a doormat but eventually left him.

Books about Picasso are two a penny, but this one was less about Picasso and more about Gilot and her refusal to become a victim to an all-powerful, all-consuming man. I was captivated.

On returning to New York, I had an irrational urge to contact Gilot. Ostensibly, I had nothing in common with this sophisticated French painter, yet after reading her book I felt some sort of kinship with the author. (As often happens with the best books.) Although she'd written *Life with Picasso* over forty years earlier, Gilot was still alive and living in America. But where in America, I had no idea. Despite loathing the notion that coincidences are "meant to be," I do occasionally believe in happenstance. Rolling the dice, I dialed the directory. Shockingly, there was an F. Gilot living on West Sixty-Seventh Street. I called the number. After the phone rang five or six times, a frail-sounding woman with a French accent answered. It was Gilot herself.

After apologizing for calling her out of the blue, I uttered something fulsomely complimentary that I instantly regretted. Uncomfortable talking on the phone, Gilot ignored the compliments but gave me her mailing address and suggested that if I had anything of consequence to say I should write a letter to her. She gave me a curt goodbye and hung up. As someone who can never end a phone conversation without a gratuitous "talk soon," I found Gilot's directness a blast of fresh air. And another reason to admire her.

That morning I had a dozen meetings. Intending to knock off a quick letter to Gilot before they started, I was still at my desk three hours later, unable to write the first sentence. Of course, it would have been easier to write the letter if I *hadn't* liked the book. (As all critics know, it's far easier to write about something you dislike than something you love.) On my fifteenth attempt, I finally typed out my three-sentence letter. (When in doubt, keep it short.) A week later I received a beautifully handwritten reply encouraging further correspondence. A series of letters then began, between an ex-girlfriend of Pablo Picasso and a longshoreman's son from Bethnal Green.

After leaving Picasso, Gilot married twice. First, briefly to a French actor, then for twenty-five years to the love of her life: Jonas Salk, the man who developed the first safe vaccine for polio. The couple were very happily married until Salk's death in 1995.

Two months after our correspondence began, Gilot invited me to dinner at her apartment, above a restaurant appropriately named Café des Artistes, on West Sixty-Seventh Street. Hanging on the apartment's stark white walls were a few paintings by Picasso but many more by Gilot herself. Around the table it was just Gilot, a friend of hers and me. I couldn't believe I was sitting next to Picasso's old girlfriend.

After two glasses of wine, Gilot began telling stories about Picasso's friends Matisse, Braque and Derain. It seemed incredible that these mythical names entered the conversation. (It was like something out of Woody Allen's film *Midnight in Paris*.) Unfortunately, I was so captivated by Gilot's expressive, birdlike face that I didn't take her stories in and, as a consequence, have no memory of them. It was strange to think that the woman opposite me had sexual intercourse with somebody born in 1881.

Although meeting Gilot put me within touching distance of Picasso, I was glad El Maestro wasn't there; I'd far rather have dinner with Gilot than with the bullying genius himself.

Picasso, Matisse, Braque, Derain, Françoise Gilot. That dinner was the most extraordinary I've ever had. And all because I picked up an abandoned book. The pleasures of happenstance . . .

. . . The misfortunes of happenstance. When Monica Lewinsky walked into Balthazar in 2014, many of the customers snickered and made vulgar comments. A week earlier, I'd read an article that Lewinsky had written for *Vanity Fair* in which she came across as sensible and terrifically brave. The article, "Shame and Survival," was an account of her affair with President Clinton and its shocking aftermath. Shocking because this former White House intern was publicly humiliated and branded a tramp for having an affair with the president. *The Wall Street Journal* called Lewinsky a "little tart." Most Americans joined the chorus, as did, to their eternal disgrace, almost every feminist movement. ("My dental hygienist pointed out she had third-stage gum disease," said Erica Jong. Betty Friedan dismissed her as "some little twerp.")

Several months after Lewinsky began working at the White House, the twenty-two-year-old made the mistake—not entirely uncommon for a twenty-two-year-old—of falling in love with her boss. Only in this case, her boss was president of the United States. After the relationship was uncovered, the president claimed on television that he "did not have sexual relations with that woman, Ms. Lewinsky." Hillary Clinton called "that woman" a "narcissistic loony toon."

Until I read the *Vanity Fair* article by Lewinsky, I hadn't realized how badly her reputation had been defiled by the press—particularly by the *New York Times*—and how unconscionably she'd been treated by the president. The vile reception she received from some of Balthazar's customers that night revealed how nearly impossible it is to revive a tarnished reputation. It also made me ashamed to be the restaurant's owner.

According to my staff, Lewinsky was exceptionally decent to wait on. She also left one of the biggest tips of the night.

27.

Following the success of the restaurants I'd built with Lynn, I had a string of six places I'd built without her that did even better. These included Balthazar, Pastis and Minetta Tavern. In 2009, I felt I couldn't put a foot wrong and, against the advice of Søren Kierkegaard, started believing I was the master of my own fate—the quickest way to court disaster ever invented.

In 2010, I put several million dollars into building Pulino's, a large upscale pizzeria on the Bowery. Just as I was feeling impervious to failure, I had the biggest failure of my restaurant career. Pulino's was a monumental flop and I was totally to blame. It was my idea to build a high-end pizzeria in what I thought was a perfect location—the corner of the Bowery and Houston. I couldn't have been more wrong.

The reviews were diabolical. I'd had bad reviews before, but they never stopped the customers from coming. But with Pulino's, to quote Sam Goldwyn, they stayed away in droves. I've noticed that when a loving relationship turns sour, everything you do to improve it only makes it worse. It was the same with Pulino's. No matter what I did to enhance the food, fewer and fewer customers came through the door.

In my world, there's nothing quite as sad as an empty restaurant at prime time. And the excuses one makes! The snow, the Jewish holidays, the marathon, the Grammys, the midterm elections, Martin Luther King Day . . . There was always some justification for Pulino's being empty. What I never mentioned was the truth: I had lost my touch.

Desperate to prove Pulino's failure an anomaly after my run of ten successes, I spent a million and a half dollars of my own money transforming this unsuccessful pizzeria into an unsuccessful French restaurant, Cherche Midi.

Initially, Cherche Midi worked. It received positive reviews and restored my self-confidence. Temporarily, that is. Because after six months, it began to run out of steam. A sure sign your restaurant is slipping out to the China Sea is when servers begin leaving you to work in busier restaurants. Cherche Midi's best waiter left because he wanted to take care of his ailing grandmother in Dayton, Ohio. Ten days later I saw the bastard waiting tables at a restaurant on Sixth Avenue.

While acting in a stage production of *Peter Pan* at sixteen, I was told by an older actor that once the theater enters your bloodstream, it's there forever. At the time, I dismissed this as rubbish, but today I think there might be some truth to it.

Although I'm enthusiastic about films, my connection to the theater runs deeper. During the three years I worked at One Fifth, I spent much of my spare time trying to write a play. Once I'd finished it, I had the gall to stage an amateur production of this three-act play in Lynn's downtown loft. *The Appointment*, as it was pretentiously titled, had a cast of just two men, which meant I could afford to hire professional actors. The audience of twenty consisted of friends and two producers. It "ran" for two nights and though neither producer liked it, and the play sank without a trace, the overall experience wasn't quite awful enough to deter me from writing another one.

Ideas for plays don't come thick and fast to me. The idea for my first play came in 1976. The next one came thirty-two years later. This was three years before Alina and I moved to England.

By the time we'd settled into our London house in 2011, I'd accumulated over a hundred pages of notes for the play, but not a single word of dialogue. Determined to change this, I converted the storage room in our new house into an office. Suddenly, the dialogue gushed out. After ten days of writing, I had completed five full pages. At this rate, the play would be finished in three months. I was euphoric.

Then disaster struck. Someone offered me a million dollars *not* to write the play. Not exactly. Someone offered me a million dollars to build another Balthazar in London. Having gone way over budget renovating our house in Notting Hill, I was tempted. Of course I wanted to write the play, but not as much as I wanted an excuse *not* to write it. This million-dollar offer killed two birds with one stone. It also killed my soul. And my brand-new office remained forever empty.

The man behind the Balthazar offer was coiffured businessman turned restaurateur Richard Caring. Caring knew precious little about restaurants, but a whole lot about shafting people.

Building Balthazar in London in 2011 was the most difficult time I've ever had putting a restaurant together. I hadn't worked in London for almost forty years and, like Austin Powers emerging from a time capsule, had underestimated the city's changes during that time. Crucially, I'd forgotten that the English and Americans were poles apart when it came to work ethic. In my experience, the English are lazier and complain more. I also wasn't prepared for how vile the press could be about a returning Englishman who'd earned a measure of success abroad.

After eighteen months of continuous problems, Balthazar finally opened. The reviews were terrible. Some were so personal they reminded me of why I had left London in the first place. An editor friend at the *Observer* magazine, Allan Jenkins (a lovely man), telephoned me three days before the review was published in his paper and advised me to avoid reading it. Unfortunately, there's no worse way to discover a bad write-up than by being cautioned not to read it. Although the *Observer* review wasn't quite as hellish as I'd imagined, it was awful nonetheless: "A lobster and truffle risotto . . . was thin, underseasoned and curiously prissy. . . . Service is notable for being like frogspawn in spring: bloody everywhere."

It wasn't the criticism of the food that most bothered me. It was the reviewer's desperation to be funny. W. H. Auden said, "One cannot review a bad book without showing off." This is also true of London restaurant critics. In particular the minuscule journalist Giles Coren ("Not a memorable mouthful to be had. Like all New York restaurants").

The morning after the Sunday reviews, I had to do what all restaurateurs—and theater directors—dread the day after disastrous press: face a despondent staff. Though the impulse is to crawl under a small rock, you must feign optimism and understate the calamity. It's like the captain of the *Titanic* telling its crew the ship's collision with the iceberg caused superficial damage only.

The same day, playwright David Hare—whom I knew a little—emailed and without a single reference to the bad reviews made a booking at Balthazar that night. For a writer whose plays are often accused of lacking heart, this was a most compassionate gesture.

Balthazar in London survived its appalling reception and is still busy today. Three years after the restaurant opened, I had a stroke and never heard from Caring again. Although I own twenty-five percent of the restaurant, I've nothing to do with the place anymore. Not long after I was hospitalized, most of the staff I'd hired—including the chef and general manager—were fired. Since Balthazar opened in 2013 I haven't received a dime in profits. After canceling my salary without explanation, the parting shot of the integrity-free Richard Caring was to buy the English rights to my restaurant Pastis. Oddly enough, this duplicity didn't anger me. I knew the deal when I accepted a million dollars from Caring. You can't form a partnership with a pit bull and then be shocked when he bites you. All the same, I wish he'd change his barber. (Caring, that is, not the pit bull.)

Of the many thousands of employees I've worked with, one stands head and shoulders above the others: Roberta Rossini Delice. Roberta was one of the original Balthazar servers, and its best. A week after opening, she knew the restaurant's menu and its hundred wines backward. She also had a check average that was thirty percent higher than all the other servers'. But what made Roberta really special was how much she *cared* about the customers. She'd rather the guest leave her a five percent tip and go home happy than leave her a fifty percent tip and go home dissatisfied. After four months, I promoted Roberta to floor manager, and four years later to my director of operations. These days she's my number two and a partner in Minetta Tavern. Although post-stroke I still make the major decisions, it's Roberta who puts them into practice twelve hours a day. Since the first day she began working with me in 1997, Roberta and I have never had a single argument. In managing over five hundred people, Roberta is scrupulously fair and, like all good managers, would rather be respected than liked. I'm the other way around: with my staff, I'd rather be liked than respected. That's my Achilles' heel. And why I need Roberta. Without her I'd be lost. Luckily, she's never sick. Except that's not true.

Augustine opened in October 2016. One night during its opening month, Roberta turned white and became strangely dizzy. Fearing she was having a stroke, I called an ambulance. But she insisted I cancel it. As I looked at this ball of energy slumped in a chair, I selfishly thought not of her health, but that my workload would double if she were ever sidelined.

Three weeks later the opposite happened: I suffered a stroke and Roberta's workload doubled.

It's a reflection of her talent—as well as my relative unimportance—that the restaurants didn't close after my stroke. In January 2017, I handed their control to Roberta and my two oldest children, Harry and Sophie. I felt blessed having two children who were willing to sacrifice their own careers to help sustain their father's. Though this dreamy coalition functioned perfectly for the first six months, ultimately it didn't work. Both Harry and Sophie left the company quite disillusioned with me, which was my fault entirely. Though I'd told my children that they—alongside Roberta—had total control, it didn't turn out that way. As soon as I recovered from the immediate trauma of my stroke, I began interfering with their decision-making. I tried as hard as possible not to get involved, but I just couldn't stop myself. Having had full control of Balthazar for twenty years, I didn't find it easy to watch others run it slightly differently. No excuse, but if King Lear had been a restaurateur, he would have acted just like me. (Though he might have taken the escargots off the lunch menu.)

* * *

In March 2017, five months after Augustine opened, the *New York Times* finally reviewed it. The moment I read, "Augustine has the prettiest, giddiest interior [McNally's] ever done," I knew the food would be slammed. Just as beautiful women have a hard time being taken seriously, so it is with restaurants. The reviewer Pete Wells condescendingly gave it one star. The five months leading up to the review, Augustine had been packed every night. The day the review came out, it was half full. I was done for.

No one likes failure, but for Americans it's worse than bladder cancer. Loyal customers who before the review had praised the food to the skies abruptly canceled their reservations. And those who did come seemed embarrassed by the number of empty seats around them. The only thing New Yorkers like less than a crowded restaurant is an uncrowded one.

My usual response to a negative review is to talk to the staff in person and raise their morale by telling them stories of great restaurants that survived one-star reviews. But since I was terrified of my staff seeing me in my post-stroke condition, going to Augustine was out of the question. Being badly handicapped, I was more demoralized than my staff and therefore in no fit state to give a pep talk. Instead, I took the cowardly route. I fired the chef by email and began looking for someone else to take over the kitchen.

Augustine had taken two years to build and cost $4.5 million. After the review, morale plummeted, cooks left and the place began to leak money. I'd gone from having ten successful restaurants in a row to three failures in a row. I'd not only lost my touch . . . I'd also lost my way.

28.

In April 2017, my oldest brother, Peter, died of colon cancer. He was seventy. He'd known for some time he was dying and handled it with the same absence of self-pity he did most things.

Peter was the most moral one of my family but also the most socially awkward. Which trait came first, I couldn't say, but it seems the two often go hand in hand. My brother Brian has the opposite character— little moral conscience but boatloads of charm. Or so I believed, until Peter's illness became terminal, when Brian shocked me—and himself, too, no doubt—by taking meticulous care of Peter every day of his last four months.

In school, Peter had been exceptional at art. He painted most of his life but never spoke about it until he was over sixty. Leaving school at sixteen, he took a job as a trainee stockbroker at the London Stock Exchange. Promotion came quickly to my brother, but lacking the patience for a conventional job, he quit the Stock Exchange and in 1967 hitchhiked to Israel to work on a kibbutz.

Proficient in languages, Peter soon became fluent in Hebrew. Life on the kibbutz suited him. In a small community, everyone's accountable for their actions and there's no hiding one's work ethic. Peter worked hard and couldn't stomach those who didn't. Someone on the kibbutz with ties to Israel's intelligence service must have recognized Peter's stoicism and talent for languages because after eighteen months, he found himself summoned to an office in Tel Aviv for a meeting with a nameless bureaucrat. The bureaucrat was a recruiting officer for Mossad. The one meeting turned into several, and over the next few weeks, the purpose of the meetings was spelled out. My brother immediately agreed to be sent to Europe to spy for Israel.

Peter spoke German, and after eight weeks of intensive training, the nameless bureaucrat enrolled him in Frankfurt University to secretly observe German and Arab students who were believed to be dissidents. This was the early seventies, when the Baader-Meinhof Group, a German anti-Zionist gang, was terrorizing Germany.

Peter thrived as a spy but didn't remain one. After spending two years in Germany, Mossad asked him to transfer to Egypt. He later told me he refused the offer due to the shortage of available women in Egypt. Regrettably, my brother left the one job outside the kibbutz that gave him a sense of purpose, and never recaptured it. For the rest of his life Peter worked as a black-cab driver in London, a job in which, luckily, he only had to deal with people through a rearview mirror.

The last time I saw Peter was in the Cotswolds. I knew he was dying. He did, too, but went out of his way not to elicit sympathy. I remember thinking how fortunate I was to be in such good health. Eighteen hours later I had a stroke and never saw Peter again.

Four months after my stroke, he wrote an email to Alina and me, knowing full well he had less than a month to live.

It seems your trip to NY was a good move—if only to make the way forward somewhat clearer.

Of course, I'll be disappointed if Keith & I don't end up painting together off a jetty on Lake Waramaug.

At the moment it looks as if I'll be going back with Brian to Connecticut; a completely impractical decision fraught with danger, but probably the best given the circumstances.

If I can make the journey I'd be quite happy to be left with 2 or 3 weeks to see family & friends—& perhaps to knock out 3 or 4 paintings.

Anyway, love to you all.
Peter

Floating not Drowning. Martha's Vineyard, July 2023.

Pravda—a Constructivist-inspired bar where affairs began and married women
never took their husbands—opened in 1996.

With Balthazar's original chefs, Riad Nasr and Lee Hanson, in 1997.
Courtney Winston

ABOVE: With playwright Alan Bennett, Paris, 1996.

LEFT: On a break from cycling from Paris to Saint-Tropez, 1998.

My huge payroll! Balthazar staff, 2022.

Coffee at Balthazar, 2005.
James Hamilton

My dad at Balthazar, 1998.

On top of the world, with Sophie, Isabelle and Harry. Montana, 1997.

Playing chess with Harry on the Vineyard, 1999. Sophie and Isabelle clearly riveted by the game.
Les Gillings

With my daughter Isabelle in 2004.

With Oliver Sacks,
Martha's Vineyard,
2005.

Sharing a joke with
Jonathan Miller in his
house on Gloucester
Crescent, 2016. *Tom Miller*

George and Alice with
Alan Bennett, 2012.

Wedding day, 2002. With Alina's sister, Glenda, and my old friend Les Gillings.
Les Gillings

Alina with George, 2004.
Les Gillings

Hiking with Alice and George in Devon (Simonsbath), 2012.

With George and Alice, 2010.

Alina and me covered in clay, Martha's Vineyard, 2005.
Les Gillings

George with my dad on the stoop of our Eleventh Street brownstone, 2007.

Martha's Vineyard, 2000. Post–5K road race. Seated: My school friend Les Gillings and Harry. Standing next to me are Alina and Sophie. *Les Gillings*

Roberta Rossini Delice. My restaurants would have closed down long ago without her. She began as a server in 1997 and ended up as my partner in Minetta Tavern.
Minh Cao/du soleil photographie

With my codesigner of over thirty years, Ian McPheely, building Pastis Miami, 2022.

Morandi is my only Italian restaurant. It opened in the West Village in 2007 and is still there today.

The second Pastis opened in June 2019. The first restaurant I built after my stroke.
Louise Palmberg/Gallery Stock

ABOVE: With Alina at Minetta Tavern, 2010. In the left booth behind us is Jay McInerney. In the right booth is Jerry Seinfeld with his wife, Jessica. *Peter van Agtmael/Magnum Photos*

LEFT: Minetta Tavern photos. My dad is the boxer in the dark shorts. *Victoria Dearing*

ABOVE: Schiller's Liquor Bar, 2003. *Phoebe Vickers*

LEFT: Standing in front of my biggest flop, Pulino's, in 2010. *Phoebe Vickers*

Beauty and the Beast. Sophie's wedding, Martha's Vineyard, 2016. *Gabriela Herman*

Sophie and husband Adam Pritzker at Augustine, October 2016.

ABOVE: Hiking with George in the Lake District, 2016.

RIGHT: George on Martha's Vineyard, 2016 (the last bike ride the two of us took together).

With Alice at Sophie's wedding on the Vineyard, 2016.

The day I stopped being an Englishman in New York, 2022.

Favorite room I ever had a hand in designing.
The Cotswolds house, 2017. *Paul Raeside/OTTO*

With Tom Stoppard at Minetta Tavern, 2022.

With Anna Wintour. Balthazar, 2023.

Chef Laurent Kalkotour with unknown singer, Minetta Tavern, 2023. *Victoria Dearing*

With great American film director Woody Allen. Minetta Tavern, 2022.

With George in my Thompson Street apartment, 2022.
Victoria Dearing

I think . . . therefore I am. George at the end of a long shift tending bar at Balthazar, 2024. *Olivia Montalto*

With my youngest child, Alice, 2024.

With Harry, 2021.

With Lynn
Wagenknecht.
The Odeon, 2024.
Ryan Lavine

With my sister, Josephine,
and brother Brian at the
Odeon, 2024.

With Isabelle on
Martha's Vineyard,
2024.

SoHo, NYC, November 2024. *Corry Arnold*

At Minetta Tavern, Washington, DC. December 2024. A week before we opened. *Corry Arnold*

My two catalpa trees, Martha's Vineyard, 2024.

Peter loathed sentimentality and enjoyed reading authors who felt the same way. One of these was Auberon Waugh, the son of novelist Evelyn Waugh. There was a Waugh quote Peter often referred to: "Sentimentality is the exact measure of a person's inability to experience genuine feeling." I tend to agree with this.

Peter had more genuine feeling than most people, including me and the rest of my family. He just didn't know how to express it. The only people he showed affection to were his nieces and nephews, whom he adored unconditionally. He occasionally had a girlfriend for a week or so, but the same stoicism that made him an excellent spy rendered him unfit for a romantic relationship; he never married.

Peter was the only man I knew who spent the bulk of his teenage years in London's Swinging Sixties without a trace of them rubbing off on him. He was born in the wrong period, and for someone with such fierce independence, died the kind of death he would have been ashamed of.

A week before Peter died, Brian wrote me this email:

I'm not sure what to do. Today I found Peter three or four times collapsed in his room, obviously in an effort to get to the bathroom because of his terrible diarrhea. Each time he has failed to make it, in large part because he is disoriented and not mentally acute anymore. He soils himself horribly, all over his body, in his hair, everywhere in fact. I have to bathe him with sponges and towels, clean him, clean the carpet, the bathroom, the sheets, the bed. Picking him up and carrying him back to his bed can take 15 minutes and afterward I often have to throw away my own clothes. And the smell is sickening and permeates everything.

This is what happens when one "battles" cancer.

Peter died in New Milford, Connecticut. I'm sure that if assisted suicide had been an option, he would have taken it. To give dignity to the dying, assisted suicide should be made legal for the terminally sick. Especially for those with as much integrity as my brother had.

29.

For the first four months after my stroke, feelings of shame prevented me from seeing anyone outside my family. I rarely left the apartment and didn't step into any of my restaurants for over a year. I couldn't bear the staff to see me looking this way, and the idea of bumping into a customer I knew was mortifying. Whenever my phone rang, I'd shudder and refuse to answer unless certain it was one of my family calling. Besides, my voice was now so badly impaired I was difficult to understand. I still am.

I once answered my phone by accident, and it was television interviewer Charlie Rose. Rose had recently made headlines for being fired from his job at PBS for allegations of sexual harassment. It was now so awkward for him to make a reservation publicly that he felt forced to do it privately, through Balthazar's owner.

I didn't know Rose well, but he regularly ate at my restaurants, often by himself. I've always warmed to people who dine alone and Rose was no exception, particularly as he was always so gracious to my staff.

Like me, Rose was now trapped in his own form of purgatory. Embarrassed for him to hear my mangled voice, I barely spoke. Since he had no idea about my stroke, I hoped he didn't mistake my lack of conversation as a sign of judgment. Although I detested the actions he was accused of, I nevertheless felt sympathy for Rose, who was now ostracized from a society he craved, and until recently had been the epicenter of.

I've no clue how the call ended because I was distracted by the absurdity of the situation: two New Yorkers divorced from their own worlds, each trying to communicate some vital information to the other, but failing.

* * *

In October 2017, as a result of the Harvey Weinstein allegations, the #MeToo movement burst into life. I fully support #MeToo, but I'm marginally uncomfortable with the McCarthyist element of it. Any movement based on exposing people runs the risk of incriminating the innocent. For every twenty Weinsteins, who thoroughly deserve their exposure, there's potentially one innocent who does not. Unfortunately, the mere accusation of sexual harassment (or child molestation) is so powerful that the innocent are tarred for life. And just as those who've suffered from sexual abuse must have the inalienable right to due process, those accused of the crime must have the same right also. Without it, democracy fails.

In the same year that the #MeToo movement began, while recovering from my stroke, I was sued for sexual harassment myself. That summer, while vacationing on Martha's Vineyard, I asked a woman who'd worked for me in New York to be my temporary assistant on the island. Ava Meadows (not her real name) was one of a team of people I'd worked with on various restaurant projects over the previous fifteen years. She was knowledgeable, conscientious and terrifically resourceful. Meadows's job on the Vineyard was to be purely organizational.

A month before arriving, Meadows told me she was soon going to make a permanent move from New York to Pennsylvania and helping me on Martha's Vineyard would be the last time we'd work together. This saddened me, as I'd always enjoyed working with her. During the two weeks she assisted me on the Vineyard, my physical therapist Martin Spollen and his wife, Chen Jie, were there also, as well as two of my children, Harry and Isabelle. In the daytime I'd exercise with Spollen, and at night the six of us would have a long, enjoyable dinner together.

I'd rarely socialized with Meadows before and was glad to see her so relaxed. However, I was surprised that drinking a few glasses of wine brought out such strange opinions from her that everyone at dinner became slightly embarrassed. Among the more bizarre was a belief in flying saucers and extraterrestrial life, and one conviction that all loonies seem to have in common: that the moon landings were created in

Hollywood. I found these weird views hard to reconcile with Meadows's informed thoughts on other subjects.

Each day, after Spollen had given me therapy in the swimming pool, I'd hobble to the outdoor shower three yards away and, assisted by a hospital intern, take a shower and change. One time when the intern was sick, I was obliged to shower without assistance. Beforehand, I asked Ava if she could hand me some clothes after my shower. I made a point of telling her that I'd be wearing both my swimwear and a towel. She said she was uncomfortable with this and I immediately apologized and asked Harry to help me instead. At dinner, I once again apologized to Ava. I thought that was the end of it. Particularly as that night she mentioned wanting to return to Martha's Vineyard later that summer to work for me in the same capacity.

The next month, Ava moved to a town in Pennsylvania ninety miles away from New York. She then threw a spanner in the works by asking if she could rescind her resignation and continue working from her new home several hours away. As Ava's main job consisted of sourcing materials for restaurants under construction, it was necessary for her to be on-site a lot of the time. Living ninety miles away would make this untenable.

Unable to agree to Meadows's request to work from home, my director of operations, Roberta Delice, offered her a decent severance package. In retrospect, I made a mistake by staying out of the negotiations. Apart from the emotional turmoil of my stroke, I was under considerable financial stress brought on by the uncertainty of rebuilding Pastis. My health couldn't take the additional strain of negotiations with Ava. Unsurprisingly, in trying to avoid stress, I brought on a ton more.

Three months later, a certified letter arrived from Ava's lawyer claiming that I had "made the most egregious and offensive act of sexual harassment toward Ms. Meadows. And when Ms. Meadows refused Mr. McNally's advances, he illegally terminated her employment in retaliation for her not acquiescing to his sexual overture."

When you're wrongfully sued for sexual harassment, it's hard to find the right words of denial without appearing hyper-defensive. When the director Jonathan Miller was asked what he feared most in life, he replied, "Being tortured for information I don't have." That was how I now felt.

I was eager to talk to Ava. I felt sure that if we met in person, she'd agree that this claim was pure fiction. My lawyer, however, said it could be dangerous for me to have contact.

Oddly enough, I was just as upset by her lawyer's depiction of my character as I was by the accusation itself. It wasn't that I was incapable of infidelity, but the truth is I'd be more likely to promote a woman who had the good sense to reject my advances than to fire her. To be accused of trying to initiate an affair by asking a woman to help me shower was ridiculous on many levels. Not least of which is, post-stroke, I'm deeply embarrassed by my crippled body. But to say this and be believed, in these politically correct times, is next to impossible.

The one saving grace of the allegation was the cheesy novelette wording of the lawyer's letter. "McNally seized the opportunity to exert his authority over Ms. Meadows and asked her to help him bathe. In other words, McNally asked his female employee to help him disrobe, view him naked and caress his body parts." If the accusation didn't have such potentially dire consequences, I would have found this trashy Jackie Collins–like phrasing hilarious. In many ways, considering my paralysis, I should have been flattered to have been thought capable of such poetic lovemaking.

To drop this unfounded charge, Meadows was demanding $500,000. My instinct was to fight her in court. Like the character I'd played in *The Winslow Boy* fifty years earlier, I was desperate to prove my innocence. Unfortunately, the American legal system is so convoluted that to prove my innocence lawfully would cost me four times more than to settle out of court. More worryingly, by challenging the accusation, I'd be exposing myself to the press and, such is the weight of sexual allegations, that even if found innocent, I'd have to bear the stain forever.

The five months it took to resolve matters took its toll on me. I woke up every morning petrified I'd see my name in the papers. Not for my sake, but for my children's: I'd hate them to think their father could be capable of such a repellent act. What's more, they would have to suffer their friends' whispers.

One redeeming feature of this whole sordid episode was how much Alina supported me. She didn't once question my innocence. This meant more to me than she would ever know.

But what if Ava Meadows's allegations had been true? And she, like hundreds of thousands before her, had been fired for not agreeing to her boss's advances? Or if she did agree, she'd have to live with the remorse forever. It wasn't so long ago when the sexually abused had no voice at all, and the abuser held the extra piece on the chessboard. If the accused had enough money or power, the truth could be kept out of the newspapers. With history favoring the accused in matters of rape and sexual harassment, it's understandable if the #MeToo movement is occasionally overzealous.

After months of haggling, the case was settled in the spring of 2018. I paid Ava Meadows $220,000, which, hopefully, was enough for her to cover the deposit on a flying saucer. Almost $100,000 of this sum went to the avaricious lawyer who helped Ava interpret my innocent request for fresh clothes as a squalid incident of sexual abuse.

When the matter was once and for all over, Ava Meadows officially withdrew her allegation of sexual abuse: "Ms. Meadows withdraws the allegations of gender harassment she previously asserted in her demand letter to Keith McNally. Ms. Meadows understands that there was no intention to make her feel uncomfortable."

Since I believe that the more repugnantly someone behaves, the greater one's responsibility is to understand the person, I later wrote Ava an apology for the way our friendship ended. She wrote to say that she, too, was sorry. All the same, I wanted to throttle her lawyer.

30.

The larcenous nature of my stroke has meant that I've been robbed of the ability to speak fluently. These days it takes me so long to reply to someone that I live in a perpetual state of *l'esprit de l'escalier*. I'm able to think of an appropriate response as quickly as ever, but it now takes me an age to haul up the words. Where once I had the authority to summon whole sentences on command, I now have to trudge through the brain's equivalent of the British Library to retrieve a single word. The medical term for this is aphasia, and in America alone over two million people suffer from it. I also have dysarthria, a weakness of the muscles used for speech, causing my voice to sound slurred and imprecise most of the time. With so many things going wrong with my speech, I'm just grateful my accent hasn't changed to Australian. Or worse, South African.

Though I've always valued language, these days with my voice being close to incomprehensible I appreciate it even more. Words I once merely enjoyed now give me inconceivable pleasure. Conversely, words and phrases I used to dislike I now detest beyond reason. High up on the list of the words I loathe are those often wielded by parents toward their children—none more so than "quality time." Did Aristotle's parents spend quality time with him as a child? Boredom is an integral part of life and learning how to deal with it when you're young is crucial. Kids need to be bored in order to find their own way of contending with it. We should no more relieve them of boredom than of education. Learning to deal with boredom *is* an education. (Quality time is the opposite.)

Another word I can't bear in connection with kids is the adjective "proud." For decades parents weren't proud of their offspring unless they achieved something considerable—like passing a difficult exam or being selected for the school's swim team. Nowadays, every child who makes a simple drawing is considered a budding Michelangelo: "I'm so proud of you!" announces the misty-eyed parent five times a day. When did effort turn into achievement? When was the bar set so disturbingly low? What's so wrong with saying "pleased," "happy," "thrilled," even "over the moon"?

Being "proud" of your child carries a hint of possessiveness and seems to say more about the parent than the child. Perhaps I'm fearful of the word because it was instilled in me from a young age that pride comes before a fall. And to some extent, I still believe this.

In my thirty-nine years of parenting I've only once used the word "proud" with my kids. Isabelle, my youngest child with Lynn and the feistiest of my kids, was being bullied by her teacher at the Lycée Français and to his face she called him "a fucking bastard." She was eight years old at the time. The night she told me, I said, "I'm so proud of you, Isabelle, for calling the teacher a fucking bastard."

Though they won't admit it, most parents carry a best-case scenario of their children's future. When I used to brag that I was more concerned with my children's happiness than with their academic success, I knew I was lying. Of course I wanted my kids to be happy, but like many parents, it had to be on my terms. It had to include excelling at exams, learning an instrument, reading Flaubert and succeeding in the sciences—all the things I didn't achieve at school.

It's only when our children are seriously unwell that we come to our senses. That the years we spend fretting over schools, grades, exams and colleges—fuel for our own toxic ambitions—mean nothing, mean fuckall compared to our children's health. I learned the hard way with Isabelle.

Isabelle was always funny, independent and outspoken. From a young age she also suffered from major depression. She was just three years old when Lynn and I divorced. As a consequence, I saw her far less often than I wanted to. From Isabelle's perspective I was an absent father during her adolescence.

As Isabelle's depression increased, she began seeing a psychiatrist who recommended "an open therapeutic community" hospital in Massachusetts called Austen Riggs. (The musician James Taylor, who also suffered from depression, wrote most of the song "Fire and Rain" when he was a patient at Austen Riggs.)

At sixteen, Isabelle was Austen Riggs's youngest patient in fifty years. I attended her family therapy days there twice, but beyond that I didn't allow myself to become further involved. Harry, her twenty-year-old brother, more or less took over my parental role. Unforgivably, I remained detached from my young daughter's problems.

Isabelle was subsequently admitted to another clinic, which was just as beneficial as Austen Riggs. Unfortunately, I never knew its name because, disgracefully, I never visited her there. Not once. This was a critical period in Isabelle's life and disgracefully I went AWOL.

With no help from me, Isabelle had the strength of character to manage her depression and carve out a successful career as an actress and writer/director. In 2018, when she discovered I was quite depressed myself, she offered to put her career on hold and join me in England. This kind, selfless gesture only emphasized how distant I'd been when Isabelle most needed me. I still can't believe I didn't visit her in the second clinic. This has plagued me ever since.

Being deprived of the use of my more dominant hand has forced me to learn to type with my left. Correspondence has always been a major part of my life, but since my stroke it's become crucial, because writing is the only time I feel I'm not being prejudged on appearance. Consequently, it's the only time I feel normal.

Due to my aphasia, I not only have a hard time spelling but have a tendency to leave out key words. One of these is, inexplicably, the word "not." This has resulted in some deeply embarrassing memos to my staff. ("If a customer forgets to leave you a tip, do, I repeat, do ask him for one.") To avoid making similar mistakes, I have to comb through each email before sending it off.

Two years ago, I emailed my brother Brian, explaining what agony spelling now causes me—primarily words with more than one syllable. It took me fifteen minutes to spell the word "syllable." I tried "sybelle," "sybabell," "sibelle" and "sillable." I must have written "syllable" correctly two thousand times, but now it was beyond me. Then it got worse. I couldn't spell the word "agony." The closest I got was "angony." I stared at "angony" knowing for sure it was spelled wrong but was unable to fix it. Furious at myself, I resorted to Google. The ignominy of aphasia.

31.

During my stay at NewYork-Presbyterian, someone told me about a mysterious rehab clinic in San Diego that had reportedly worked wonders for stroke patients. Like other unconventional practices I'd heard of, it was owned by a charismatic figure with less-than-perfect credentials. Even though I questioned the clinic's credibility, I trusted the therapist who'd recommended it. Unfortunately, it was full for five months and I was wary of booking a clinic I was unconvinced by so far in advance. Nevertheless, I decided to go once Alina promised to travel from London to join me there.

In May 2017, Harry accompanied me on a flight from New York to San Diego. Knowing that Alina was still refusing to see him, Harry offered to drive to LA for a few days to give us some time alone. If I'd been more principled, I wouldn't have agreed to Harry's generous offer, but I was desperate to see Alina.

It had been two months since I'd last seen her—our longest break in twenty years. In order to make her arrival special, I planned to have a romantic dinner waiting for her in my hotel room. The only trouble was, ordering food on the phone when you're suffering from aphasia is no easy matter. After repeating "roast chicken for two with dauphinoise potatoes" four times without being understood, I was reduced to ordering two chef salads.

Although the dinner went well enough, there was a hint of sadness about it. I felt something had changed between us. The next morning I began my treatment.

The clinic's interior managed to be both elegant and soulless—a feat only a professional designer could achieve. All of the clinic's therapists were women. And each appeared to be devoted, in a kind of Squeaky Fromme way, to its weirdly seductive owner. In my experience, all post-stroke treatments outside conventional medicine seem to have two unifying elements: they're wildly expensive and are seldom operated by a bona fide MD. Like the sham massage I'd had six months earlier, the treatment at the San Diego clinic proved to be just as fraudulent, but on a far grander scale.

The therapist assigned to me concentrated on my paralyzed right hand. Her goal, she said, was to alter its permanently clenched-fist position into a fully open one. For such a sophisticated-looking clinic, her method appeared quite primitive, and consisted of reams of white paper, Scotch tape and a small wooden paddle. After laying my hand flat on the board, she Scotch-taped the white paper around it and for the next hour performed a dozen or so exercises on my "mummified hand." At the end of the hour, she unwrapped the paper from my flat hand, squeezed it back into a fist and held it there for thirty agonizing seconds. When freed from this forced pressure, my fingers would (of course) automatically move a little. The Squeaky Fromme character called this involuntary movement "fantastic progress." I called it a fucking scam. But half the patients there swore by it.

One of the clinic's stranger rules was that patients could only purchase therapy aids, such as a foot or arm brace, made by one particular company. I later discovered the major shareholder of this company was the same Svengali-like figure who owned the clinic. After five days of unconventional therapy, I returned to New York in exactly the same condition as before I left—only $7,000 poorer. (Including hotel, car rental and airfare for three people, it was more like $15,000.)

On her second night, Alina broke down. We were in bed. She was facing the other way when I suddenly heard whimpering. I touched her shoulder and asked what was wrong. She wouldn't say, just continued sobbing. Ten minutes later she turned to face me.

"How come in twenty years you've never taken an interest in my family? Every time you're with one of them you act like they're beneath you."

"That's not true," I said.

It was true. From day one, I never wanted anything to do with Alina's family. Every time they visited us on Martha's Vineyard, I found an excuse to return to New York. For some reason I didn't want to be around them. I'd been the same way with Lynn's family. I knew why. And it had more to do with me than them. But I wasn't willing to go into it that night.

Alina then told me that fifteen years before, her father was on Martha's Vineyard and had to stay in a motel because she was too scared to ask if he could stay with us. I had no idea. Hearing this now made me feel sick to my stomach.

I wished I could start over again.

Alina cried herself to sleep that night.

The next day, I didn't go to my morning therapy session. We stayed in the hotel room and talked. Things got slightly better between us. But not completely.

On her third and last night, Alina wanted to take me for supper in La Jolla. I hadn't eaten in public since my stroke. It was a twenty-minute drive from downtown San Diego. On the way, we stopped to look at some seals close to the harbor. It was a warm evening, but as the sun went down it became unexpectedly chilly. We drove around downtown La Jolla for half an hour searching for a decent restaurant until we finally found one. But I suddenly went into a panic. Now that we'd found a restaurant, the boldness I'd conjured up to eat in public left me and all I wanted to do was stay in the car.

We ended up eating takeaway crab rolls in our rented Toyota Camry, stationed in the far corner of an empty parking lot. We ate in silence. It was a melancholy way to end the evening.

Six weeks after my stroke, the little toe of my right foot had swollen to the size of a golf ball. It also forked unaccountably to the right, the result of excessive spasticity. As no podiatrist in the city could reduce its swelling, the rogue toe had to be accommodated by cutting a large hole in my sneakers, leaving it exposed to the air and fully ostracized from its neighbors. My doctor said that if I wanted to wear regular shoes again, I'd have to make a choice between amputation and an operation to straighten the toe. I hesitated for half a second then chose the operation.

The procedure would be painless but due to another restaurateur being in my hospital ward, the experience turned into torture.

A year earlier I'd received a newspaper article from Drew Nieporent—owner of Nobu and several other restaurants—regarding the alleged sexual indiscretions of the celebrated hotelier André Balazs. Considering I barely knew Nieporent and Balazs was a friend, it seemed offensive that he should send me this story. I sent him a terse email the next day, adding a postscript that he should never contact me again. Few things are quite so vile as the conspicuous glee some people take in the downfall of a competitor. Nieporent was clearly reveling in Balazs's potential un-doing. Unfortunately, the degree of satisfaction I received in taking the moral high ground made me feel just as guilty as I knew Nieporent to be. All the same, I was glad to be rid of him. Only I wasn't. Nine months later, I would have another encounter with Drew Nieporent.

After advertising for a new chef for my restaurant Augustine, the most qualified applicant was a chef called Markus Glocker. Unfortu-nately, Glocker was the chef and partner of Bâtard, a restaurant owned by Nieporent. I met Glocker and after an hour of discussing food, of-fered him the job. He accepted, but only on the condition that he remain at Bâtard twenty percent of his time. Usually, I wouldn't agree to this, but I admired Glocker so much I thought it worth sharing him with another restaurateur. Even one that I'd haughtily disowned nearly a year earlier.

My ill-starred path with Nieporent was to be crossed one more time. I was in Mount Sinai Hospital's pre-op ward, waiting for my wayward toe to be operated on, when I heard someone in the bed opposite boast-ing to an audience of nurses: "I'm a great friend of De Niro's." Only my nemesis Drew Nieporent would boast of a connection to "De Niro" while awaiting medical attention.

After the nurses left his bedside, Nieporent looked like a man who was scared to be alone. I felt quite sorry for him and began wondering if I, too, lying in the bed opposite, seemed to others as forlorn and adrift as Nieporent now did to me. Like seeing a brand-new sports car broken down on the side of the highway, there's something pathetic but mildly reassuring about a semi-public figure reduced to ordinariness.

Despite my increasing sympathy for Drew, I couldn't bear the idea of him recognizing me and tried to block his view by raising my left leg awkwardly in front of my face. When the anesthesiologist arrived at my bedside, he curtly asked me to drop my contortionist-like pose. As soon as I'd lowered my leg, he thrust a needle into me. Succumbing to the anesthetic, the last, fading words I heard were those of the restaurateur telling a mystified Jamaican nurse that he could book her a "good" table at Nobu "anytime she wanted."

Most neurologists believe the future of stroke recovery lies in stem cells. In September 2017, the University of California, San Francisco was coordinating a stem-cell trial for a limited number of stroke patients. Thousands applied, but only a few were chosen. I was one of the few. I'm embarrassed to say that on hearing the news that I'd been accepted, I had a momentary feeling of superiority, not dissimilar to that of being hand-picked to enter a fashionable nightclub. The velvet rope is unhooked and one glides in without a moment's thought for the rejected masses. Only in this case, it wasn't a nightclub that beckoned but a surgeon's drill boring into my skull.

Although stem-cell technology has existed since the 1980s, its use for those suffering from chronic motor disability, like me, was relatively new at the time. The trial I was to undergo was still at an experimental stage, and one third of the patients were to be administered a placebo. If I was to go through the rigmarole of having my skull drilled into, a placebo was the last thing I wanted. (Whether not wishing for a placebo decreases your chances of getting one is difficult to say.)

What persuaded me to forge ahead was the news that a patient with a similar condition had regained most of the use of her paralyzed limbs after undergoing a comparable trial. It meant the door wasn't entirely closed on me.

The surgery was to take place in Chicago and would consist of a small hole being drilled into my skull, directly above the damaged area of my brain. The neurosurgeon would then inject either the absence of cells—a placebo—or 2.5 million or 5 million cells into the impaired part of my brain. The stem cells to be used in the trial came from the bone marrow of two anonymous adults. As the transplanted cells infiltrated my brain, their role was to trigger rejuvenation of the damaged tissue. It would be similar to dropping a division of elite troops into a foreign country to galvanize the population into revolution. Except this foreign country happened to be on the left side of my head, and I wasn't sure I had enough food in the fridge to feed that many troops.

Alina offered to come on the trip and stay with me during the procedure. The four days we'd spend in Chicago would be our happiest since my stroke. They would also be our last good times together.

Just before the procedure began, I was asked to sign a document agreeing not to sue the hospital if something went drastically wrong. Alina was next to me as I badly scrawled my name. Signing this document made me realize how dangerous this procedure was. It also made me realize how much I loved Alina. How pitiful that I discovered this only when faced with my possible demise.

Once in the operating room, the neurosurgeon's assistants wedged a helmet-like device tightly onto my head, which made me resemble a character from *Mad Max*. This was called a stereotactic guide and was being fitted to allow precise delivery of the valuable stem cells. Fastening this metal contraption to my head took thirty harrowing minutes, and when secured I felt as if my head was jammed into a particularly unforgiving vise. I was fully conscious for the entire shebang.

After his assistants had done the heavy lifting, the esteemed neurosurgeon arrived and, like an executive chef entering a kitchen at the last minute, added the final flourish—in this case, the all-important injection of stem cells (or not).

The drilling itself didn't hurt that much and was, like most things that are highly anticipated, quite anticlimactic. The *sound* of the drilling, though, was another matter and inconceivably gruesome. Every time I've heard drilling since—of any kind—I want to throw up.

As a consequence of my stroke, my right arm is so spasticated it often freezes into a sling-like position, giving me the imperious look of a Napoleon portrait. In those eighteenth-century paintings, Napoleon's right hand is regularly thrust under his tunic as if soothing a sudden bout of heartburn.

Prior to the twentieth century, such a pose used to be considered a symbol of good breeding. Good breeding clearly isn't behind my pose. Not because I'm trying to conceal my working-class roots, but because my spasticity is involuntary and I have absolutely no say in the matter. However, via periodic injections of Botox, I'm able to temporarily alleviate my arm's stiffness and reduce the imperious Napoleonic look.

Botox is a type of purified botulinum toxin used medically to relax muscles, and used cosmetically to smooth out undesired wrinkles. In both cases, a minute quantity is injected into the muscles in order to untighten them. Botox became FDA approved for cosmetic use in 2002 and for extreme spasticity, like mine, in 2010. I had my first series of acutely painful injections of this drug at Mount Sinai in March 2018. This procedure was administered by "Dr. James Sutcliffe."

Inexplicably, most of the New York doctors I've met are obsessed with the city's restaurants. Many appear so restaurant savvy that it's a wonder they have time to practice medicine. Perhaps there also exists a whole raft of New York busboys who, when they're not clearing plates from restaurant tables, specialize in rare and unusual areas of medicine.

Dr. Sutcliffe was no different from the other restaurant-obsessed doctors, except he'd reveal his insider's knowledge of the restaurant world while injecting my limbs with Botox. Perhaps his intention was to take my mind off the excruciating pain, but instead he increased it by unconsciously praising my competitors:

"The new Italian restaurant two doors down from Morandi is jammed every night."

"That place your ex-chefs opened just got three stars in the *Times*."

"Eater says the Carbone boys' new French bistro has the best fries in town!"

In 2021, I stopped having Botox injections. The pain of the injections was just about bearable, but the agony of listening to my competitors being praised to the skies was not. I never went back.

32.

It's often said that a near-death experience puts things into perspective. After my stroke, the only perspective I had was the certainty of not having one.

When you're sick, everyone bangs on about the importance of family, yet it was work, not family, that pulled me out of my despair. During a personal crisis, the importance of work is often undervalued. "Take time off work," people typically say when someone's depressed. My advice would be to work more, not less. When all else seems lost, work—of any kind—provides the one thing we need to keep going: a sense of purpose.

What gives me a sense of purpose is restaurants. Since 1980, I've built and operated nineteen of them, fourteen of which I've put together with my codesigner, Ian McPheely. I say "codesigner," but it's clear to everybody working on our projects that my contribution—though not insignificant—is thirty percent, tops. Fortunately, McPheely never mentions this. Nor does he mention my inability to read architectural plans, or my ignorance where plumbing, electricity and air-conditioning are concerned. What I bring to our partnership, I believe, is an eye for lighting, a passion for texture and a clear understanding of negative space.

Five months after my stroke, I asked Ian to send over the Pastis floor plan that we'd begun working on a year earlier. If I wasn't clinically depressed at this point, I wasn't far off. Over the next few weeks I spent two or three hours alone with the plan each day, altering it here and there until I thought the whole thing might work. Somehow, putting the plan into better shape also put me into better shape. I started to feel less unhappy about my physical limitations. Whether this was a consequence of doing something mildly creative or because I was so absorbed in what I was doing that I forgot about my condition, I don't know. But for the first time since the stroke I had the urge to return to work. I emailed Ian and asked him if we could meet.

It had been six months since I'd last seen Ian and I wondered what he'd think of the changes in me. We'd been through a lot together and though we shared a certain closeness, neither of us ever acknowledged it.

Ian landed in the construction business by accident. When we first met, he was an artist who supplemented his painting by doing a bit of renovation. Nowadays it's the other way round. How much he still paints I don't know, because I'm not comfortable asking him. For some reason, I have a hard time talking about personal matters with Ian. As I do with all those I work with. I'd rather stick to more tangible things. But I feel that way with most people. When I used to go on dates (two hundred years ago), I'd always make sure we watched a film first; then afterward I could be certain we'd have something definite to talk about.

I'm at sea with the abstract and the nonrepresentational. That's why I like to begin conversations with something concrete. I don't do well with silence. Not regular silence, but the sort that comes from unsaid words hanging in the air. A dangling conversation type of silence. Being in an elevator with a stranger is a nightmare for me. Even when a conversation goes well I'm always thinking of ways of ending it without offending anyone. My life is dictated by conversations I'm dying to get out of. I'm the least hospitable person in the hospitality business.

If Ian was shocked by my condition, he didn't show it. Then again, he didn't have time to. Eager to keep the conversation factual, I whipped out the new floor plan and put it in front of him. He paused as if expecting pleasantries, but realizing I wasn't going there, turned his attention to the plan. Never one to rush things, Ian studied it before speaking. He liked the plan and, as always, found ways of improving it. We worked on the floor plan for an hour before calling it a day and agreeing to meet again at the end of the month.

Over the next six weeks, I finished the plan and made the decision to rebuild Pastis. I was in from the cold.

When Dick Robinson had invested $2.5 million in Balthazar, he barely knew me, but the risk paid off and after fifteen years his investment was returned tenfold. Robinson also invested in the original Pastis, Schiller's, Morandi and my very profitable bakery business. Sharing the same liberal values, Dick and I had become close during our long collaboration.

And although I would refer to Robinson as my business partner, he never made any decisions in the running of the business. He supplied the investment only, a function so vital that no project would exist without it, but one easily forgotten when successful. Dick had a gentle, old-fashioned demeanor and invested the old-fashioned way: with a firm handshake. The money would usually arrive a week before building began, and only after the restaurant had opened would we get around to the tedious business of formulating a contract.

In 2015, I showed Dick an eight-thousand-square-foot space where I planned to build the new Pastis, and asked him if, once again, he wanted to be my investor. I estimated Pastis would cost $6 million to build. Dick immediately said yes and we shook hands. The two of us had been partners for eighteen years and in all that time we'd never had a single disagreement.

Six months after my stroke, I felt well enough to return to work, and in May 2017 I phoned Dick Robinson to tell him the good news. As he was in the same boat as me—he'd also signed a $1 million guarantee on the building of the restaurant—I thought Robinson would be overjoyed by my return to work. Surprisingly he said nothing. It was only after I hung up that I understood his silence.

If I built Pastis, Dick would have to make good on his promise to invest an additional $6 million. Yet the person he'd made the promise to two years earlier didn't sound like the same man now slurring his words on the phone. Dick found himself torn between his principled, decent side and his more canny business side: whether to fulfill a promise made to a friend and restaurant partner of twenty years or go back on his word to invest $6 million in a half-paralyzed stroke victim. I understood Dick's dilemma. I wasn't sure what I'd have done if the roles were reversed. All the same, if Dick went back on his word, he'd be throwing me under a bus.

Over the next three months, I contacted Dick many times asking if he still planned to invest in Pastis. It was always the same answer: he'd let me know by the end of the week.

In September 2017, two days before my brain surgery in Chicago, and after three months of evasiveness, Robinson's lawyer called my lawyer to say that "his client" wouldn't be investing in Pastis. This was hard to take. If my savvy business partner had lost faith in my ability to run a restaurant, I must be in pretty bad shape. I tried not to get angry at this man who'd made more than $40 million profit off my labor, but I was furious with him. In an effort to stay calm, I recalled the words of Socrates that we must do no wrong even when we are injured ourselves. But, of course, Socrates said this before the invention of baseball bats.

By going back on his promise, Dick Robinson had left me hog-tied and heading for disaster. Unless I could persuade someone to invest $6 million in a badly stalled project, I'd have to pay my landlord the $1 million penalty and walk away from Pastis. In my condition, it was hard enough coming up with a complete sentence, let alone a slew of honeyed phrases to impress a potential investor. In desperation, I turned one more time to my daughter Sophie and asked her if she could help me find another investor.

Sophie contacted several financiers and restaurateurs, but on being told I'd had a stroke, each one politely declined. After four or five rejections, Marc Packer, the owner of a glitzy nightclub called Tao, expressed interest. Sophie met with Packer, and after a month of negotiations they reached terms. Just before the signing, however, Packer changed the agreement significantly in his favor. I had no choice but to reject it. Revising terms at the eleventh hour is a common business ploy, and I suspect the move was premeditated. Regardless, the deal was off and I fell into a bad slump. Before my stroke, there wasn't a restaurateur in the city who wouldn't have been eager to form a partnership with me. Now there wasn't one.

I had delayed telling my Pastis landlord that Robinson had pulled out. But now that a second investor had bailed and my prospects of finding another were almost zero, I saw no reason to hold back. Bobby Cayre was a typical New York landlord, and I imagined that once he knew what had happened he'd demand his pound of flesh. I was wrong. Cayre reacted with surprising sympathy and even offered to help find me an investor. Although this was good news, I felt oddly disappointed that it didn't fit the narrative I had of him as a cutthroat landlord.

However, Cayre's behavior wasn't entirely altruistic. He owned a vast number of buildings in the neighborhood, and a successful Pastis would be bait to attract more high-end stores to the area. All the same, I felt he genuinely liked me. And at this point the feeling was mutual.

In February 2018, Cayre talked to the restaurateur Stephen Starr about becoming my partner. I'd never met Starr but knew he was a prolific Philadelphia restaurateur.

Cayre introduced Starr to Sophie, and the two discussed my predicament. A good judge of people, Sophie told me she liked Starr and suggested I meet him. Without Sophie's help during this daunting period, I'd never have built Pastis.

I'd first heard Starr's name in 1996 when Harry's ice hockey team played a match in Philadelphia. We'd traveled to Philly the night before the game and the whole team stayed in the same hotel. After the kids had gone to bed, a group of dads decided to go out to dinner and asked me to join them. Having a phobia of all-male groups, I declined, saying I had to work. In fact, I was going to have dinner with a former Lucky Strike waitress at a martini bar she'd recommended. I don't remember much about the bar but was curious enough to ask who the owner was. It was Stephen Starr.

The ex-waitress and I spent the night together (and we actually dated for six months afterward), but due to the early-morning match, I had to leave her apartment at 5:30 a.m. As I tiptoed into the hotel lobby with a takeaway coffee, I bumped into one of the other parents. Imagining I'd risen early out of conscientiousness after a night of "working," the highly impressed father said, "The early bird catches the worm."

At eight that morning, the boys played their hockey match and won easily. The father was right. The early bird does catch the worm.

I met Stephen Starr for the first time at Balthazar in March 2018. We had a coffee in a wooden booth opposite the bar. Although I wanted Starr to invest in Pastis, I was more concerned about him understanding my speech—but the anxiety only made my speech worse.

Starr was quite intimidating. But for a man who owned forty restaurants, he was surprisingly unsure of himself, and his uncertainty quickly put me at ease (as uncertainty often does).

I took out my crumpled floor plan of Pastis and laid it on the table. The new restaurant was intended to resemble the original but not be identical to it. Starr put on his black-rimmed reading glasses to look at the drawing and was swiftly transformed into a more appealing man. Contrary to convention, I've always found women more attractive with their glasses on than off and felt the same about Starr.

"Are you passionate about the project?" he first asked me. After I nodded yes, he asked a few questions about the layout. I answered as if talking through a gas mask. Luckily, he seemed less concerned with the quality of my voice than with the effectiveness of my floor plan. He then repeated the question:

"Are you passionate about the project?"

"Yes," I replied, and suddenly the Treaty of Versailles was completed. Over coffee at Balthazar, Stephen Starr and I became partners. He agreed to come up with the $6 million and left the meeting.

Starr told me later that this was the most expensive coffee he'd ever had.

Now that Starr had agreed to invest, I needed to come up with the goods. When nobody wanted to invest, I was certain that Pastis would succeed, but now that somebody did, I wasn't so sure. It's like telling Scarlett Johansson how great you are in bed because the chances of sleeping with her are a billion to one. Unfortunately, it's far easier to be confident about something you never expect to happen than something you do. (My unwritten play is a masterpiece.)

The original Pastis had been so successful that between 1997 and 2013 it took in an average of $17 million a year. Lightning rarely strikes twice, and no matter how good the new Pastis would be, it would never match people's memory of the original. But that's the nature of reproduction: the better you know something, the more critical you are of its successor. When an actor is replaced in a play, the public invariably prefers the first actor. Whenever I change a long-standing dish at Balthazar, regulars always complain it's not as good as the original. I feared the same would happen with the new Pastis. But there was a long way to go before I'd have to face such a luxurious problem. Not least, there was the matter of acquiring a liquor license—no easy matter in New York City.

Few restaurants survive without a liquor license. When I opened the club Nell's in 1986, the State Liquor Authority (SLA) had a monopoly on granting liquor licenses. The SLA was so powerful back then that it had become untouchable and, like most agencies that are untouchable, was also susceptible to corruption. I obtained a liquor license for Nell's partly by indirectly paying off someone connected to the SLA, a common practice among restaurateurs in those days.

Payoffs came to a stop in the new millennium when the SLA ceded most of its power to the city's neighborhood community boards. The criteria for issuing licenses then became more ethical and were often based on how much a drinking establishment would affect local residents. Although I totally agreed with this shift in power, it made it much harder for restaurants to acquire liquor licenses. And without a license, Pastis wouldn't last a week.

The hearing to decide the fate of Pastis was scheduled to be held by Community Board Two on April 12, 2018. Three weeks before the hearing, I flew from London to New York for an unofficial meeting with fifteen or so residents who lived close to the site. Stephen Starr joined me. To have a shot at receiving a license, we needed to prove to these residents that we were going to be conscientious neighbors.

The meeting took place in the conference room of the Standard Hotel, close to Pastis. It would be my first time speaking to a large body of people since my stroke. With my voice out of joint, I felt as if I was about to give a piano recital with half the keys missing. My first sentence came out so garbled it embarrassed everyone at the meeting. But at least it clarified my condition. After that, I mumbled, more than garbled, my way through the next two hours.

The residents' main concern was how noisy Pastis would be at night. Knowing that the original Pastis had been an active part of the city, they also asked me how similar the new version would be to the original. In replying to this question, it struck me how much of my answer could have applied to my own body. I wondered if this crossed anyone else's mind at the table.

I knew the meeting was swinging in our favor when one of the residents asked if the new Pastis would have any vegan dishes on its menu.

Even though the residents couldn't officially support Pastis at the meeting, I sensed the majority of them would do so at the critical board hearing in ten days' time. I left the hotel confident that Pastis would receive its license—which put me in a great mood on the next day's flight back to England.

One undeviating pattern I've noticed in my life is that great moods are always followed by minor disasters. This time would be no different, except the disaster wasn't going to be minor.

33.

Unstable marriages become miserable marriages when one's living in the country. Our dream house had taken two and a half years to renovate, and in September 2017, Alina and I finally moved into Great Brockhampton Farm deep in the English Cotswolds.

I had just returned to England from my stem-cell trial in Chicago, and after ten months of hospitals, clinics and rehabs, was ready to spend the rest of my days in our beautiful house three miles from the village of Broadway.

When Alina and I bought Great Brockhampton Farm, it was a ninety-year-old stone house with an interior that had been "modernized" in the seventies into something joylessly suburban. The formality of its dining room expressed a sad, aspirational quality that made me wonder which of the changes Alina and I were about to make would have us looking equally pathetic to the next owner.

Building began in the spring of 2015. Our project manager came with a crew of four jacks-of-all-trades who each had the surname Little. Of course, the Littles were related to each other, and their surname bore a strange resemblance to their character. The Littles worked as discreetly as dormice: even their jackhammering sounded subdued.

Although I'd renovated several houses before—and renovated them meticulously—I put more money and effort into Great Brockhampton Farm than any place in the past. And as usual, there were no lengths I wouldn't go to in order to make the house perfect. And by perfect, I mean imperfect and undesigned-looking. I believe my obsession with design stems from a need to keep chaos and bad news at bay. If I can just get the lighting right, penury, divorce and my kids' bad grades will be like water off a duck's back. But this time I went too far. In buying eight hundred subway tiles in a Brooklyn salvage yard to line the walls of my shower, and flying to Connecticut to purchase eighteenth-century pine floorboards, the cost of renovating the Not So Great Brockhampton Farm had shot perilously through the roof. But I wasn't the only person responsible for reckless spending.

Alina had hired, and befriended, a landscape designer called Mia, who, at one point, made the mistake of excavating an enormous hole for a swimming pond without official permission. When the authorities got wind of this illegal crater, they demanded we instantly fill it in. Three days later, the hole was no longer a hole and Mia immediately applied for a permit to dig another one. The local council agreed and the next day the diggers excavated the land all over again. It was like *Groundhog Day*. Of all the projects I've worked on, renovating the Cotswolds house is the one I most regret. Everything that could go wrong did go wrong and more. During the course of building my perfect house, I went broke, had a stroke and two of my restaurants went bust. But the worst was about to come.

Midway through the renovations, Alina had enough of city life and suggested we rent out our London house and live in the country year-round. Having no clue how deadly living full-time in the country can be, I agreed. Despite the house being in a remote part of the Cotswolds, Alina and I convinced each other that the area's beauty more than compensated for our loneliness. It didn't and we both knew it. But in the eight months we lived there, neither of us ever admitted it.

With George away at boarding school, it was just the three of us: Alina, Alice and me. With autumn closing in, Alina told me she was going to sleep with thirteen-year-old Alice. It was to be a temporary arrangement. Eight months later, nothing had changed.

Of the three of us, it was Alice who was most affected by the isolation. She had no friends in the countryside and just five other children in her class at school. Never one to complain, Alice internalized her sadness and started spending more time alone in her room. I sensed I was losing touch with her, and being allowed to sleep so often with her mother—which had become seven nights a week—only increased the distance between us.

The more time Alina and I spent together, the more we aggravated each other. Of course, this happens to all married couples by degrees, but in our case it was compounded by the abrupt change in our circumstances. Not knowing how to deal with my post-stroke needs, Alina became increasingly frustrated, and in my humiliation at having to rely on her for the simplest of chores, I'd look for reasons to reproach her. I remember just one happy day during our whole time together in the Cotswolds.

A few weeks after moving in, the two of us drove to a twelfth-century church in a village called Swinbrook. Though an anti-royalist, I'd always taken an interest in England's aristocratic Mitford sisters, and three of them, Nancy, Unity and Diana, were buried there. We parked the car and I hobbled across the graveyard looking for the headstone of Nancy, the oldest of the Mitfords, whose novel *The Pursuit of Love* has been revered in England by many different generations, mine included. Not counting the dead, Alina and I were the only people there. We located Mitford's grave and I remember being shocked by how neglected it was. The grass around it was overgrown with weeds and the headstone itself was badly eroded and pitted with lichen. In the 1930s, Mitford had been considered London's brightest young thing. Now she was just a box of bones in a flowerless grave. This austere scene must have affected Alina, too, because as we stood looking at this lonely, seldom-visited grave, she uncharacteristically took my hand.

A month after the stem-cell surgery, there was no change in my condition. Either I'd been given a placebo or the experiment had been a failure. Whatever the reason, I no longer felt I had any chance of improvement. My right side would remain paralyzed and my speech slurred until the day I died.

Not long after we moved to the Cotswolds, the searing back pain I'd felt intermittently in New York had become continuous. An obsessive hiker, I considered it a cruel joke to be surrounded by some of the best hiking trails in England now that I was unable to walk five yards. I could see why Chekhov labeled his most tragic play, *The Cherry Orchard*, a comedy. To escape the loneliness, Alina rented a flat in London close to Notting Hill tube station, where the three of us could meet George on weekends. Since my stroke, George had been having a difficult time at school and was desperate to spend the weekends in London.

The first time I saw the flat I noticed it only had two bedrooms—one for Alina and Alice and one for George. There was no bedroom for me. Instead, I had a makeshift bed in a corner of the living room. Although it would be a little awkward not having my own bathroom, I was surprisingly fine with this arrangement. The penny was still far from dropping.

November 26, 2017, was the first anniversary of my stroke. Up until then, I'd worn the same Tiffany watch every day for thirty-eight years. Needing both hands to attach it to my wrist, I'd been unable to wear the watch since the day of my stroke.

For many years my wrist bore a trace of the thin leather strap. For the last twelve months, the tan line created by the strap was becoming imperceptibly fainter with each passing hour. I dreaded the day when this reminder of my former self would fade into nothingness.

Winter nights in the English countryside are bleak and oppressive. The pitch-dark nights of December were especially hard on our relationship, most of all after Alice went to bed, when Alina and I were left alone at the dinner table. Never a big drinker, Alina would become argumentative after a second glass of wine, which she'd pour the second Alice left the table. Within five minutes she'd be lashing out at me for past injustices. Admitting they were true only inflamed the situation. Desperate for me to fight back, Alina would insult one of my older children. The times when I couldn't take it, we'd have a screaming row. I often wondered what Alice thought. She always claimed she never heard us fighting, but as her bedroom was directly above the dining room, I was sure she could. Hearing my parents argue in another room was one of the ugliest memories of my childhood. I just hope Alice doesn't feel the same way about hers.

No matter how foul the insults, nothing stopped me from loving Alina. I suppose proof of loving a long-term partner is that regardless of how badly they behave, you never lose sight of the person you first fell in love with. I realized that Alina was losing sight of this person in me when, at dinner one night in the Cotswolds, she refused to take a bite off my fork. Something she used to take pleasure from she now found repugnant.

Like many people with low confidence, Alina had suppressed a crucial part of her nature throughout our marriage. When the knives came out in the following months, she'd claim I was responsible for this. Perhaps I was, but I believe Alina suppressed it further by not taking a job once George and Alice went to school. The only thing my suicide attempt taught me was the importance of work. At its very least, work takes your mind off contemplating how pointless life is.

A consequence of Alina's poor self-esteem was never thinking she had something valuable to say. She only felt good about herself when taking care of our children. My stroke, and five months' absence convalescing in New York, forced Alina to take the initiative. It also led her to reassess the role she had taken in a marriage in which she'd allowed me to make all the major decisions: a marriage where she had lost her voice.

As with all deteriorating marriages, the flaws in our relationship were aggravated during the holiday season. Despite George being home from boarding school, Christmas 2017 was a melancholy affair. No amount of exchanged presents could heal the rift that now existed between us. Alina, who'd once hung on to my every word, now couldn't bear to hear me speak. There wasn't an opinion of mine that she didn't contradict. When I mentioned that the salmon she'd bought was a little oversalted, Alina tore into me: "No, it's not!" I struggled to reply, but before my words saw daylight, she had jumped all over them. Suddenly, our roles were reversed. It was Alina who now possessed all the words. Ironically, she only discovered her voice the moment I'd lost mine.

During one of her rants, I snapped and went for the jugular. I insulted Alina's new best friend, our landscape gardener Mia, by mocking the shape of her body. Alina didn't respond; she just stared at me. We both knew I'd crossed the line. There was a long silence. Alina bowed her head. Something had broken.

A year earlier, Mia had asked Alina to assist her in landscaping our fifteen acres in the Cotswolds. It was the lifeline Alina needed to feel good about herself. The work was very physical, and she loved it. And she adored Mia for having faith in her.

Mia and I didn't get along from the start. I found her manipulative. All the same, by giving Alina a job, she'd made her happy. That's why I insulted Mia in the most vile way that night. I was jealous of her. Jealous that she was able to make Alina happy—something I could no longer do.

After my insult, there was a long silence. Eventually, I got up and went to bed. I woke with a start an hour later. Sensing something was wrong, I went downstairs. Alina was huddled on a kitchen chair, knees under her chin, trying to make herself as small as possible. She was listening to the Cat Stevens song "Wild World," tears rolling down her cheeks.

The house in the Cotswolds is the only house I've lived in in which I've never had sex. Since the day Alina and I moved there, we'd never slept in the same bed. One night in April 2018, Alina surprised me and suggested we sleep together. Though we didn't touch, I thought this might be a turning point in our relationship. It was, but not in the way I'd hoped. The next morning, Alina woke early to drive Alice to school. Two hours later, just as I was waking, the door burst open and a tall woman wearing a long SS-type overcoat shoved some papers at me:

"Sign these!"

"Who are you? What are you doing here?" I screamed.

"Your wife wants to divorce you. Sign these!"

Desperate, I called for Alina, who came into the room with a composure that scared me.

"It's true. I want to divorce you."

Like my stroke, divorce came out of the blue.

A more perceptive person would have seen the signs. I'd naively thought that our sleeping together was a sign that things were improving. Instead it was a Judas kiss.

Two days later, I discovered that Alina had begun divorce proceedings four months earlier and that the Himmler figure who'd burst into the bedroom was a process server from the law firm she'd hired. Over the next ten days, I pleaded with Alina that we see a marriage counselor. She refused. "There's no going back," she said.

I found the idea of Alina holding secret meetings with her lawyer to prepare for our divorce as disturbing as the divorce itself. It was difficult not to compare this subterfuge with the subversive action my body had been plotting for several months before my stroke. In both cases, the convergence of the two—the furtive groundwork with its unthinkable outcome—plunged me into despair. Of course, Alina's actions were probably no different from those of many women planning a divorce. But to me, in my susceptible state, it felt like the two forms of guile were connected.

I dreaded the next few months. Most of all, I dreaded having to tell the children.

In the majority of divorces, both partners believe they're the victim. The real victims are the children, of course. No matter how well they seem to take their parents' breakup, or adjust to their new circumstances, all children struggle with their parents' divorce—and continue to struggle, by varying degrees, for the rest of their lives.

In the US, almost half of all marriages end in divorce. The earliest known divorce laws were written on clay tablets around 2000 BCE and cost the divorcé half a sheep. Mine was written on five hundred pages of foolscap and cost me millions of dollars.

The day after being served divorce papers, I hired a lawyer. Knowing that Alina had signed a prenup before our marriage, I wasn't too concerned about the financial settlement. But I was concerned about receiving joint custody of George and Alice, and fearing that in my semi-paralyzed state the courts might decide against it, I asked a friend if she could suggest a good divorce lawyer in England. She recommended Baroness Fiona Shackleton.

Although ninety percent of our laws are based on morality, when seeking a divorce lawyer we never look for one with impeccable morals. Most of the time we seek a lawyer whose reputation will terrify the opposition. Baroness Shackleton was such a lawyer. Known in the press as the Steel Magnolia, Shackleton had taken on many high-profile cases and had represented Prince Charles and Paul McCartney. Tall and commanding, the baroness had a deep, authoritative voice, which in my world would have had maître d's scrambling for the best table. With her aristocratic bearing and seat on the Conservative bench in the House of Lords, Shackleton symbolized everything I loathed about England's class system. It's unsettling to have one's assumptions contradicted but, against the odds, I ended up liking her.

Although Alina refused to see a marriage counselor, she did set up a meeting with a man who held the lofty title of Civilised Separations Specialist. "Nick Arnold" was a conceited Australian in his early fifties. Handsome, single and looking much younger than his years, he was the kind of man who volunteered his age just to bask in the inevitable response. In the first meeting he talked soothingly of our need to "evolve" as parents as we entered the next "chapter" of our lives. (The moment he used the words "evolve" and "chapter," I knew I didn't like him.) Arnold always ended the session with the phrase "Let's circle back on this next week." Circle back. There wasn't a cliché going that Arnold didn't embrace. Alarmingly, Alina didn't see it. In fact, she became so captivated by Arnold's platitudes that after a few sessions she began nodding in agreement long before he finished a sentence. There's nothing as disturbing as seeing the woman you love find another man more appealing—even more so when he's a phony. The contrived serenity of Arnold's voice reminded me of the computer, HAL, from *2001: A Space Odyssey.* Unfortunately, next to Arnold's manner of calm reassurance, I came across as a raving lunatic.

At one point it was agreed that I should see Arnold alone. When Alina was present, his shirts were always blue to match the color of his eyes. On the day I met Arnold, his shirt was bottle green. He also seemed uncomfortable and could barely look me in the eye.

It was suddenly obvious to me what was going on—they were having an affair.

I spent the rest of that day feverishly going over each second of our recent visits to London: Alina's habit of suddenly popping out for coffee every weekend after receiving a phone call now looked very suspicious. Overcome with jealousy, I searched for proof of my wife's loyalty while at the same time desperate for confirmation of my suspicions. To some extent, there's nothing quite as satisfying as finding evidence of one's partner's infidelity.

The following weekend, twenty minutes after Alina left the apartment for coffee, I called Nick Arnold's mobile number. He always picked up. If he didn't, it would be proof he was with Alina. On the second ring, he picked up. At that moment, Alina walked in with two coffees. One was for me.

Sometimes popping out for coffee means just that.

34.

Though each of my five children was affected by my stroke, George was the one most visibly so. Auden once wrote that trauma was good for children and suggested they should be loaded with as much of it as they can bear. George was thirteen when he witnessed my stroke. Auden was right about many things, but wrong about trauma being good for children.

Nine months after my stroke, George's teachers noticed that he was struggling at school and suggested he see a psychologist. Alina tried but failed to find one, which I felt was odd as she was seeing a shrink at the time and regularly praised the benefits of therapy. (Unfortunately, I was in no shape to help with this.) Alina's inability to find George a psychologist only increased the tension between us.

During the next year, George's grades plummeted and he began having physical fights with other boys. In the fall of 2017, Alina and I were summoned to the school for a meeting with three of George's teachers to discuss his behavior. Brighton College is one of England's most academically rigorous schools, with many of its students going on to Oxford or Cambridge. To soften its exacting reputation, Brighton is quick to advertise its gentler side. "A school where confidence, kindness and curiosity are championed" was the first line on its website that year. This was bullshit. The teachers at Brighton were merciless, and none more so than the three who faced Alina and me that morning. They told us point-blank that George was lazy and delinquent, and that if his grades didn't improve they would expel him. We were stunned. Then angry. There's nothing that makes your blood boil as much as someone criticizing your child—even if they're right.

In eighteen months, George would sit for the first of his eight GCSEs (General Certificate of Secondary Education). These formidable exams are graded from 1 to 9, with 9 being the highest. Brighton expels anyone with an average grade of 6.5 or less.

If Brighton College was as compassionate as its website proclaimed, it would give more attention to those with low grades, not kick them out. The school justifies charging colossal fees because of the high percentage of its pupils who go on to esteemed universities. This percentage would drop if the school made allowances for pupils like George who really require its attention. Instead of helping the imperfect students—those who most need improvement—Brighton expels them. One sometimes forgets that private schools—like private medicine—are first and foremost businesses, and none more than Brighton College.

Sitting at the head of the table that day, the teachers predicted that George's average score in his GCSE exams would be 6.5. The hint of smugness on their faces triggered the worst in me. I blurted out that they were wrong and that George's average would be 8. I said I was certain of it. Alina apologized for my outburst. (You know your marriage is down the tubes when your wife stops supporting you in public.)

I left the meeting angry and determined to help my son with his exams. Or rather, help with half of them, as I knew nothing about physics (my worst subject at school), chemistry, math or biology. And although I knew less than I pretended about history, English language, religious studies and English literature, I did know *some*. But in the coming six months, I was going to know a lot fucking more.

In our melancholy Cotswolds house, I spent the majority of the fall and winter reading everything I could on the Russian Revolution, the Cold War, the Bible, *Romeo and Juliet* and J. B. Priestley's *An Inspector Calls*. I wrote long, detailed essays on each subject. Satisfied that the essays were written in an unfussy language that a sixteen-year-old would understand and perhaps enjoy, I'd send them off, one at a time, to George at school. For whatever reason, Alina disapproved of the endeavor and would roll her eyes every time I asked her to print out an essay for me (which was every day). Perhaps she thought I was doing this more for myself than George. If so, she was right.

In May 2019, George sat for his GCSE exams, and a few weeks later, Alina and I attended parents' day at Brighton College. Although none of the five hundred or so parents gathered there knew about our impending divorce, they probably got a good idea from Alina's body language. As I walked precariously across the courtyard with the aid of a cane, Alina walked ten feet ahead. Aware of my embarrassment, George took my arm and—in full view of his peers—helped me across the yard. For the school's "troublemaker" to do this took considerable courage. It's a pity an act of decency like this counts for nothing in the results-driven world of English academia.

Nine weeks later, George's GCSE results arrived. The teachers who had predicted his average grade would be 6.5 were wrong. His average grade was 8. Curiously enough, George achieved his best result in physics. So much for my help.

35.

The day before he married us, Reverend Southworth asked Alina and me to name the other's most disagreeable trait. "How long do I have?" Alina jokingly asked.

She then said my worst trait was not being mentally present. I said hers was not following through with tasks. We both left the meeting agreeing to work on our individual flaws but never did, and this led to our undoing.

Although I give the appearance of being a good listener—sympathetic posture, furrowed brow, constant eye contact—half the time I'm not there, I'm across the room observing matters. This is what Alina was referring to when accusing me of not being present. This inability to join in is my Achilles' heel. Whether it's an intimate conversation, dancing at a party or singing a hymn in church, I simply cannot participate. In restaurant terms, it means when a waiter recites a list of the day's specials, I'm so not present I can't even remember a single dish. Whether this comes from self-consciousness or self-absorption, I don't know. But it's definitely a problem.

The longer we were together, the more irritated I became at Alina for not following through with things. I once read that everything that irritates us about others can lead to an understanding of ourselves. Instead of understanding more of myself, I pushed Alina further and further away from me. Her so-called "flaw" still persisted but my need to endlessly point it out like some irksome messenger caused increasing resentment. Fittingly, one of the few things Alina did follow through with was divorcing me. She finally got to shoot the messenger.

* * *

A life without memories would be a life worse than death. Alina and I had accumulated thousands of happy memories during our twenty years together. What would happen to them now that our relationship had ended? Was there a memories guidance counselor to help keep them intact? (And would he have an Australian accent?) How does one prevent the excess bile of a hostile divorce from seeping into one's memories and tainting them? If it was necessary for Alina to shred her memories of me in order to move on—and surely it was—could the process be reversed in the future? What did it matter anyway? With the slippages of time, all memories—like all living things—eventually fade and disappear. Ultimately, everything becomes nothing.

It's surprising how many couples divorce soon after moving into their dream house. One submits to life's struggles through fastening onto some future goal. These goals are often cooked-up fantasies to help us bear the daily grind. A mere eight months after we moved into our newly reno-vated house, Alina asked for a divorce. Though we continued living in the same house, from that moment on we were unofficially separated. We were also leading double lives. When the children were present, we were happily married parents. In their absence, we fought badly and plotted our lives as single parents.

The days when the four of us were together became hard to take. Be-fore Alina asked for a divorce, the kids seemed to be growing up so fast. Now they appeared oddly vulnerable. Perhaps instinct warned them that bad news was looming. George, who rarely mentioned our summer plans, started talking incessantly about the family's summer vacation. Just as wives, on some level, can sense their husbands' infidelity, perhaps children can sense their parents' impending divorce.

Although George was two inches taller than me at the time (it's now seven, the bastard), he started wearing my clothes—shirts, socks, pants, underwear. I loved this idea, but his enthusiasm caused me a severe shortage of underwear. At one point I bought him some new socks, but they remained untouched.

Alice's behavior also changed. She often became scornful of me, which was alarmingly similar to her mother's behavior.

Despite our arguing, Alina reluctantly agreed that we should all spend the summer together on Martha's Vineyard. The children seemingly had no idea about the divorce. We planned to tell them soon after our arrival.

This would be our last holiday as a family.

Since 1993, I've spent all but two summers at my house on Martha's Vineyard. In order to catch the flowering of the two magnificent catalpa trees in front of my house, I make a point of arriving on the first day of July. That summer of 2018, they flowered unnaturally early and I missed them.

As soon as we all arrived at the house, George and Alice began running around the garden like six-year-olds. Watching them horse around in front of the catalpas brought back memories of past summers and things we'd do together: swimming in the ocean, taking a bike ride or simply kicking a ball around in front of the house. Things that were now impossible for me. That was the moment I first thought seriously of suicide.

I couldn't face being unable to take an active part in my children's lives anymore. Surely better to end it now and leave them with memories of an active father, rather than of a bystander in a wheelchair. Besides, my back pain was killing me. Like the hairline crack that leads to the plane's engine failure, what had started as a dull ache eighteen months earlier had now become unendurable.

From the moment we arrived on the island, Alina wanted to tell the children about our plans to divorce. Though I knew it had to be done, I wanted to delay this turning point in their lives for as long as possible. Alice and George had been on the Vineyard three days when we called them into our bedroom. They had no idea. They were smiling as they entered the room.

Following the Russian Revolution, the czar and his family were put under house arrest near the Ural Mountains. One night, they were abruptly awakened and told to go to the basement to prepare to be escorted to a safer location. The five children were happy to leave and rushed excitedly down the stairs to the basement. Once there, they were all murdered. I thought about this macabre incident as George and Alice came smiling into our bedroom. Alina and I broke the news.

Alice was silent and appeared unmoved. George was angry and demanded to know why. Hearing George's question, I broke down and blurted out that it was Alina who wanted the divorce, not me. Alina looked at me disdainfully and left the room. Alice followed swiftly behind.

Alina was right to be disgusted, as my behavior was hideously self-pitying. Clearly, there's no good way to tell children their parents are divorcing, but to break down and blame one's spouse is the most despicable.

After Alina and Alice left the room, George and I lay on the bed, holding each other as tightly as possible, weeping.

The next morning, Alina informed me that she'd rented a cottage ten miles away where she planned to spend time alone or with the children. Two days later, she took the children to her Vineyard "bolt-hole" to stay the night. This happened half the nights of the week.

Those nights in my large summer house without George and Alice plunged me into a dark place. I realized I was living a life feeding off scraps. All my life I'd been told I was lucky. But it turned out I'd drawn the short straw. I decided to commit suicide.

Over the next four weeks, I stopped taking most of my sleeping pills and began hiding them in my desk drawer. I also wrote to my brother, who was then living in Vietnam, asking him to buy me some sleeping pills on the black market. In telling Brian that my month's supply had run out, I discovered how easy it is to lie, and lie convincingly, when you're desperate for drugs. Two batches of black market Ambien arrived by express mail from Saigon within five days.

Taking only a quarter of my sleeping pills, I found it impossible to sleep more than an hour a night and as a result became slightly hallucinatory. This somehow made it easier to harass Brian for more drugs. Paradoxically, my desperation for sleep was aggravated by hoarding the very pills intended to give me permanent sleep. By the first of August, I'd accumulated thirty-eight Ambien—enough to "do myself in," as my mother would say.

The worst thing about dying is how easily life goes on without us. Garbage still gets collected. Lawns continue to be mowed. Elections still get held. No matter how monumental my death was to me, for the rest of the world it would be, at best, a faint murmur.

The American educator Horace Mann once wrote: "Be ashamed to die until you have won some victory for humanity." I wonder if lowering the price of Monday's lunch special counts as a victory for humanity.

From the time my five children were young, I'd made it a tradition on the Vineyard to watch a film together after dinner. The criteria being any movie in black and white or great American films made in the 1970s. Or any film they especially hated the sound of. Before they'd reached double digits, each of my children had watched most of the movies made by Hitchcock, Kubrick, Truffaut, Woody Allen and Billy Wilder together, as well as *Shane*, *Sexy Beast*, *The Third Man*, the Naked Gun series and, of course, *The Graduate* and *Dog Day Afternoon*. Watching a good film with one's kids is as close to paradise as it gets in this godless, fucked-up world. But by the last week of July, the pain in my back was so excruciating that sitting through a film with them was out of the question. That's when I knew it was time to throw in the towel.

I intended to do the deed when my family was off the island. A friend of George's was staying with us and Alina and the kids planned to take the boy to the airport in Boston, put him on a plane to London and then spend the night in Boston.

But the day before they were to leave, someone had mysteriously moved the stack of sleeping pills I'd been hiding. Fearing that my plan had been discovered, I decided to take the pills that night.

Though each one of us has a last day on this earth, not many of us get to choose it. Mine would be August the Third, 2018.

That night I went to bed early. Alice was in her room. Anxious to avoid anything emotional, I simply called out goodnight through the closed door. In the hallway, I bumped into George. While believing that this was the last time I'd ever see him, I was desperate for him not to know it: I just hugged him in my usual way and said goodnight. Once in my bedroom, I sat at my desk and emailed him a quote from *Hamlet*:

Dearest George,

Doubt thou the stars are fire,
Doubt that the sun doth move,
Doubt truth to be a liar,
But never doubt I love.

Dad xxx

After sending it off, I sat at the end of my bed and thought about the silence that would soon consume me and wondered if it would be like the one that followed the *Titanic*'s sinking. I thought about how my stacks of unread books would remain stonily unread. But most of all I thought of my five children and how sad it would be not to see them again.

I locked the bedroom door and methodically transferred thirty-eight Ambien and fifteen painkillers into a bowl and scooped the pills into my mouth in handfuls, washing down each mouthful with water from a small plastic bottle. Then it was done. The line "Things we can't untie" from a Leonard Cohen song drifted into my head. Other songs too. I then became inexplicably anxious about my catalpa trees because I wasn't sure who was going to take care of them in my absence. And then . . . nothingness.

Fourteen hours later, I surfaced from oblivion, in Martha's Vineyard Hospital, hooked up to an IV, with George and Alina staring at me. One in relief, the other in contempt. If I had any hopes of Alina loving me again, the withering look she gave me right then dispelled them forever. It was clear she wanted no more to do with me.

Lynn, Harry and Brian, meanwhile, were on their way.

In the States, the only way one can leave the hospital after attempting suicide is by going directly to a psychiatric facility. After spending two days recovering from my overdose, I was to be driven to McLean Hospital outside Boston.

On the day I left, George and Alice were waiting outside the hospital to wave goodbye. Their last view of me that day was being stretchered horizontally into an ambulance. Their tentative waves were heartbreaking to watch.

It rained the whole way. Lynn accompanied me in the ambulance. Brian and Harry followed in a rented car. Floods and traffic jams caused delays, making a two-hour journey take four and a half hours. When our ambulance pulled up outside McLean, the entrance was in such near darkness that it appeared austere and unwelcoming. I felt uneasy entering the place.

It was then that Lynn told me something that struck me to the core: Isabelle had been admitted here ten years earlier. This was the hospital I'd refused to visit more than a decade ago. This was the place that had plagued me for so long. This was my appointment in Samarra.

36.

McLean is the most famous psychiatric hospital in America. With its manicured grounds and mock Tudor buildings, it resembles an elite prep school more than a hospital. Founded in 1811, its original name was the Asylum for the Insane. Eighty years later, recognizing the dangers of calling a spade a spade, it was renamed McLean Hospital. Since then, it's had a roll call of famous patients, including poets Sylvia Plath and Robert Lowell, musicians Ray Charles and James Taylor, and writer David Foster Wallace. Oddly enough, the man who designed the hospital's grounds—as well as New York's Central Park—Frederick Law Olmsted, also wound up as a patient there.

We arrived so late at McLean that only the guards and wardens were still awake. The ward I'd been assigned to was in a cold, institutional building with an oppressive atmosphere that reminded me of Orwell's *1984*. Even its name—SB1—had Orwellian overtones. There was something vaguely sinister about the place.

I'm not often scared, but I was that night after Lynn "signed me over" to a severe-looking female warden. Given five minutes to say goodbye to Lynn, Harry and Brian, I prolonged it as long as possible because I didn't relish being alone with the warden.

After they left, Ms. Psycho searched my body for anything that could be used to kill myself with. Then she searched my bag. I got the feeling that nothing would have pleased her more than to find an enormous machete. But there wasn't much in my bag because, hoping to return to George and Alice on the Vineyard in the next few days, I'd packed lightly.

SB1 was a psychiatric ward for adults who were a danger to themselves or other people. It was like a Victorian madhouse. There was no daylight, and what meager windows existed were barred and thickly curtained. The blankets on my bed were filthy, and the bathroom—which I shared with eight geriatrics—was squalid.

In my small, airless room, a man in his mid-eighties snored loudly in a bed two feet from mine. But it wasn't his snoring that kept me awake. It was the guard opening the door every fifteen minutes to check I hadn't hanged myself. As he did so, a sickly fluorescent light from the corridor seeped into the room.

For the first three days, I was only allowed outside for ten minutes, and each time under strict supervision. The food cooked on the miserable premises looked more depressed than the patients.

I was required to attend several one-hour group sessions each day. A typical session had me sitting, eyes closed, in a circle with nine other patients listening to brainless New Age music for thirty minutes. When it was over, we each had to describe to the therapist—and everyone else in the circle—how the music made us "feel." (Murderous, in my case.)

One of the more humiliating aspects of my life post-stroke is that I require assistance to shower. At SB1 it was doubly humiliating because the place was so short-staffed that I more or less had to plead with one of the aides to help me wash.

I was assigned to the head psychiatrist, who met with me for fifteen minutes each day. Dr. M. was a vain man but not an unpleasant one, who dressed for effect. He wore socks that matched the color of his shirt, and a trilby cocked stylishly to one side. His flamboyance was at odds with such grim surroundings. If you were inside SB1 for attempted suicide, Dr. M. held immense power over you, because he had the final say on when you could leave.

On the fifth day, I was given my own room. It reeked of recirculated air. The bedsheets were changed every day, but each fresh set felt grimier than the last. It was insufferably hot, and in order to sleep, I needed to throw off the rancid sheet and sleep naked. Unfortunately, this wasn't so easy, because patients with their own rooms were required to leave the door open and exposed to the corridor. The idea of the psychotic-looking warden watching me sleep naked was so unsettling that I slept under a filthy sheet for the next six nights.

I was desperate to get out.

By making bootlicking references to his wise counseling, I fooled the conceited Dr. M. into believing I no longer wanted to kill myself. This wasn't true. After my dreadful experience in SB1, I wanted to do it more than ever.

Dr. M. promised to let me out of SB1 as long as I agreed to have additional therapy at another dormitory on the campus. Luckily, a spot had become available in the most prestigious (and most expensive) program at McLean: the Pavilion. Although moving to the Pavilion reduced my chances of returning to Martha's Vineyard that summer, remaining in SB1 was unthinkable. The eleven days spent in the living hell of SB1 were the worst days of my life, and my reward for not ending it.

Moving the next day to the Edwardian-sounding Pavilion was like tunneling out of San Quentin and ascending into the Four Seasons. Except the Four Seasons costs $900 a night and the Pavilion $3,500 a night. Even though the profits from my restaurants were rapidly dwindling, I had no choice. I couldn't put up with another second sharing a bathroom with eight other depressives.

As a car drove me across McLean's sprawling campus to the two-story Pavilion, the relief from having left SB1 was so immense that I felt almost euphoric. It's strange how often the relief from discontinuing something can be so satisfying. I've spent half my life waiting for things to end: The end of school. The end of a family get-together. The end of a relationship. The end of a social event. The end of winter. And recently, the end of my life.

From the outside, my new residence had the air of a country club. Leading up to the main door was a whitewashed porch with a couple of empty wooden rocking chairs. On the ground floor were eight en suite bedrooms, two counseling rooms where the therapy sessions took place, a small kitchen and a dining room. On the second floor were the administrative offices. There were neither security guards nor bars on the windows.

The patients of the Pavilion were there voluntarily. Though many suffered from emotional instability, psychosis or substance abuse, all suffered from depression. Most stayed at the Pavilion for two weeks. I stayed two months.

After the rattrap of a room I'd slept in at SB1, my room at the Pavilion was a sanctuary. Spacious and bright with a desk full of books, it could easily have been a writer's retreat in the Berkshires. It was a testament to the importance the immediate environment has on our welfare. Best of all, it was adjacent to the kitchen.

After unpacking my clothes, I headed for my first therapy session. I knocked and entered one of the ground floor's two counseling rooms. A psychotherapist called Dr. Jay Bonnar introduced himself and asked me to take a seat. The joyless-looking Dr. Bonnar then retreated into silence. One of the things I dislike about shrinks is the way they manipulate silence.

Bonnar blinked first: "What's on your mind?"

The thing on my mind was seeing George and Alice before they returned to England. They were ninety miles away, but in two weeks they'd be three thousand. Seeing my kids was crucial. Being analyzed to death was not. I cringed at the idea of "opening up." At the same time, I was anxious to talk about myself. Dying to, in fact. I felt competitive and wanted to show off and impress the shrink. But like everybody I'm anxious to impress, Bonnar wasn't having any of it. That didn't stop me from trying. As the words tumbled out, I felt simultaneously fraudulent and sincere, totally genuine and a complete phony. I felt like myself.

Bonnar didn't have to ask many questions to receive a windfall of information. If he asked the color of my socks, I gave him the name of the manufacturer and its history. For someone who admires terseness, I talk a lot. Or can do, given the right circumstance. And sitting opposite this psychotherapist was the right circumstance.

By the end of the session, Bonnar said he was concerned I might try to commit suicide again. He was right. Killing myself in a place as quaint as the Pavilion would be a breeze. Like Matt Dillon and Kelly Lynch in

Drugstore Cowboy, I could break into the pharmacy and steal enough drugs to kill me several times over. Bonnar then said something that jolted me. He said that children who lose a parent to suicide were far more likely to kill themselves than the children of parents who don't. That stopped me in my tracks. I didn't know what to say.

That night I was plagued by thoughts of my mother, but one thought stood out—her last visit to New York to see me. It was 1994, and she came alone. A week before she left London, I sent my mother a long list of things we'd do together in New York. We both knew this would probably be her last trip to the States.

I met her at the arrivals gate. She looked older than I remembered, but as always happens with those we've known for a long time, she slowly reverted back to her former self. The face I was looking at after a few minutes became the same one I'd looked at when I was ten years old.

My mother had been separated from my dad for a few years. She must have been quite lonely because the first thing she said at arrivals was that she'd missed me. It caught me off guard because she'd never said it before. I knew what I was supposed to say but couldn't say it.

We took a taxi from the airport to my apartment in SoHo. She was so happy to see me she talked nonstop. As the cab edged closer to my apartment, I began thinking that her coming was a mistake. We stayed together in my small apartment on Thompson Street. Even though I'd been divorced from Lynn for a couple of years, my life was still in turmoil.

My mother planned on staying two weeks; we were going to do something together each day. On the fourth morning in a row of me canceling that day's activity, my mother fell into a slump. The next day she switched her ticket and left that evening.

We drove in silence to JFK. At the airport, her departure gate was so far from check-in she had to request a wheelchair. As we sat waiting for assistance to arrive, I apologized for the way I'd treated her. I gave her the pathetic "this is a really bad time for me" excuse. She said nothing. Just looked at me blankly.

A porter arrived to take my mother to the gate. I hated myself even more once I saw her in a wheelchair. Every line of her body seemed to have altered. She looked stricken and alarmingly old. The last image I have of my mother in New York is of her slouched in a wheelchair being pushed through airport security. That image kept me up all night after my session with Jay Bonnar. I don't know why.

The morning after my first session, I met the Pavilion's team manager, Marc Zuckerman, a clinical psychologist who supervised each new patient's evaluation period. Being confronted by another shrink, I felt a lot less defensive than usual. How much of this was due to having Jay Bonnar's spiel about suicide on my mind, or Zuckerman's sympathetic manner, I'm not sure. But for once I listened without whipping up a biting response. I liked Zuckerman a lot and could understand why he was such a central figure at the Pavilion.

He believed I was chronically depressed but thought the suicide attempt was linked to my severe back pain. I couldn't see how: surely it had something to do with the depression—it was psychological, not physical. Zuckerman explained that the "father" of American psychology, William James, believed our bodily changes often formed the basis of our emotional experiences. By this logic, happiness could be the result of smiling, something I rarely do when I'm happy. I wasn't buying Zuckerman's theory at all. Nevertheless, I agreed to see a specialist masseuse he recommended. I've always admired people who do things immediately after talking about them. There and then, Zuckerman made an appointment for me to see someone that afternoon. Her name was "Amy Byrne," and her practice was a twenty-minute drive from McLean.

On the drive to my appointment, I feared that this masseuse might be as phony as the Indian masseur I'd seen after my stroke.

Byrne's "practice" was a spare room in her suburban bungalow. Suddenly I had my doubts about her. But it wasn't the spare room that put me off having the massage. It was the room's walls. They were chock-a-block with photos of Donald Trump. Trump outside the White House. Trump with Kanye West. Trump with Roseanne Barr. Trump with Simon fucking Cowell. The idea of being naked next to photos of Donald Trump so nauseated me that I wanted to leave that instant.

After introducing herself, masseuse Byrne asked me to strip and lie under a sheet on the massage table. In her mid-fifties, she had a raspy smoker's voice and a slim figure. The slim figure accounted for her wearing skirts embarrassingly short for her age. She was working class with a string of ex-husbands and a surprisingly sharp sense of humor. Byrne was the first person to make me laugh about my stroke. She was also the first masseuse to locate all of my back's trigger points in under four minutes. She might have had a rough voice but Byrne's hands were like velvet. She gave me the most remarkable massage I'd ever had. The drawback was her politics. As she massaged my rhomboids, she'd voice her support for the NRA. Normally I'd lash out at someone defending the National Rifle Association, but when that someone's relaxing your trapezius, it's hard to speak your mind. It was the same when she asked me if I thought Trump was good for the country's national security. It's not easy to stick to your principles when someone's making your lumbar area feel like jelly.

After seeing Byrne once a week for two months, I had minimal back pain. Since leaving McLean, I've had several different masseuses. Each shared the same liberal politics as me, but not one of them softened my back muscles like Byrne did. Unfortunately, the less support I heard for the NRA, the more severe my back pain became.

Though I've learned to live with being handicapped, I haven't come to terms with it and probably never will. Contrary to popular belief, and the feeling of many of McLean's therapists, I don't believe there's closure after serious personal loss. Grieving isn't a corridor one passes through on the way to well-being. By degrees, I grieve every day for the physical person I used to be. The intensity may differ, incidents may make me happy, but the loss is always there. Grieving isn't a finite process with a beginning and an end. Regardless of what the experts say, closure is always ajar.

The truth is that nobody gets over anything. Eventually the accumulation of all the things we never recover from registers in microscopic detail upon our faces.

* * *

Although Lynn and our daughters, Sophie and Isabelle, came to visit me at McLean, Alina did not. Zuckerman wanted her to be part of a group therapy session, but she refused. She'd closed the door on me, or as Zuckerman called it, she had "checked out." I didn't blame her.

One person who made an unexpected visit was my lawyer, Baroness Fiona Shackleton. This titled, upper-class woman dropped everything and, without charging a penny, flew from London to Boston to check on my health. It was bizarre to see the six-foot baroness striding imperiously down the ward of my psychiatric hospital, but strangely reassuring. Her spontaneous gesture helped me through a horrific time. It also taught me not to make assumptions about people. It's never about wealth, religion or politics. It's always about the individual. Always.

Although I've learned to judge people (like Fiona Shackelton) for who they are and not what they've achieved, it's not the way I judge myself. Unfortunately, I need to "achieve" things to feel halfway decent about myself. I'd give anything not to feel this way.

One afternoon, just before returning to England, George visited. We talked about my suicide attempt. Without making eye contact, he told me he was the one who'd found me. I was shocked. That wasn't the way I'd planned it. On the day of my overdose, I'd asked my best friend on the island, Fernando Parada, to knock on my door at 11 a.m. I imagined I'd be stone dead at this point and wanted Fernando to find me, not one of my children. That day, George—though normally an idle layabout on holiday—rose unusually early and came to my bedroom around eight. Finding the door locked, he knocked, gently at first, then much harder. Fearing the worst, he called out to Alina in the next bedroom with Alice. Alina told Alice to stay in her room and began frantically searching for a key. Meanwhile, George climbed onto the roof. Through the dormer window he saw me lying on the bedroom floor unconscious. If George hadn't woken uncharacteristically early that morning I probably would have died.

An ambulance and two police cars arrived, and for the second time in less than two years George witnessed his father being carried off in an ambulance. He asked one of the medics if I was going to die. The medic said no, he didn't believe so.

While telling me this story, George clenched his fists the whole time. We lay on my bed and talked. I think he felt good about me staying at McLean. I told him the worst was over. He smiled for the first time that day.

Prior to McLean, my fear of analysis kept me away from psychotherapy. Growing up in working-class London in the '50s and early '60s, I never knew—or had even heard of—someone seeing a psychologist. Just as seat belts were once considered unmanly, people from my background believed seeing a shrink was a sign of weakness. But being working class wasn't the real reason I feared analysis. It was my absolute horror of losing control. It's why I'm scared stiff of recreational drugs and why I'm desperate to create my own environment. I'm terrified of losing control.

During my two months at the Pavilion, I had more than seventy sessions of psychotherapy. I also met with neurologists, neuropsychologists, physiatrists and cognitive behavioral therapists. Slowly, I began dismantling the wall I had built up around myself and set about listening. I went from fearing my sessions starting to dreading them ending. I stopped wincing when I heard the words "mindful" and "contextual." I stopped being an observer. I stopped for my children's sake. I stopped because I didn't want them to see me being stretchered off to a hospital yet again.

Each evening at six, the eight Pavilion patients would sit down for dinner together at a long communal table. The food was served family style and it was surprisingly good. A typical meal would often include a delicious bowl of fresh lettuces, tagliatelle with tomatoes and greens, with a choice of grilled filet mignon or pan-roasted salmon. For dessert, patients could choose between apple tart, crème brûlée or key lime pie. It was definitely not average hospital food, but at $3,500 a night, the check wasn't an average check, either.

However much I enjoy fresh food, I usually prefer it the next day as leftovers. One of the advantages of my room being next to the kitchen was having such easy access to the fridge at 3 a.m. I've no idea why food tastes so good in the middle of the night, but it does. Before I die, I'd like to build a restaurant serving nothing but leftovers.

Unfortunately, I had to stop raiding the fridge at 3 a.m. because in my second week at the Pavilion the night nurse caught me eating the next day's marinara sauce, which I mistook for the marinara sauce left over from the night before. At three in the morning it's hard to tell the difference.

From the day of my stroke until my suicide attempt it had been impossible for me to fall asleep without taking sleeping pills. Miraculously, at McLean I didn't need them anymore. I was no longer addicted. Oddly enough, once I stopped taking sleeping pills my dreams became more intense. They varied, but one that began at SB1 occurred repeatedly.

I'm in London playing soccer in the back garden with George. There's no hint of my paralysis as eleven-year-old George and I are running around laughing and tackling each other. I'm deliriously happy until I wake up and realize that it's just a dream. And then it's agony.

The dream continued at the Pavilion, but toward the end of my stay, I began to view it differently. Not as a bleak reminder of something I was now no longer capable of, but as a unique period that helped form my extraordinary relationship with my son. Whether this turnaround was a direct result of therapy I'm not sure, but I don't believe it would have happened without spending time at McLean.

37.

Initially, I was dying to leave McLean, but after a couple of weeks I became unopposed to staying there. Although there was no pivotal moment when this change took place, the two months I spent at the Pavilion were conducive to quiet reassessment. Out of this reassessment came an odd desire to reevaluate a few books I'd read in my more impressionable years. I believe I learned as much about myself from rereading as I did from the sixty or so sessions of psychotherapy I took at McLean. But, of course, without the therapy I wouldn't have been motivated to reread these books.

The literary critic Harold Bloom once wrote that "there is nothing more profoundly healing than the act of solitary reading." I never really thought about this until my stay at McLean.

The first books I reread were Hemingway's *The Sun Also Rises* and Jane Austen's *Pride and Prejudice*. Reading *The Sun Also Rises* at twenty-two, I was bowled over by how good it was. I found *Pride and Prejudice*, which I read at twenty-three, artificial and silly. Rereading the Hemingway book, I winced at the dialogue and found parts of it embarrassing. With Austen it was the opposite. Second time around I thought *Pride and Prejudice* was a masterpiece and couldn't believe I'd ever thought otherwise.

In my twenties I'd viewed Hemingway's masculinity as a sign of seriousness and Austen's light touch as a sign of shallowness. Forty years later, I thought the reverse. Reading Austen today, I'm surprised how often I change my opinion about her characters, as I'm constantly reassessing their moral worth. Unfortunately, it wasn't until I was past sixty that I discovered this is what most good books do. At least, they can if we're not afraid to change our minds. As I pile on the years, I realize more than ever the importance of changing one's mind. The fact that politicians rarely do speaks volumes.

Just after I began rereading books in earnest, I stumbled across something written by the editor Clifton Fadiman, which gave me another reason to reread: "When you re-read a classic, you do not see more in the book than you did before; you see more in yourself than there was before."

After a month of rereading at McLean, I began to think that so many books I'd read in my twenties were wasted on me. But on reflection I don't think that's true. Changing your opinion about something gives your revised opinion more depth.

I'm embarrassed by how slowly I read. By the time I've read one book, many of my friends have read two. After my stroke I stopped being embarrassed by this. Having bigger fish to fry put my slow reading into perspective and made me realize that it's not how much you read, it's how much you absorb. It's better to read one book that takes root than five that don't.

Many of the authors whose books I connect with seem to have suffered traumas when they were young. Though I don't believe that suffering makes you more legitimate or virtuous, I do think the internal isolation that follows profound suffering can provide access to the uncharted areas of one's inner life. If the trauma of my stroke and suicide attempt didn't give me the same access, it did give me something so close to it that I felt compelled to write about it.

In my third week at McLean, I received a highly sympathetic letter from Alan Bennett suggesting that I "write things down." That was Alan's understated way of encouraging me to write about my suicide attempt. He often used the tradesman's entrance to discuss weighty topics. A few days later, Sam Sifton, a food editor at the *New York Times*, emailed to ask if I'd write an article explaining how I operated three restaurants in my post-stroke condition. (No less inefficiently than in my pre-stroke condition, I wanted to reply.) Sifton had no idea about my suicide attempt—few people did—but two years earlier he'd overseen an article I'd written for the *Times* on opening my fourteenth restaurant, Augustine.

I agreed to write the piece for Sifton. The trouble was, once I started I couldn't prevent incidents connected to my stroke and suicide attempt from flooding the page. Knowing that this wasn't what Sifton wanted, I eventually passed on the *Times* article. Two days later, I took a stab at what Alan had suggested and tried to write about my attempted suicide. This time words didn't "flood" the page. Nothing did. Ironically, when I'd been commissioned to write exclusively about restaurants, other areas of my life spilled out. But now that there were no constraints, these *other areas* refused to appear. They became, in restaurant parlance, "no-shows." (Usual excuses: "the rain was nonstop, the kids had a fever, the Uber didn't show.")

Gradually, the "no-shows" began arriving.

Although suicide was no longer foremost on my mind, I still had some dark moments at the Pavilion. I decided to use them as inspiration to write about the truth of my attempt to kill myself. Only it wasn't the truth. Just as suffering doesn't necessarily ennoble the character, truth doesn't necessarily emerge from dark moments. Raw truth is rarely the real truth. To make sense of trauma, I believe there must be a kind of incubation period. One's subconscious needs to be given time to sift through the remains of trauma in order to rake out the truth. (And even then I wouldn't be certain it's the real truth.)

I began writing every day. It was a terrific release. I'd be at my desk at 5:30 a.m. or earlier. I couldn't wait to start. Suddenly, I had a purpose.

For the first month, I found it hard to write about things I didn't understand. It wasn't until my last week at McLean that I realized it didn't matter. That understanding comes through writing, and not always the other way round. How this minor breakthrough came about I'm not sure, but during my last week at the loony bin I began to feel a little more confident about things. I was also conscious how lucky I was to be alive. I felt like I was now playing with house money.

* * *

All of the Pavilion's rooms had a phone with a line to the nurses' station. Although I sometimes woke in the middle of the night feeling nauseous, it was never serious enough to call the night nurse. Besides, since she'd caught me in the kitchen stealing marinara sauce, I was too embarrassed to face her again. But three days before leaving, I woke up at 2 a.m. with a headache so strong I was forced to call her. She arrived five minutes later with two Tylenol, but it was a different nurse. Apparently, the one who'd reprimanded me had left and been replaced. The new nurse was in her late thirties, with dark shadows under attractive brown eyes. It was a rule at McLean that you had to take pills in front of the nurse who administered them. "Nurse Cole" watched me take the pills, and after swallowing them I made her laugh by immediately asking for a dozen more. As she was leaving, Nurse Cole noticed the book on my bedside table and told me she'd just finished reading it. It was Saul Bellow's *Herzog*, a book I was struggling with.

She asked if I liked Bellow. I said yes, *very much so*, with the kind of conviction that implied I'd read every book Bellow had ever written, when in fact this was the only one. Nurse Cole reeled off about five Bellow books she'd read and asked which ones I liked most. Embarrassed to be caught out, I quickly changed the subject and asked if she'd studied literature at college. There was a pause: "I never went to college," she said sheepishly. "Nor did I," I said.

We talked for half an hour—mainly about books. "Grace" had read a lot, far more than me. She worked as a night nurse, she said, not because she wanted to help people, but because the job gave her half the night to read. Although this may have accounted for the very dark shadows under her eyes, it wasn't true. Several patients told me on my last day that Nurse Cole was the most caring nurse at the Pavilion.

As Grace was leaving, I said I'd need two more Tylenol the following night around the same time. "I'll bring you six dozen," she said, and we both laughed. Laughter, to paraphrase Auden, is the first sign of attraction.

The next night, I called her at two in the morning but she didn't arrive until three. "There was a gallbladder incident with Mrs. Finkelstein in 5B," she explained. We talked for about an hour, during which she returned to 5B every fifteen minutes or so to check that Mrs. Finkelstein was still alive and kicking. (Unfortunately, she was.) After one visit, she came back holding a cup of hot chocolate and a slice of angel food cake. She told me she was married.

"So am I," I said. "But I'm getting divorced." It felt strange saying this, and even stranger that this was the last time I was going to see Grace. She was off the following night, and I would be leaving McLean for good—hopefully—the day after. A friend of mine was taking me to Boston to see a neurologist. I'd be staying overnight in a hotel before flying home to New York the next morning.

I enjoyed talking with Grace so much that night I didn't want the conversation to end. Around four in the morning she said she must get going, otherwise she might be fired. The long silence that followed said a lot. Reaching for my house money, I broke the stillness and asked if she wanted to have lunch with me at my hotel in Boston. She looked me in the eye and said yes. I was ecstatic.

The charge you experience when someone you're falling for first reveals an interest is the most thrilling feeling in existence. Beside myself with anticipation, I slept no more than an hour that night.

Two days later, there was a gentle knock on my hotel room door. Initially, it was jarring to see Grace out of uniform, but I soon got used to it. She looked at the menu while I poured her a glass of white wine. "Just half a glass," she said. Not wanting to appear too eager, I poured myself the same (though I really wanted a full one). Grace didn't talk much. I got the feeling she wished she hadn't come. After a bit of prompting she opened up. She lived in Brockton and had married young, she said. Five years after she had twin boys, her marriage started to go south. Her husband was a welder with a gambling habit so bad he couldn't be trusted. Seven years earlier he'd got them into such debt that Grace had had to borrow money from her father, which she'd only paid back eighteen months before. She'd wanted to leave her husband after that, but the boys adored him, she said. If things didn't get better after they went to college, she was going to find a place for herself. There was a pause.

"We sleep in separate beds, you know."

I nervously asked, "For how long?"

"Seven years." I found Grace devastatingly attractive. Leaning toward her, I put my hand on her cheek, but she took it away instantly. I suddenly remembered the incident with the French girl from the London strip club and felt foolish. I turned around and took the last sip of wine. I now wished I'd poured a full glass.

"Let's lie on the bed," she said.

This shocked me.

The bed was unusually high and I had trouble hoisting myself onto it without effort. I thought of Jon Voight in *Coming Home*. Grace pretended not to notice. Lying on the bed, I became less self-conscious. Except I could only touch her with one hand. With our faces almost touching, she caressed my neck and I stroked her hair. And then we kissed. A long, sensual kiss. She pulled away and said, "You're the first man I've kissed in seven years." I was about to say, "You're the first woman I've kissed since trying to kill myself," when she suddenly kissed me again.

We stayed on the bed kissing, talking and touching, and I thought of the Maupassant line: "A lawful kiss is never worth as much as a stolen one."

After about an hour she said she had to go. I walked her to the door and, placing my cane on the nearest wall, we kissed again. It was heavenly. And then she left. As soon as the door closed, I wanted to write to her *that second* to say how beautiful she was. But of course I didn't.

First thing the next morning I had my appointment with the neurologist. In the taxi to the airport I emailed Grace to say how much I'd enjoyed our lunch. And how brave she had been to meet me. I wanted to say a lot more but I thought it better to gauge the warmth of her reply first. As soon as the New York shuttle landed, I switched on my phone to check her reply. There wasn't one. I waited a few hours and wrote again, this time more intimately. Again nothing. The next morning I woke early and opened my laptop.

Grace had written back: "Keith, please don't contact me anymore. Please respect my wishes."

I respected her wishes and didn't write.

I never saw her again.

38.

After spending a month on Martha's Vineyard and nine weeks at Mc-
Lean, I'd been away from New York for over three months. I returned
to the city in the fall of 2018 only to discover that my local barbershop
had turned into a Baskin-Robbins. Why do changes in the landscape ac-
celerate as one ages? You take a quick shower and another Duane Reade
opens. You wake from an afternoon nap and there's a new president. The
second you hit sixty, life becomes the unstoppable bus in the film *Speed*.

During my stay at McLean, construction on the new Pastis began. A
few days after returning to New York, I visited the site. Being ignorant
of building matters, I've always felt out of my depth on construction sites.
Even more so on sites where I'm the boss. But if I felt this way before my
stroke, how would I feel now, when physically I'm half the man I used to
be? It turned out to be the opposite. The macho-looking crew proved to
be not so macho after all. They showed more sensitivity toward my crippled body than I thought possible, and in being respectful without being
deferential, they allowed me to be myself. Visiting construction sites when
I was healthy, I'd always pretended to know more about the building process than I really did. Why I felt the need to embellish my knowledge I
don't know, but every time I did this, I came away feeling like a complete
fraud. However, on this visit, though frail and powerless, I left the site
feeling more dignified than when I'd arrived.

Desperate to see George and Alice, I flew to London the next day.
One of the most annoying things about being disabled is being classi-
fied as disabled. This happens in a most demeaning way at airports. Although I detest being in a wheelchair, I'm obliged to take one at the

terminal, otherwise it would take me an hour to walk from check-in to the boarding gate. Going through security is the worst part of the whole journey because I'm often herded together with other people in wheelchairs. There are few things that rob me of my individuality so invidiously as being lumped together with other disabled people. I don't have anything *against* people in wheelchairs—I'd feel the same way (or worse) being shoved into a room full of restaurateurs or Englishmen from Bethnal Green. I simply don't want to be defined by an aspect of myself that doesn't represent the *whole* of me, or the person I think I am inside this battered body.

But this trip was different. While lining up to go through JFK's security, something happened that took my mind off this grim wheelchair business. As luck would have it, I became intrigued by a young French-looking woman in the line opposite me. In her late twenties, she was the sultry type, with an air of rebelliousness about her. She sauntered through the body scanner so contemptuously it was clear she'd rather be sipping espresso in Paris. I imagined her at Café de Flore absorbed in an existentialist novel. She embodied everything I loved about French women. I longed to be with her.

This changed drastically as the woman picked up her personal belongings from the conveyor belt. Unexpectedly, this French-looking woman put a large cowboy hat on her head and began speaking with a strong Texas drawl. My longing immediately turned into loathing.

The fact that I became so disdainful of a woman because of a mere accent and a hat made me realize how shockingly guilty I was of a prejudice I'm constantly praying strangers don't feel about me. My voice is so defective these days that people find me very hard to understand. If it meant I could talk normally again, I'd be ecstatic to have a Texas drawl. (Not so sure about the cowboy hat, though.)

Seeing George and Alice in London was quite emotional. Between the news of their parents' divorce and my suicide attempt and subsequent stay in a nut house, my kids hadn't had an easy summer.

We met in the "weekend" flat Alina had rented a year earlier. George teared up when he first saw me, but Alice was unmoved. This was surprising as the last time she'd seen me—nine weeks earlier—I was being stretchered into an ambulance en route to McLean. Not long after we spent this weekend together, three years would go by during which Alice would barely speak to me.

From a young age, Alice had always been highly principled, with a character so incorruptible that beside her I felt like an imposter. She was often silent, and in my more anxious moments, I interpreted this as an unwillingness to talk to me. Although she loved me, Alice possessed an instinctual closeness to Alina that was missing with me, which no doubt accounted for her taking Alina's side during our arguments.

Though my first weekend with Alice and George was not a total success, I nevertheless dreaded them leaving. Now that I was officially separated from Alina, memories of my first divorce resurfaced. The inescapable gloom of Sunday evening would always be intensified by the knowledge that my allotted time with the kids was coming to an end. The usual repacking of the overnight bag, the hurried kiss goodbye and the utter forlornness of Sunday nights being alone in the apartment without them.

To improve my relationship with Alice and provide a less hostile environment for her and George to grow up in, Alina and I agreed to see a "relationship specialist" together. Her name was Tanya Haynes. Unlike Civilised Separations Specialist Nick Arnold, Haynes was straightforward and her language—like that of many people who are direct—was free of clichés.

Our first session began in November 2018. I hadn't seen Alina since the day after my suicide attempt three and a half months earlier. Seeing her in the waiting room took my breath away. I was still in love with her. But we were here to stabilize our children's lives, not to repair a broken marriage.

Haynes was considerate without being reverential and always made sense. Alina and I immediately respected her. The sessions would begin unemotionally but at some point they would become so intense that one of us would break down. Usually Alina. I did so less often, because I was unable to break down without observing myself breaking down. After nine weeks at McLean, I thought I was through with this "observing" myself rubbish. I was wrong. Leopards don't change their spots no matter how much therapy they have.

Alina was completely raw during these sessions. She was stripped bare to the bone and scrupulously herself. I suddenly admired Alina in ways I'd never done before. And though she sometimes accused me of things that were patently not true, she did so with conviction because she believed them to be true, not because she wanted to score points or curry favor with Haynes the way I did.

During these sessions there wasn't a second when I wasn't conscious of Haynes listening to us. Even at my most self-critical, a part of me was always angling to impress her.

Alina and I saw Haynes every week that I was in London, but after seven months, Alina abruptly ended the sessions. I had one or two meetings alone with Haynes because I needed her advice on how to respond to Alice since she'd lately stopped replying to my emails. Haynes advised me not to confront Alice and not to get angry if she didn't respond. I took her advice and for three years bit my tongue every time Alice didn't reply to my calls or emails. Even when she didn't respond for a month or more, I resisted saying anything contentious and always signed off by saying how much I loved her. It wasn't easy, but after a few years my persistence began to pay off.

Alice now lives three blocks away from me in Greenwich Village and we see each other regularly. But despite how well we get on, I'm not so blind to think that the hard work is behind me. Just because you turn a corner with your kids it doesn't mean you're out of the woods. Quite the opposite. No matter how great the relationship is or how old they are, you're never out of the woods with your own kids. Not even when you're dead and buried.

Getting married is like boarding a train without knowing its destination. I thought my train was heading for Kansas. Who knew it was going to end up with a leather-coated SS officer serving me divorce papers in

bed? For one thing, I really wouldn't have thought Alina capable of en-
gineering such a stunt. But I was wrong. I was wrong because I was so
wrapped up in myself in both marriages that I didn't have a fucking clue
how either wife was *really* doing. I also had no idea how people behave
when they're driven to leave their spouse the way Alina was with me.

Acting uncharacteristically is par for the course when you're desperate to leave your spouse. A fucking necessity. "I could accept him having
sex with another woman, but not *my best friend*," says the wife, shocked
out of her skull. The shock isn't so much the husband's behavior as the
wife being shocked by it. Sometimes the only way one can leave a long-
term partner *is* by acting abominably. But the one left seldom takes this
into account. He or she would rather get as much leverage as possible
from their spouse's supposedly "bad" behavior than search for its true
cause. Instead of looking into the mirror, they dine out on feelings of aggrievement. Aggrievement is one of the ugliest qualities known to man.
Not least because the aggrieved always exaggerate. I know I did.

I find it strange how many more people are sympathetic to the spouse
left in a breakup than the one who does the leaving. In literature, you seldom read about the heartbreak the person who ends the relationship goes
through. As a character in Tom Stoppard's play *The Real Thing* says, "Gal-
lons of ink and miles of typewriter ribbon expended on the misery of the
unrequited lover; not a word about the utter tedium of the unrequiting."

Though I was the one left in both my marriages, I identify far more
with the person who breaks up a relationship than the person who is broken up with. I'm not sure why that is, but perhaps it helps explain why
my favorite character in literature is the unfaithful Anna in Tolstoy's
Anna Karenina, and why I've no sympathy at all for the cuckolded husband in *Lady Chatterley's Lover*.

During my six weeks in London, I met regularly with Baroness Shackleton to discuss my divorce. I liked Shackleton and detested Alina's
lawyer, Helen Ward. But if Ward had been my lawyer and Shackleton
Alina's, I would have felt the opposite about them. Divorce lawyers are

hired hands. They go where the money is, and regardless of how sympathetic and loyal Shackleton was to me—and she *was*—I'm sure she'd have done the same for Alina if the roles were reversed.

Lawyers are the only ones who benefit from divorce. The more bile they can generate between a separated couple, the richer they become. If the same logic applied to restaurants, the less my customers enjoyed their dining experience, the more money I'd rake in.

As Shackleton mapped out in nightmarish detail the worst-case scenario of my divorce, it suddenly hit me that there was no going back. I was enmeshed in an impenetrable legal system I neither respected nor understood, and it was now going to force me to hate the person I still loved.

Ever since my stroke, I've needed a personal assistant to help me shower and set out my morning medicine of seven pills—including my antidepressant and the all-important blood thinner—and drive me around. The day after my second meeting with Shackleton, my assistant Karmen drove me from London to the Cotswolds. I hadn't been to Great Brockhampton Farm in five months and the thought of seeing it again—this home that had once held the promise of a glorious new life—filled me with anxiety.

Approaching the main door, I heard the familiar sounds of wood pigeons cooing. Once inside, the faint smell of pine and lavender brought back a rush of warm feelings that were abruptly replaced by memories of arguments and abandonment. Strange how something so inanimate can represent the collapse of one's ideals: health, marriage, finance, children's stability—all stolen by the drive to build something of beauty and lasting value. This was meant to be my last hurrah. A final gesture in almost half a century of striving to build the perfect restaurant, the perfect house, the perfect life. Perhaps I flew too close to the sun; who knows? No matter; it led to my ruin, and Great Brockhampton Farm, like my life, was now up for sale.

Next day, I hobbled out of the house, and within a week I was back in New York.

39.

I rarely have a plan, but after my release from McLean I had two: to finalize my divorce and to finish building the 170-seat Pastis. Of the two, finalizing my divorce was the more taxing.

My troubles began with the prenup. Or rather, the absence of one. Late in the game I discovered that the prenup Alina had willingly signed in New York was worthless in England. That's when the gloves came off.

Even though Alina was right in asking for half my money, the divorce process itself is so adversarial that I fought against it. At the time, I was the principal owner of five restaurants and a bakery business. Owing to the volatile nature of restaurants, and the unlikelihood that I could still operate them after my stroke, my net worth wasn't easy to assess. Consequently, the judge ordered an independent appraisal company to try to work out the value of my restaurants. After a month of plowing through my accounts—and charging me $75,000 for the privilege—the company came up with the figure of $16 million. Alina's lawyer was incensed. She believed my businesses were worth far more and asked the judge for a second appraisal from a different company. The judge reluctantly agreed and the whole thorny process began again. (And once again, I had to foot the bill.)

The second company was more thorough and even had two of their accountants grill me for several hours at my apartment. They were searching for any mental deficiencies the stroke could have caused that would decrease the worth of my restaurants. I guess they found some because their assessment was a whopping million dollars less than the first company.

Alina's lawyer was livid.

There's no such thing as an amicable divorce. No matter how determined you are to keep things agreeable, divorce brings out the worst in people. I kicked off the process by offering Alina three times what she would have received from the New York prenup, plus full child support. She rejected it. I made two more offers, each higher than the last. She rejected them both, which put us one step closer to a dreaded trial. They say divorce trials are to be avoided more than the Black Death. Since less than ten percent of all English divorces go to trial, the chances of this happening were slim. Nevertheless, we did have three pretrial hearings, each one held in London's spectacular Royal Courts of Justice on the Strand.

At the third and last pretrial hearing we finally settled. Although relieved it was over, neither of us came away from the process unscarred or with our heads held high. If both parties come away from a divorce settlement feeling short-changed—as we both did—it probably means justice was served. In July 2019, Alina and I were officially divorced. In fifteen months we had both aged five years and paid over a million dollars in lawyers' bills. Such is justice.

Since my stroke, I've lived in fear of falling. Paralyzed on one side, I can't walk without a cane. And even with a cane, every step I take is a precarious one. Falls are the leading cause of death from injuries in those over sixty-five, and though I've only had two in five years, the chances are a fall will lead to my undoing. It's the sniper on the roof.

The first of my two falls happened at Gatwick Airport in February 2019, when I was flying from London to New York with George. Though I'd normally use a wheelchair at an airport, I couldn't bear George seeing me in one so I risked hobbling with a cane—even on the airport's moving walkway. I hadn't been on one since before my stroke, and though I had no difficulty getting onto the walkway, getting off it was another matter.

Approaching the end of the walkway, where the moving floor slides underneath the grate, I became unsure which foot to lift first and in my confusion lifted neither. My right foot bounced off the grate, spinning me backward and onto the walkway floor. I lay on my back like some upturned turtle, unable to get upright while the moving contraption bounced me from side to side. (Once again, George witnessed me in a humiliating position.) Other passengers rushed to my aid. In doing so, one of them wrenched my spasticated arm almost out of its socket. This caused me far more pain than the fall itself. Nevertheless, I still flew to New York.

The next day, I took a cab to a meeting at Balthazar. The curb outside the restaurant is unusually high and as I attempted to step onto it, I lost my balance and tumbled over. As with the airport fall, the serious damage was done by a passerby who, in pulling me off the ground, yanked my paralyzed arm so hard that he unintentionally fractured my shoulder. After multiple X-rays the doctor told me my humerus bone was broken. (It might have been humerus to the doctor, but it wasn't funny to me.) Since then, I've had no falls. But it's only a matter of time.

In March 2020, in the middle of studying for his A-levels, George quit Brighton College and came to live with me in an apartment I was renting on Gloucester Road. Although I wasn't too happy about him dropping out of school, I was thrilled to have him living with me again. He was passionate about films and began making short films of his own. To make ends meet, he found a job tending bar at a pub off High Street Kensington. The apple didn't fall far from the tree.

In November that year, Alina sent me an email to say that she'd bought a house in Hawaii and that she and Alice were moving there in a month. I was stunned. This would mean that Alice was going to be plucked out of her fourth school in four years and live seven thousand miles away from her father and brother. I immediately called Alina and asked if we could at least discuss the idea. She said there was no point. They were moving to Hawaii a week after Christmas, five days before Alice's sixteenth birthday. This was significant. Once a child reaches sixteen in England, he or she can decide for themselves which parent they want to live with. (In America the age is eighteen.) I was devastated.

At the time, I wondered how on earth Alina could move so radically far away. What I should have asked was what Alina was feeling inside that prompted her to move seven thousand miles from me. But I suppose if I'd been sensitive enough to ask myself that question, Alina wouldn't have needed to move so far away.

After nine months of construction, the seemingly superficial work on Pastis began: the installation of banquettes, the hanging of mirrors, the placement of tables and chairs, choosing the length of the waiters' white aprons and the working out of the all-important lighting. Being exceptionally superficial, this is where I really come into my own and where, in the complicated building of a restaurant, I unfortunately make the most impact.

During this stage, Stephen Starr and I had our only disagreement. Starr felt the semicircular booths that Ian and I had designed were too small to seat four people. He thought they should be much bigger. I feel the same way about oversize booths as I do about oversize tables. They destroy intimacy. I asked Stephen to wait until Pastis had opened to see what our customers thought. Nobody ever complained, so we kept them the same size.

In the restaurant world, there's nothing so thrilling as the week before opening. The crew of carpenters, plumbers and laborers who've spent the past twelve months putting together the nuts and bolts of the restaurant are gradually replaced by a very different constituency of workers: waiters, waitresses, bartenders, bussers, hosts and maître d's. For three or four days, both sets of workers uneasily share the same space, but as the finished restaurant begins to materialize, those who actually built the place cede their importance to those who didn't. The baton is passed on.

Two days before the opening party, Starr and I prepared to give a speech to all 150 employees of Pastis. Before my stroke, I used to enjoy giving this semi-motivational speech, but the idea now terrified me.

How could someone so incoherent and physically crushed be fit to lead and inspire?

When the time came to deliver the speech, I stood anxiously in front of all the employees and began talking. Unfortunately, my voice was so weak that most employees only understood half my words. But they didn't need to understand every word to be inspired. The inspiration they found came from an aspect of my character that until then I'd never given a second thought: my reputation. Watching a man who for over forty years had been opening restaurants in the city, including the Odeon, Balthazar, Minetta Tavern and a slew of other semi-famous New York places, struggle to talk to his staff was perhaps an inspiration in itself. Before my speech, I understood neither the meaning nor the value of the word "reputation." Afterward, I did. And very much so.

Taking local transport across Afghanistan in 1971, I was struck by how much value the Afghans placed on reputation. To them, it was everything. You could be as strong as an ox, but if you had a poor reputation, you had nothing. My reputation's far from perfect, but I'd like to think that one of the reasons so many of my staff have stayed with me for twenty years or more is because for the most part I'm not so terrible to work for. One busboy—Wong Cheng—has been working for me for forty-four years so far. He put three kids through college and owns several houses in Queens. (I'll probably end up renting a small room in one of Wong Cheng's many houses.)

The night before Pastis opened, we threw a party for four hundred people, mostly long-standing customers who hadn't seen me since my stroke. Many were shocked by my condition. But for once it didn't upset me. For once I wasn't embarrassed by the way I looked or spoke. That night, for the first time since my stroke, I saw myself not as others saw me, but as I saw myself. I was still the same person *inside*, and despite my banged-up body and marred speech, I could still build restaurants. Most importantly, I still had my reputation. That hadn't changed. And in the end, that's all we're left with.

"Reputation, reputation, reputation! Oh, I have lost my reputation! I have lost the immortal part of myself." —*Othello*

40.

Pastis opened in June 2019. It was an immediate hit and even received two stars from the *New York Times*. What drove me to make Pastis succeed wasn't money; it was the desire to prove wrong those who'd refused to invest.

The need to get even is a great motivator for me. The trouble was that as soon as the restaurant succeeded, proving people wrong felt meaningless. Once I'd achieved what I was after, I no longer desired it. This is a major trait of mine. Whether I was born with it I couldn't say, but the first time I recognized it was the day after my marriage to Lynn in 1983.

To escape the fanfare of a wedding, we flew to LA and married at the Beverly Hills Hotel. The next morning Lynn went to Oregon to see her brother and I rented a green Ford Escort and drove to Phoenix to look at some Frank Lloyd Wright buildings. Never good with maps, I went the wrong way and ended up on a coastal road heading south. Flustered beyond measure—*so this is what married life is like*—I stopped at a gas station to get my bearings. Pulling up, I noticed another car about to leave: a sixties Volkswagen Beetle with two surfboards mounted on top. The driver, in his late twenties, had a breezy, carefree appearance, with one hand on the steering wheel and the other slung over the shoulder of his girlfriend. The girlfriend looked equally laid-back and was gazing at her boyfriend like she didn't give a fuck about anything or anybody but him. I saw the couple for no more than ten seconds but they reminded me of Bob Dylan and his girlfriend on the cover of his album *The Freewheelin' Bob Dylan*. They seemed to have the world at their feet.

I was massively unsettled. Not so much by the couple's good looks, but by what their cool demeanor and Volkswagen Beetle represented.

Throughout my eight-year marriage to Lynn, I was desperate to buy the same Beetle, but fearing Lynn would criticize its impracticality, I never did. A month after we divorced, I forked out ten grand and bought one: a jet-black 1968 convertible. It looked great and I got a terrific kick driving it. But something was missing. From the outside I was driving a Volkswagen Beetle, but on the inside I was still driving a Ford Escort. I hadn't become the person on the cover of *Freewheelin'* and never did. And since then, hardly anything I've looked forward to has matched its anticipation. Not even the birth of my children.

Before my oldest child, Harry, was born, a friend my age told me that becoming a father had been the best moment of his life. Others said the same. However, it wasn't like this for me. When each of my five kids was born, it was as if a stranger had entered the house. Of course, they mean the world to me now, but until my kids reached seven or eight months old I didn't truly connect with them. And no amount of childbirth classes before the event could help create that bond. But on the day when each one of my children was born, I played the game and, like all fathers, shouted from the rooftops that this was the greatest moment of my life.

In my twenties, some literary friends advised me to read Cervantes's *Don Quixote*. They said it was one of the best books ever written. I waded through the thousand-page "classic" without enjoying a single page, but for the next thirty years told everyone it was a masterpiece. I said this not because I loved the book but because I was *supposed* to love it.

It was only when I reached fifty and discovered that "experts" are not always right—in fact they're invariably wrong—that I felt comfortable saying what I *really* thought. That it's okay to hate New Year's Eve and adults in Halloween costumes. That it's okay to admit you're on the verge of bankruptcy and that your last family get-together was a godawful disaster. Or that *Don Quixote* is a rubbish book and that the birth of your child was nothing like it was cracked up to be. That it's okay *not* to play the fucking game.

* * *

In November 2019, my friend, the director Jonathan Miller, died.

The last time I'd seen Miller was in the spring of that year, by which point he was suffering from Alzheimer's. He no longer remembered me and barely recognized his own children. What was once an extraordinary memory was now a black hole. That encyclopedic knowledge of history, philosophy, the arts and sciences had been looted. It seemed like a perversion of nature to watch Miller, the most articulate man I'd ever met, struggle to communicate.

A director, writer and lecturer, Miller was also a doctor of medicine who, for more than sixty years, informed, dazzled and inspired. His learning was vast, but what interested Miller most was the negligible. He believed that only by recognizing the negligible could we understand the considerable. He was some kind of man.

Miller's favorite film was *The Third Man*. When I was visiting him and his wife, Rachel, at their home in 1970, he suddenly noticed that the film was showing on TV that night at 11 p.m. "You must stay and watch this," announced Miller. And so I hung around till late, when Jonathan, Rachel and I sat in front of a minuscule television set to watch this remarkable film.

Most fans of *The Third Man* harp on about the Ferris wheel scene, in which the nefarious Harry Lime—played with unseemly charm by Orson Welles—lectures his best friend on the flaws of democracy: "In Switzerland, they had brotherly love, they had five hundred years of democracy and peace, and what did that produce? The cuckoo clock!" Though Miller adored this scene, he focused on a more subtle one that he believed elevated the film to greatness.

The sequence comes early on, when Lime's melancholy lover, Anna, visits the apartment of the supposedly dead Lime. Sitting alone in his bedroom, she picks up a ringing telephone. While talking on the phone, she unconsciously opens a drawer, takes out two dice and instinctively rolls them. These unsensational few moments capture the intimate nature of Anna's relationship with Lime that words would have labored to explain. It was a stroke of genius that I would never have recognized were it not for Miller.

Being Jonathan Miller's friend was the best thing that ever happened to me.

Though Miller was Jewish, his funeral was held in a church. There was no sign of a vicar, and God—whom Miller hadn't a shred of belief in—wasn't once mentioned. With Miller's wicker coffin lying on the cold flagstone floor between the altar and the choir stalls, 350 of his friends and family commemorated him. I sat in the back row with George and Alice. At a lectern set up in front of the altar, a number of friends told stories about him, which made the funeral seem more like a memorial.

At every memorial I've attended there's always been someone who talked more about himself than about the dead person, someone who made the eulogy about *them* and not the deceased. But this was different. The stories people told about Miller were about the man himself. Some serious, some funny, but all appropriate. Though all the attendees that day seemed imbued with Miller's fiercely unsentimental presence, the funeral itself was unexpectedly moving.

As the pallbearers carried Jonathan's coffin slowly out of the church, the theme from *The Third Man* played.

In early 2020 I discovered Instagram. Before then, I'd been so clueless about social media that I didn't even know the difference between Instagram and Twitter. Once I'd figured out how it worked, I was shocked by the fictitious lives people presented on Instagram. Almost everybody appeared to have perfect marriages and "bright" kids, and to lead exceptionally undamaged lives. The kind of life I might have presented before my stretch in a psychiatric unit. Spending two months at McLean didn't necessarily make me more stable, but it did make me face the truth about my post-stroke condition. I was a disabled and incomprehensible fragment of the man I used to be and didn't plan to conceal it on this vast repository of self-deception, this modern-day Barbie's world where fewer than one in a thousand owned up to their shortcomings, this envy-producing conveyor belt of narcissism we call Instagram.

No one goes through life unscathed. Everybody hits the skids at one point. If I could be honest about my own "skids," perhaps it could help someone else deal with their own. Who was I fooling? I joined Instagram to piss people off. To yank them off their high horses, not to fucking help them.

From school onward I'd had a knack for adding moderately witty captions to postcards. Joining Instagram was an extension of this. But there was a more vital reason. Since the stroke, my voice was so slurred and garbled that it barely existed. Instagram became my voice.

My first post was in February 2020 and was "liked" by ninety-eight people. Getting carried away with myself, I immediately posted ten more. One was of an empty restaurant of mine with the caption "Minetta Tavern. Packed to the Rafters." Another was a photo of Tom Hanks promoting a new film with his customary Forrest Gump look. Underneath I wrote: "Hanks in another Boring film playing someone who's had a lobotomy. Business as usual for Hanks." Not quite Jonathan Swift, but people got the idea.

Although I enjoyed Instagram more than I wanted to, I deplored its embrace of cancel culture, and many of my posts were mild attempts to illustrate this. A number of them dealt with subjects normally taboo on Instagram. Among others, these included regular support for Woody Allen, my vasectomy (with photos), a hatred of the film *Barbie* and the humiliation of my post-stroke physical condition. Of course, owning restaurants gave me a rich source of material to write about and I'd often post my restaurant managers' dinner reports. The more disastrous the night, the more likely I was to post it. In some ways, it was only after I lost my voice that I learned to speak my mind.

Although I pretended to be indifferent to the number of followers my posts attracted, I was secretly obsessed with it. For vanity's sake, my goal was to have 100,000 followers. After eighteen months my followers had climbed from zero to 30,000, but for some reason once I reached 58,000, the numbers unaccountably ground to a halt.

There's a theory that everyone is born with a finite amount of luck inside them. Maybe it was the same with Instagram followers. It seemed so because in August 2022 I couldn't get a single new follower for two months. Then out of nowhere came a gift from heaven: James Corden. Ever the obnoxious customer, the English actor crossed the line at Balthazar one day and insulted one of my servers to the point where she broke down and cried. Exaggerating my outrage, I posted an account of the actor's bullying behavior on Instagram. By exposing Corden's abuse, it appeared as though I was defending a principle, when all I was doing was seeking the approval of my young Balthazar staff.

Within hours of the Corden post, the number of my followers shot up from 58,000 to 73,000. My post had gone viral and each hour that passed, my followers increased by 5,000. I felt like I'd hit the jackpot of a slot machine and thousands of gold coins were spilling out in front of me. That night I ended up with over 90,000 followers.

Corden called me four times the day the post came out, each time asking me to please delete it. On the last call he sounded desperate. Relishing my hold over someone so famous, I told him I wouldn't delete it. Like a little dictator, I was intoxicated with the power I'd received from having galvanized over 30,000 people. For someone who's hyperconscious of humiliation since suffering a stroke, it now seems monstrous that I didn't consider the humiliation I was subjecting Corden to. Especially as I hadn't personally seen the incident I so vividly described on Instagram. All I thought about during each of Corden's calls (and endless texts) were the gold coins spilling uncontrollably onto my lap. Despite knowing that self-righteousness is the most repugnant of feelings, in calling out James Corden, I was intoxicated with self-righteousness.

Though most of us have opinions on controversial subjects without knowing all the facts, airing them among friends is unlikely to affect or influence the subject. The world of social media is radically different. Owing to the vast numbers of reachable people on platforms such as Instagram, uninformed opinions *can* affect a subject. In giving weight to those who shout loudest—who are more often than not the least informed—social media strengthens allegations and weakens facts. It emboldens prejudice and blurs the line between accusation and truth. As a result, the presumption of innocence is no longer so inviolable as it once was, or as it should be if we want democracy to survive.

By writing about something I didn't witness, I had played into the existing prejudices of 90,000 people. By writing about something I didn't have the full facts of, I'd possibly stained the career of someone I didn't know. I'm not suggesting Corden didn't deserve the backlash from my post. (The bastard probably did.) I'm just saying I didn't see the incident I wrote about that, to some degree, jeopardized his career. If this is the power of Instagram, I want no part of it.

That's what I'd like to say. But I can't. I'm afraid the lure of gold coins is too much to resist.

Just before Christmas 2019 came reports of a fatal virus that was overwhelming parts of China. As this mystifying virus advanced west, the reports became more alarming. It was called coronavirus and was untreatable. In Europe and America there was considerable panic.

On March 1, 2020, the first case of coronavirus in New York was publicly confirmed. Two weeks later, the governor of New York banned all of the city's indoor dining. Balthazar would be closed for over a year, and two of my restaurants—Augustine and Lucky Strike—would close forever. Even though I lost a great deal of money during Covid—as it was soon to be called—I consider myself fortunate not to have lost my life. But in April 2020 I almost did.

I was living in London with George when I first showed the symptoms: weakness, fever, difficulty breathing. Two medics arrived and tested me for Covid. I was positive. They said my oxygen level was so low I should go to a hospital immediately. The closest was the National Health's Chelsea and Westminster. For the fourth time in three years, George witnessed me being hauled off to a hospital.

I knew it was serious when the doctor examining me said, "Do you want to be revived if your heart stops?" Five minutes earlier he'd told me that coronavirus was in my lungs and the only way forward was to blast them with oxygen—a risky procedure with only a fifty percent survival rate.

For the second time in less than two years I thought I might die. Only this time I didn't want to. Waiting for the procedure, I began to think how little prepared I was for death. How most of my life was still unresolved. Is it the same for most people? Do most of us die with our knots still untied, our desks still uncleared? I think so.

Half an hour before the procedure was to begin, the doctor reexamined me. Miraculously, the virus had decreased enough for the doctor to cancel the procedure.

I remained in the hospital for eight days. Most of that time I had a thin, flexible tube wrapped around my head with two prongs inserted into my nostrils delivering about six liters of oxygen per minute. During my stay, one patient in my ward died from the virus. One forgets how deadly Covid was before a vaccine was discovered. Between 2020 and 2023, over a million people died from the virus in America; in Europe the death toll was over two million.

I spent the first four months of lockdown in London. As I was accustomed to being indoors most of the time, lockdown just felt like more of the same. That the healthy were now forced to stay at home sort of leveled the playing field. Having a normal amount of schadenfreude, I found this thought weirdly pleasing. As a result, lockdown was my happiest period in years.

At the height of lockdown, in May 2020, I flew from London to New York. The plane was three-quarters empty. Driving in from the airport was like entering a ghost town. New York had the same corpse-like feeling as it did after 9/11. Except now the enemy was invisible. But even with Covid stripping the city of its energy, I was still riveted by New York. In the same way you appreciate loved ones more when they're ailing, I began to love New York even more during Covid.

An hour after returning to Manhattan, I visited Balthazar. As the main entrance was padlocked I had to enter through the back door. Apart from closing for two days in 2010, the restaurant had been open every day—from morning to midnight—for the last twenty-three years.

I walked through a back corridor to the dining room. There was something deeply unnatural seeing this once-bustling dining room so dark and lifeless. Covid had forced the restaurant's closing only three months before, but the air inside was so stale and musty it felt like thirty years. Balthazar's once-vibrant dining room had lapsed so far into decrepitude that it reminded me of Miss Havisham's house in *Great Expectations*. I couldn't imagine the place ever opening again.

Emergencies bring out the best and worst in people. Like passengers on a plane bonding during a hijacking, New York's divided restaurant industry pooled its resources and, against the odds, became united during lockdown. As the city's bars and restaurants were losing millions of dollars, people in the industry stopped backstabbing each other and linked arms. Restaurateurs, restaurant critics, food writers and even restaurant landlords began supporting each other: landlords lowered their tenants' rents, restaurant critics stopped writing sarcastic reviews and the *New York Times* suspended its polarizing star rating system. It took a worldwide virus for professional food writers to accept that not all non-chef restaurateurs were swindlers and used-car salesmen. Suddenly we were a compassionate, noncompetitive community and it felt so extraordinary I didn't want Covid to end.

But it *did* end. And once that happened, the *New York Times* returned to its segregationist-like star system, landlords went back to gouging their tenants and the sanctimonious complained about sidewalk structures. After a two-year Pax Romana, the restaurant world returned to its cutthroat competitiveness and was once again operating as business as usual. At this point, I began to long for another lockdown.

They say what doesn't kill you makes you stronger. That through suffering you attain a benevolence, an otherworldliness that somehow makes you a better and more decent person. What crap. Suffering, alone, doesn't make you stronger. Neither does it make you a more noble or tolerant person. Often, suffering does the opposite. It makes you mean and petty. The only thing you learn from suffering, *at best*, is an awareness of other people's suffering. Nothing else. Those born round don't die square.

Although my speech is shot to pieces and my right side fully paralyzed, inside I still feel the same. Just as nobody ever feels their age, I feel exactly the same way as I did before my stroke. Embarrassment is still my biggest fear. The number of moments in the day when I want to disappear down a manhole hasn't changed. I still make matters more problematic when trying to simplify them and still feel beholden to people who work for me. I still crave the kind of success I pretend to despise, and revel in a modesty I don't possess. I still think people who claim personal change comes from watershed moments are talking bull. And I still believe that only idiots think creativity comes from harmony, and only those who don't have a clue about poetry believe it's a declaration of emotion and not an escape from it.

I'm still suspicious of those who place self-expression above self-awareness and of people who have a romantic view of art. I still hate those who don't believe that the more vile the crime, the more crucial due process becomes. And I still have no time for people who bask in being right, or anyone religious who won't admit that if they were born to different parents, chances are they'd have a totally different religion. I still hate those who use knowledge as a weapon, but most of all I hate those who don't have the fucking guts to change their minds. Especially about the things they're most certain of.

And yet . . . against the odds, I have changed a little. I'm more aware that it's the unnecessary things that make life civilized. These days, incidental gestures of kindness have a disproportionate effect on me: a taxi driver's thoughtfulness, a busboy's sensitivity, a doorman's courtesy. These small, unprompted acts of decency suddenly have more resonance. And . . . since my stroke, I'm embarrassed to say I cry more easily.

By the early spring of 2021, the worst of Covid was over. In March, New York restaurants were allowed to open to fifty percent capacity. Balthazar was one of the last in the city to reopen. This was partly because

I REGRET ALMOST EVERYTHING

a restaurant with 315 employees takes longer than most places to get its wheels turning again. But mostly because after being concealed from the public for more than a year, I wanted to fling open the restaurant's doors and have Balthazar shine brighter than it had ever shone before.

After 373 nights of darkness, Balthazar's lights were switched on at 5 p.m. on March 24, 2021. Though the law stated that restaurants couldn't be at more than fifty percent capacity, that night I said to hell with the law and filled the dining room and bar to the rafters. Balthazar was packed all night. It was like VE Day. Everyone was deliriously happy. Strangers hugged each other, customers danced in the aisles and young couples left enormous tips. The whole night was a spontaneous outpouring of joy from New Yorkers claiming back their city.

I believe that for many of those there that night, Balthazar's reopening symbolized the city's reawakening after Covid. For me, after my body and speech had been ravaged by a stroke, it was a different kind of reawakening. Before that night I had never fully accepted being a restaurateur. I wasn't committed to my vocation. For forty years I pretentiously imagined I had a "higher" calling. But not that night. Not now. I may not be a playwright, but who's to say that even if I did possess the talent to write plays that I'd be able to affect—even in the most superficial way—as many people as my restaurants appear to have done for nearly half a century?

After spending years searching for my roots in London, I had finally found them in New York. Some say your roots are where you feel most like your true self. After Covid was over and Balthazar reopened, I suddenly felt most like my true self in New York.

Happenstance might have made me an Englishman, but I *chose* to be a New Yorker. And, hopefully, I'll die as one, too.

Keith McNally, Thompson Street, April 16, 2024

Acknowledgments

I'd like to thank the following people who, for better or worse, made this book possible:

Aimée Bell, Caroline Michel, John Burnham, Jennifer Joel, Jennifer Bergstrom, Sierra Fang-Horvath, Alan Bennett, Lynn Wagenknecht, Jonathan Miller, Charlotte Edwardes, Phoebe Eaton, Susan Minot, Po Ming and Tamimah Dhaher.